ARCTIC OCEAN

Fridtjof Nansen Land

Spitsbergen

New Siberian Islands

Greenland Sea

Novaya Zemlya

Kara

S i b e r i a

North Cape

Barents Sea

Iceland   CIRCLE

Yenisei River

Lena River

TISH LES

North Sea

Baltic Sea

Dvina R.

URAL MTS.

Ob River

E U R O P E

A S I A

Sea of Okhotsk

Lake Baikal

Sakhalin

Amur River

Volga R.

Irtish

ALPS

Danube

Dnieper

Black Sea

Caspian Sea

Aral Sea

Lake Balkhash

Sea of Japan

JAPAN

deira ary ds

Mediterranean Sea

Amu Darya

Hwang-ho (Yellow)

Yangtze Kiang

PACIFIC

Euphrates R.

Suez Canal

HIMALAYA MTS.

Indus R.

Brahmaputra

Ganges R.

Mekong R.

South China

Philippine Islands

Guam

OCEAN

Sahara Desert

Nile R.

Red Sea

Arabian Sea

Bay of Bengal

Salween

Irrawaddy River

Sea

Niger R.

L. Chad

AFRICA

L. Victoria

Ceylon

Sumatra

Borneo

Celebes

New Guinea

Gulf of Guinea

River Congo

L. Tanganyika

Lake Nyasa

I N D I A N

Java

Ascension I.

TLANTIC

int Helena

OCEAN

Zambesi R.

Orange R.

Madagascar

O C E A N

AUSTRALIA

Cape of Good Hope

Murray R.

Tasmania

A N T A R C T I C   O C E A N

A N T A R C T I C A

Lands and Peoples

THE WORLD IN COLOR

VOLUME II

THE GROLIER SOCIETY

NEW YORK   TORONTO

L

Volume II

TABLE OF CONTENTS

THE FLYDALSJUVET, A GORGE IN GEIRANGER FIORD

Geiranger Fiord is an inland arm of the Stor Fiord, in the northern Fiord Country, and cuts deep into the mountains. In this gorge the rocky walls rise almost vertically for thousands of feet, above a farmstead on the shelf of land at the fiord's edge. The large ocean-going vessel seems almost like a toy boat in the midst of the majestic spectacle.

THE LAND OF FIORDS

Norway and Its People

The Scandinavian Peninsula reaches down for more than a thousand miles like a giant's mitten, with a very big thumb, about to grasp Denmark. The "mitten" shuts off the Baltic from the North Sea, and a ridge of mountains running north and south divides Sweden from Norway. Did giants create Norway, here thrusting up a high peak, and there digging a deep fiord? One can believe that Thor once hurled his thunderbolts in these wild mountains. In the spray of the many waterfalls, rainbows glimmer—and long ago the old Norse gods rode daily to and fro across the Bifrost Bridge, which is the rainbow.

"THE sea unites us; the land divides us," has long been a saying of the Norwegians. It helps to explain both the character of the people and the rugged beauty of their country. Through countless ages, wind, ice and water have chiseled what might be called a single huge stone into a complex pattern of mountains, plateaus (*vidda*) and deep U-shaped valleys. Sending long probing fingers inland, the sea formed fiords; and off the coast a chain of more than 150,000 rocky islands and islets—skerries—arose. Thus an inner ocean passage was made, sheltered from gales. From early times this sea route has been known as Norvegr, or "the Northern Way."

If we sail around the coast, beginning in the southeast, our ship passes, first, through the Skagerrak (the strait that separates Norway and Denmark). Then, where the waters of the Skagerrak and the North Sea mingle, we pass the most southern tip of Norway, the headland called The Naze, or Lindesnes. Rounding into the North Sea, at about Stavanger we pass into the North Atlantic Ocean. Beyond Floroe, our course changes to the northeast. A further voyage of about 450 miles brings us to the Arctic Circle, and from here on, around North Cape, we are in the Arctic Ocean.

The highest range of mountains in the whole Scandinavian Peninsula rises along the west side and from early times has been called Kjoelen, or The Keel. The name of Kjoelen Mountains is also given to that part of the range which marks the natural boundary between Norway

and Sweden. Though the peaks of the Kjoelen Mountains soar higher in northern Sweden, the Scandinavian spine south of Trondheim Fiord lies within Norwegian territory. Between the Kjoelen Mountains and the Gudbrandsdal (*dal* means "valley"), the highland of plateaus and rounded summits is called Dovre. South of Dovre and running all the way to the southern coast, the mountain mass is called Langfieldene, the Long Mountains. Included in the Langfieldene are the Hardangervidda and the magnificent Jotunheim Mountains.

Though Norway is narrow—the width varies from about 4 to 275 miles—it has a length of about 1,100 miles. However, the coast is so deeply indented that the actual shoreline is about 12,000 miles long. Norway also has territory far within the Arctic Circle—the Svalbard archipelago, which includes Spitsbergen. These islands are in the same latitude as northern Greenland. Though one-third of Norway proper is within the Arctic Circle, the climate is surprisingly mild. This is because of the Gulf Stream, the ocean current that forms in the tropical Caribbean Sea, and swerves across the Atlantic in a great arc. To western Norway, the Gulf Stream brings abundant rainfall, mild winters and cool summers. However, on the eastern side of the mountains in southern Norway, the climate is drier, with hotter summers and colder winters.

The visitor to Norway by ship or plane generally lands at Oslo. It is a crisp, spacious city, with many green vistas and no slums. From the inner harbor, where

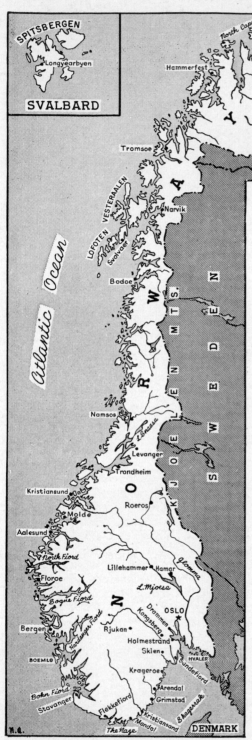

HOMELAND OF THE NORWEGIANS

passenger ships and freighters from all over the world ride at anchor, the city rises toward rounded hills clothed in pine and spruce. Conspicuous at the edge of the water front is the City Hall, a square-looking structure with two towering wings. The very modern appearance of this big building is in sharp contrast to the gleaming white Royal Palace, classic in design, that surmounts a near-by hill.

A town named Oslo was founded around 1050 at the eastern side of the harbor. However, in 1624, Christian IV, king of Denmark and Norway, established a town on the western shore, after the old town burned down. There he laid out a city with broad avenues and rectangular blocks and named it for himself, Christiania. In 1924 the Storting, the Norwegian Parliament, voted to restore the old Norse name of Oslo.

A rocky peninsula, on which Akershus Castle stands—it was a fort and a royal residence long ago—divides the port in two: Bjoervika, the old town, to the east; and Pipervika, to the west. An inviting park stretches from north of the castle to the Storting (Parliament House), and within the park is the National Theater, which Norway's foremost playwright, Henrik Ibsen (1828-1906), helped to make world-famous.

On the outskirts of Oslo, in the park at Frogner, is the lifework of the sculptor Gustav Vigeland, who died in 1943. Starting as a design for a fountain, which is in bronze, the group was added to year by year, the later works being carved in granite. The central piece alone—a column fifty feet high—has 121 intertwined human figures.

On the Bygdoe Peninsula, to the west of Oslo, is the fascinating open-air Norwegian Folk Museum, where the visitor steps into the Norway of medieval times. Among the old wooden buildings is a stave church. Carved in the portals are intertwined dragons, a favorite Viking design, which was often used in ship carving. The steep gables of the stave churches give them an oddly Oriental look. Why such a style developed under Gothic skies and in Norway is a mystery. In a building near the Folk Museum are several ships that tell stories covering centuries of adventure on the high seas: high-prowed Viking ships—the Oseberg, the Gokstad and the Tune; the celebrated Fram, on which Fridtjof Nansen and Roald Amundsen explored the Arctic and the Antarctic; and the fragile Kon-Tiki raft, on which Thor Heyerdahl and five companions made a 4,000-mile voyage across the South Pacific in the interests of twentieth-century science.

Oslo Fiord is wider and has more gently sloping ledges than the western fiords. The eastern shore—Oestfold County— is a fertile and thickly populated region of green meadows and large tracts of forest. Timber has always been one of Norway's most valuable raw products, and since the Middle Ages one of its chief exports. Norway's largest river, the Glomma, flows through Oestfold on its way to the Skagerrak. Just south of the mouth of the Glomma is one of the larger skerries off this coast—Hvaler—where fishermen and coast pilots like to gather and spin their salty yarns. In summertime, farther up the east shore, white sails fly before the wind in the regattas held at Hankoe.

On the western side of Oslo Fiord— Vestfold County—cliffs and sandy beaches mark the shoreline. Vestfold is a bustling center of industry and shipping. The largest whaling ships in the world come from the small ports here; and the town of Sandefiord is the main base of the whaling fleet. Holmestrand, called the

Norwegian Information Service

OSLO'S HANDSOME MODERN TOWN HALL

As one comes into Oslo by water, the massive building at the edge of the inner harbor draws the eyes at once. The twin towers give this part of Oslo a twentieth-century skyline; and the Town Hall is a meeting place of modern Norwegian art. Sculptures relieve the severe lines of the exterior; and inside there is a series of large murals of Norwegian life.

Norwegian Information Service

A BIT OF OLD NORWAY IN THE TELEMARK COUNTRYSIDE

On many farms one may still see a *stabbur*, a storehouse raised above the ground to protect a family's provisions from dampness and wild beasts. Usually such storehouses were two-story buildings, with an outer staircase leading up to a gallery around the upper floor. Some of those still standing have been in continuous use for more than six hundred years.

"aluminum town," is a center for one of Norway's most important industries.

Aluminum is produced from a clay called bauxite, and to extract the aluminum requires tremendous amounts of electric power. In Norway, electric power means hydroelectric (water) power. As the rivers cascade down to the sea from the mountains, the rapids and falls have given Norway a greater amount of hydroelectric power in proportion to population than any other country in the world. Thus far only about a fifth of this power has been developed. Norway does not have bauxite. Nevertheless, the falling-water resources and their nearness to ice-free harbors make it profitable to send the clay from other countries to be processed. In turn Norway exports aluminum metal and articles made from it.

Fanning out north of Oslo and cutting deeply into the mountain plateau are the Eastern Valleys, U-shaped, sprinkled with sparkling lakes, and divided from each other by rolling highland moors. The valley farthest to the northeast, Oesterdal, is sometimes called "Norway's hidden valley." It once seemed far more remote than it does today, and few travelers glimpsed its brooding conifer forests car-

peted with leafy mosses, its deep mirror-like tarns and foaming rivers, including the upper course of the Glomma. Elk still slip through the woods, and occasionally roe deer. Among the many game birds is the capercailzie, which figures so often in Norwegian folk tales.

The largest and most important valley is the broad, fertile Gudbrandsdal, which spreads between the Dovre and the northern end of Lake Mjoesa, the largest lake in Norway. Though narrow, it is almost sixty miles long. The gateway to the Gudbrandsdal is the town of Lillehammer, on the lake. Sigrid Undset, who won a Nobel Prize in literature, lived just outside Lillehammer. Her greatest book, KRISTIN LAVRANDSDATTER, is considered the most important Norwegian literary work of the twentieth century. The scene of the trilogy is thirteenth-century Norway, but the characters are seen through modern eyes. Kristin is one of the most alive and memorable women in all fiction.

The Gudbrandsdal, Norway's "valley of valleys," and the region between it and Oslo contain the most fertile and level stretches of land and make up the chief farming district of Norway. Mountains and forests leave only about 4 per cent of

MC LEISH

IN THE NORD FIORD some of the cliffs fall so steeply to the water's edge that only goats can scale them. The Norwegian fiords run inland for many miles, and though in some places they may be only two hundred yards wide, the water is so deep that ocean liners can steam up them, passing some of the finest scenery in the world.

the total area of the country suitable for raising crops. Nevertheless about one-third of the Norwegian people earn their living by farming in combination with forestry. (Along the coast a farmer may also be a fisherman.) Agriculture and lumbering have this close relationship because many of the farmers themselves own the forests. Besides, the farms are quite small: more than 90 per cent are less than 25 acres in extent; and only about 40 farms in the whole country are 250 acres or more. Though thrift and skill and the widespread use of fertilizers make the crop yields exceptionally high, not enough food-stuffs can be raised to meet the needs of the population. Only in the production of potatoes is Norway self-sufficient. Taking just two items, the country must buy from other nations about 40 per cent of its cereals (grains) and 15 per cent of its fodder (for livestock).

Saeters and Modern Creameries

The raising of livestock is an important part of the farmer's work. To this must be added the raising of fur-bearing animals, particularly silver foxes. Norway has developed its own breeds of cattle and horses, among them the Doele cattle that are raised in both the Gudbrandsdal and the Oesterdal. In addition to forests, many farmers own mountain pastures in common, where their cattle and sheep are put to graze in summer. In times past, milk was churned into butter and cheese was made in mountain dairies—the lonely saeters that, in Norwegian folklore, are often haunted by trolls. Today, however, the raw milk is sent to creameries in towns and villages. Norway, with other Scandinavian countries, was a pioneer in the co-operative movement. Most simply, this means that those who produce a certain article—milk or cheese, for instance—band together in an association that markets and sells the article without benefit of a middleman, or distributor. In Norway, the marketing of agricultural products is handled almost entirely by co-operatives.

There are several valleys, west of the Gudbrandsdal, in the enchanting lake district of Valdres. One of them extends to the slopes of the Jotunheim range—the name means "Home of the Giants"—where the mountains of Norway soar highest. Here Galdhoepiggen lifts its rocky summit 8,098 feet above sea level. It is the highest mountain in Europe north of the Carpathians. However, a near-by peak, Glittertind, appears even higher because of its thick cloak of eternal snow.

South of the Valdres district is the Hallingdal, through which the railway between Bergen and Oslo passes. The route provides a thrilling moutain ride, and from the train one sees a cross section of the magnificent Norwegian landscape. To the east of the Hallingdal lies a road-less forest called Vassfaret, where an occasional bear still lurks.

The farthest south of the Eastern Valleys is the Numedal. Its chief town is Kongsberg, which was an important silver-mining center as early as 1800. Metal for Norwegian coins still comes from these mines. Of more interest in the Numedal today are the number of stave churches still standing in their original settings. The one at Uvdal has a gorgeous "rose painting," and is an outstanding piece of Norwegian folk art.

The Norwegian Riviera

From Stavanger to Krageroe the coast of southern Norway is called Soerlandet, or the "Norwegian Riviera." Indented by many bays and tiny fiords and protected from the open ocean by thousands of skerries, the Soerlandet lures all those who love salt water and sun. From centuries-old ports along this coast—Arendal, Grimstad, Kristiansand, Tvedestrand—generations of mariners have braved the perils of the sea.

Telemark, Home of Skiing

Telemark, in the central part of South Norway, is a district of winding valleys. On many of the farms one may still see examples of the folk architecture that developed during the Middle Ages. Among these wooden buildings, adorned with carving, is the *stabbur,* a storehouse that rests on pillars.

Norwegian Information Service

RJUKAN—FOREST-CLAD RAVINE AND CHEMICAL PLANT

The little cable car carries workers from the plant to the high surrounding plateau. Extracting nitrogen from the air, this factory produces fertilizers, of great importance to agriculture. The process of nitrogen extraction was developed by Norwegian scientists. It uses enormous amounts of electric power, made possible by the country's vast water-power resources.

11

SETESDAL COSTUME. One of the loveliest valleys of South Norway, the Setesdal is also a region rich in folklore. The farmers and their families still enjoy many of the songs and dances of their forebears. Richly embroidered clothes such as these are donned today only on special occasions, sometimes for a wedding in the old style.

12

BECKETT

HARDANGER WOMEN used to wear a headdress called a "skaut" made of white linen. The bodice is beautifully trimmed with beads, and the buckles of the belt are silver. This charming costume is rarely worn now save on holidays. The Hardanger folk are among the foremost in Norway in attempting to preserve their traditions.

The glittering white cap of Mount Gausta dominates Telemark. Near this peak is the town of Rjukan, which is a center of Norway's important electro-chemical industry. This is another industry that has grown along with the development of water power. Vast quantities of cheap electricity have opened the way for the production of chemicals, of "heavy water" (used in atomic-energy plants), and for the extraction of nitrogen from the air, a process worked out by Norwegian scientists. The factories at Rjukan are among the largest in Norway and—a unique combination of beauty and utility —they nestle at the bottom of a deep, forest-clad ravine.

Telemark is also the home of skiing, the national sport, and has given its name to a kind of skiing technique. Skis have been in use all over Norway for at least a thousand years, though skiing was not considered a sport until the middle of the nineteenth century. During the four "white" months, Norwegian boys and girls learn to glide over the crust almost as soon as they can walk. Easter is a special skiing holiday, when the worker in office or factory takes his family to the mountains for the sport. It is not surprising that Norwegian skiers usually take the lead in the Winter Olympics.

To the west of the mountains lies the breathtakingly beautiful Fiord Country. At the same time that the glaciers of the ice age were scouring out the deep Eastern Valleys, similar valleys were formed on the west coast separated by rounded mountain ranges extending toward the ocean like huge fingers. After the ice age the coastline began to sink, and the sea flooded the valleys to form the fiords. After the period of sinking, a slight rising occurred so that a shelf of lowland pushed above the water in the south as well as in the west. Today the greater part of Norway's population lives on this shelf. When it was formed, the chain of skerries also appeared that forms a natural breakwater along the coast.

The fiords are extremely deep. In places in Sogne Fiord, the water has a depth of more than 4,000 feet. At their mouths, the fiords are broad and smiling, with farmlands on either side; but gradually they narrow and the walls rise sheer and ever higher above the water. In many places the sides are so nearly vertical that large ocean-going vessels may ply within a few yards of the fiord's edge. On the steeper slopes there is little soil, but elsewhere there are groves

Scandinavian Airlines

COLORFUL GARB FOR FUN ON ICE AND SNOW

Many of the intricate designs are traditional, developed by generations of Norwegian women, busily clicking their needles through the long winter dusk. The star pattern (at left on the rack) comes from the Selbu area near Trondheim.

of pine and birch, where graceful red deer may be seen now and then. The islands that stand sentinel in the open sea look barren from a distance, but in sheltered coves and in crannies in the rocks there are thickets of oak and birch, aspen and rowantree.

Some of Norway's most important cities are at the mouths of the western fiords. Stavanger is a quaint old seaport, bustling with shipping and trade. It is the center of the fish-canning industry. During the summer a constant stream of smacks bring silvery cargoes of brisling to the quays. Brisling are small fish, and those canned are sold as "sardines." From Stavanger one may sail inland, weaving in and out among the teeming isles of Ryfylke and beyond into narrow fiords. One of the most enthralling of these is Lyse Fiord, where farms perch, at the edge of steep walls, hundreds of feet above the water. On such farms, the sturdy, sure-footed "fiord horse" does yeoman service.

One of the loveliest fiords of all is Hardanger, between Stavanger and Bergen. In the springtime the orchards along the shore are a drift of white blossoms. Farther inland, upland pastures show green and lush. Rising above the head of Hardanger Fiord is a lake-studded plateau rimmed with snow-covered peaks —Hardangervidda. On the edge of it, the power of both Laatefoss and Voeringfoss (*foss* means "falls") has been harnessed in superb engineering feats.

Although the colorful costumes of old time are rarely worn any more and the folk costumes are disappearing from everyday life, the visitor to the Hardanger

Burton Holmes from Ewing Galloway, N. Y.

THE HANSEATIC WHARF ON BERGEN'S WATER FRONT

In these gabled buildings the German merchants of the Hanseatic League once bargained for fish in exchange for grain. Bergen has been an important port ever since that medieval period. Today modern docks line the busy harbor, a haven for ships of all flags.

region may be lucky enough to witness an old-fashioned wedding. The women in the bridal party wear white blouses, and over them stiffly beaded or embroidered bodices; and knee-length skirts of black or dark-blue homespun. The men may be decked out in bibbed trousers with elaborately embroidered vests, and broad-brimmed hats, or sometimes tight-fitting knee breeches, scarlet vests with silver buttons and silver-buckled shoes. If the people live inland, the bridal procession winds down a country road led by a fiddler playing the curious eight-stringed "Hardanger fiddle." (Four of the strings are set below the others, and they give out rich overtones when the fiddle is played.) Bride and groom follow, riding in state, the bride wearing a crown, a tradition that has come down from medieval times. The crown, wrought of silver, is probably a family heirloom. If the fiord is near by, the procession will be made up of a number of small boats.

Bergen was already an important city in the Middle Ages, when merchants settled there from the free towns of the

A MIST OF SPRAY hangs over the gorge into which the Maan Elv, a Norwegian river, makes its great plunge of 345 feet—hence the name Rjukanfos, or Reeking Falls. When the sun is shining on the spray, a rainbow bends its seven colors over the abyss. The photograph shows a portion of the Norwegian plateau, two to three thousand feet high.

GLACIERS, such as the one of which we see the edge in this photograph, wind down the sides of some of the mountains in the Horunger group, near the eastern end of the Sogne Fiord. These enormous U-shaped valleys were carved out by the vanished glaciers of the ice age, which cut several hundred of them along the coast.

17

Hanseatic League in northern Germany. Side by side with gabled buildings, including the Hanseatic Wharf, that date from this period, and even earlier reminders of the Vikings, are modern hotels and restaurants and shops.

Though industry is taking a more important part in the life of Bergen today, it is still one of Norway's chief shipping centers. The country's prosperity has long been dependent on world trade; and before World War II, Norway had the fourth largest fleet of merchant ships of any country in the world. During the heroic but doomed struggle against the Germans in April 1940, seven-eighths of this fleet managed to escape to Allied

ports. Thereafter it carried men and supplies to every theater of the war; and numbers of the ships and the Norwegian seamen who manned them were lost. One of Norway's chief problems after the war, therefore, was to rebuild its merchant marine. Norwegians could take pride in the fact that by 1951 their shipping was greater than it had been in 1939. Norway now ranks third in world shipping.

The largest and deepest of the fiords, and perhaps the most wildly magnificent, is Sogne Fiord. It winds inland for 110 miles, where it meets the cold fingers of the Jostedal Glacier, the largest ice field in northern Europe. The really high mountains of Norway—the Lom, the

Burton Holmes from Ewing Galloway, N. Y.

OLAF TRYGVESSEN STILL STANDS GUARD OVER TRONDHEIM

The market place is in the center of Trondheim, at the base of a statue of King Olaf Trygvessen, who founded the city in 997. A daring Viking chief, his romantic story weaves through Norwegian legend and poetry. Olaf's vessel, the Long Snake, was the mightiest in the north. During a fierce battle in 1000, Olaf fought on until he was about to be overwhelmed and then leaped into the sea.

Jotunheim, the Hemsedal and the Voss— lie in a semicircle around the innermost arms of Sogne Fiord.

The most northerly part of the Fiord Country consists of the districts of Moere, Romsdal and Trondelag. Kristiansund is the most important town of Moere, and most of its citizens are sea fishermen. Aalesund is the chief fishing center and one of the most important in the world. Inland, the streams, their headlong rush to the sea broken by numerous falls, teem with trout and salmon. Hare and ptarmigan may be flushed on the upland moors; and elk roam in the forests around Lake Snaasa. The forests of this region are second in value only to those of South Norway. All supply the country's tremendous pulp and paper industry.

Trondheim, Once Called Nidaros

The city of Trondheim, in Troendelag, is almost exactly in the center of Norway from north to south. It was founded by King Olaf Trygvessen in 997 as the capital of Norway and was then called Nidaros. The spires of Nidaros Cathedral dominate the modern city's skyline: and Norwegian kings are still crowned in the beautiful medieval building.

Beyond Troendelag lies North Norway, the Land of the Midnight Sun. The greater part of it is within the Arctic Circle. At North Cape, the farthest tip of Norway, the sun never sets from about May 14 to July 30. In the winter the shimmering curtain of the aurora borealis, or northern lights, brightens the long nights with unearthly splendor.

To North Cape by an Ancient Route

One of the most exciting experiences in Norway is to take a trip in summer on one of the comfortable coastal steamers that ply the Northern Way between Bergen and North Cape. A wall of rocky cliffs, rising sheer from the icy Arctic waters, the headland stands out in lonely grandeur. The round trip on the ship takes about twelve days. However, you can vary the tour by returning overland. There are excellent roads and railways.

Not far south of North Cape, on the island of Kvaloey, is Hammerfest, the most northerly town in the world and the center for Finnmark, as the far northern region is called. Only about 70,000 people live in this district, on the weather-beaten coast or on lonely homesteads separated by vast stretches of moor. Here, in the brief summer months, under long hours of sunlight, plants grow so fast that one can almost *see* them sprout.

South from Hammerfest, the next important town is Tromsoe, the "Capital of the Arctic." It, too, is on an island. The Northern Lights Observatory is here and near by there is a Lapp camp. Narvik, further down the coast, is the chief port for shipping iron ore. Most of the country's considerable iron-ore resources are in North Norway.

Swinging out into the ocean, northwest of Vest Fiord, is the chain of the Lofoten Islands. They are the headquarters of the tremendous fishing industry of North Norway. Cod is the chief catch. Tons of it are exported, fresh or frozen, dried or salted. The herring fisheries are the next most important after cod, and a large part of this catch is canned. Since it was discovered some years ago that cod-liver oil is extremely rich in vitamins A and D, the oil has become an important item in Norway's international trade.

The Norwegian People of Today

Their mountainous and sea-girt country —almost an island—has molded the Norwegians in many ways. For all its beauty, the land requires hard labor of its inhabitants. Toil and hardship have made them sturdy and self-reliant; and the constant challenge of sea and mountain has made them proudly independent. From the dawn of their recorded history they have also had a great respect for law and order.

From about 800 to 1050, the people along the coasts of northwestern Europe trembled in fear of the bold Viking raids. Nevertheless, many Norsemen went to trade (dried cod was even then an item for barter) and in search of homes. Norse colonies were set up in Iceland, Scotland, the Faeroes and along the French coast (Normandy!) and in Ireland. Where-

NORWEGIAN LAPPS, who number about twenty thousand, live under the protection of the government. The Lapps are the most primitive of all the European races. Those of Norway can be divided into the Mountain Lapps, who wander about with their huge herds of reindeer; the Coast or River Lapps, who are fishermen and sailors; and the cattle-breeding Lapps. The Mountain Lapps are almost completely dependent on their reindeer, which supply them with food and clothing, household utensils and means of transport.

IN THE FOLK MUSEUM at Oslo is an old wooden stave church, probably built in the thirteenth century. The church was placed in this outdoor museum in 1884, among other exhibits that show us how the people of Norway lived before modern times. These churches are considered to be the most remarkable timber buildings in Europe and, though they were built centuries ago, there are about twenty in existence. The many roofs give them an Oriental appearance that is enhanced by the dragon-like terminals to the gables.

21

SVOLVAER, HOME OF THE LOFOTENS COD-FISHING FLEET

From January into April, the harbor swarms with thousands of vessels of fishermen who have gathered from all parts of the coast. It is then that the cod come to their spawning grounds at the base of the mountainous Lofotens. Nowhere else are such large quantities of cod found in so small an area, and the catch is enormous. More than half of it is salted.

ever they settled, they brought a respect for law. The feudal system, by which the great mass of European people were held in thrall during the Middle Ages, was never established in Norway. The peasants continued to live as free men. It is an interesting sidelight on the period of colonization that ancient Norse literature —the sagas, the eddaic and scaldic poems—found its richest expression in Iceland.

By 872 Norway was united under a single chief, Harald the Fair-haired. The kingdom was made even stronger by Olaf Haraldsson (Saint Olaf, 1016-29) who brought Christianity to Norway.

However, colonies were lost, and civil strife and the terrible Black Death swept away three-quarters of the Norwegian population during the thirteenth and fourteenth centuries. So in 1397 Norway was forced to submit to a union with Denmark and Sweden, from which Sweden gradually broke away. The Dano-Norwegian union nevertheless lasted until 1814. In that year Norway wrote a new constitution

and agreed to join a union with Sweden. But throughout the nineteenth century the Norwegians strove by peaceful means for independence. Writers, composers and painters were inspired to produce works that would be thoroughly Norwegian in feeling, without the old Danish influence. Interest in the old folk arts took on new life. Asbjoernsen and Moe made their wonderful collection of folk and fairy tales, which until then had been handed down by word of mouth. Woven through the haunting music of Edvard Grieg (1843-1907), Norway's greatest composer, are threads of old folk melodies.

The union with Sweden ended in June 1905, when the Norwegian Parliament declared Norway's independence. For king, the Norwegian people elected Prince Charles of Denmark, crowned as Haakon VII.

The government of Norway is a constitutional monarchy. There are several political parties, of which Labor is the strongest. Norway was one of the first countries to develop a broad social-security program, which includes insurance against unemployment, illness and accident, and retirement pensions. The welfare services for children reach the most remote homes. Boys and girls have regular medical and dental examinations; and necessary treatment is usually free.

Other progressive nations have copied the "Oslo breakfast," served to the city's children at school before classes begin. It is a scientifically balanced meal, of whole milk, whole-grain bread, vitamin-rich spreads, and fresh fruit or vegetables in season—plus cod-liver oil!

Norway has a splendid public-education system. Boys and girls from the age of seven must go to elementary school for seven years. On remote farms and in little isolated schools, the radio helps to bring the children into closer contact with the outside world. In the last two grades of the elementary schools and in the sec-

ondary schools, English is usually taught as a second language. Oslo University is the mother institution of all the other Norwegian academic colleges.

The "big moment" in the lives of Norwegian children comes on Christmas Eve. It begins with a traditional dinner of boiled codfish and rice porridge. In the country a bowl of porridge is set out, in the barn, for the brownie who, according to legend, watches over every family. Boys and girls remember the birds, too, and for them a sheaf of oats is hung from the ridgepole. There is no lingering over dinner, for under a lighted tree gifts await the children—perhaps skis or ice skates, and mittens, sweaters or scarfs knitted in unique patterns that have come down through the centuries. As the joyous evening draws to a close, boys and girls join hands around the glowing tree and sing old Norwegian Christmas carols.

NORWAY: FACTS AND FIGURES

THE COUNTRY

Bounded on the north and northwest by the Arctic Ocean, on the west by the North Atlantic, on the south by the North Sea and the Skagerrak, and on the east by Sweden, Finland and Russia. The distance from north to south is about 1,100 miles; and the coastline, including the fiords and the shores of the islands, is about 12,000 miles. The total area is 126,099 square miles, and the population is about 3,250,000. The Arctic archipelago of Svalbard (which includes Spitsbergen), which is under Norwegian sovereignty, has an area of 23,980 square miles and a population of about 2,000.

GOVERNMENT

Hereditary and constitutional monarchy with legislative power in the hands of the Storting, or Parliament, for which women are eligible. The executive is represented by the king, who acts through a Cabinet. The constitution, which has been modified at various times, dates from 1814.

COMMERCE AND INDUSTRIES

Country unsuited to agriculture, and only 3.6% of the whole area is cultivated. Forests (mostly pine) cover 24% of the total area and are one of the chief natural resources. Cod, herring, mackerel, salmon, whale and seal fisheries are important. The mineral deposits include silver, copper, pyrites and iron, and coal is worked in Spitsbergen.

The principal exports are wood pulp and paper manufactures, edible animal products, base metals and articles made of them, oil seeds and fats. The principal imports are machinery, transport equipment, ships, base metals and articles made of them (different from those exported), fuel, oil, textiles and cereals.

COMMUNICATIONS

On January 1, 1950, the total registered merchant marine (ships above 100 gross tons only) was 2,126 vessels, 5,122,000 gross tons. Ships under construction on this date totaled 1,690,000 gross tons. Total railway mileage is 2,780 miles, mainly state-owned. There are 39,602 miles of telegraph and telephone line. Radio broadcasting is state-controlled and there are 22 stations.

RELIGION AND EDUCATION

The Evangelical Lutheran Church is the national church and the only one endowed by the state. The clergy are nominated by the king. There is freedom of religion for all denominations.

Education is compulsory and primary schools are free. There are 2 kinds of secondary schools, and a number of vocational and technical institutions. There are 2 universities, Oslo and Bergen.

POPULATIONS OF CHIEF CITIES

Oslo, capital, 418,449; Bergen, 109,320; Trondheim, 57,128; Stavanger, 50,320; Drammen, 26,994; Kristiansand, 24,343.

© E. N. A.

THE MIDNIGHT SUN, which, north of the Arctic Circle, never sets on Midsummer Day, tints sea and sky with the pale radiance of a dawn that wanes and waxes through the cycle of the nights. As in Norway, the Feast of the Sun survives in the annual Festival of St. John. On that day people dance around poles garlanded with wild flowers. They also decorate streets and houses with branches of white birch, and kindle fires on hill tops around which they dance and sing. This pagan festival survived when the people became Christians centuries ago.

24

THE HOME OF THE GOTHS

By Forest, Dale and Waterway through Sweden

Sweden, one of the lands of the midnight sun, a land of lakes, forests and rapid rivers, is rich in iron mines, paper mills and intricate electrical appliances. To it perhaps five thousand years ago came a tall, blond Aryan people who had never bowed to alien rule nor mixed their blood with that of other races. Sweden was one home of the Goths, whence hordes of "barbarians" swept over Europe from north to south and from east to west in the first centuries of the Christian era, conquering all who opposed them, even to the legions of the Roman emperors. Although few in number, the Swedish people have left their mark upon the world—for there is not one of the great ruling races, with the exception of the Japanese, that cannot, through Gothic ancestors of centuries ago, claim kindred with the Swedes of to-day. Prosperous Stockholm is a city of high culture and advanced social legislation as well as great natural beauty.

SWEDEN, facing eastward with its back to Norway, shows in its polished granite slopes and coastal islands and the basins of its snow-fed lakes the work of the last ice sheet. Centuries before the Goths swarmed out of the north to the invasion of the Latin countries, the ice in its advance down the eastern slope of the Scandinavian peninsula gouged out a chain of depressions through the very middle of Sweden. It also embroidered the entire coastline with ragged islands and peninsulas that range in size from the tiniest of pine-clad rocks to the two huge stretches of farmland, Oland and Gothland. These islands are called the Garden of Skerries, and many of them have been made even more charming by the presence of summer villas. You would enjoy the sail through the labyrinth of wooded isles and islets along the coast of Bothnia.

The Swedes came of the same Viking stock as the other Scandinavians. Though St. Ansgar preached in the ninth century in Sweden, the natives continued their pagan sacrifices to Thor and Odin until British missionaries converted them in the twelfth century. The first Swedish overlords chose Upsala as their seat of government. Stockholm originated in the effort to defend an islet with stocks from invading Danes. Ironically, it was because King Eric IX refused to cut short his attendance at Mass when a Danish army arrived that he fell victim

to them in 1160. He later became the patron saint of Sweden. Byzantine coins, dug up amid the ruins of ancient Visby, on the island of Gothland, indicate that ancient Sweden had an extensive trade. Her vast copper mine at Falun was opened in 1284, and she had furs and fish for export. Several thousand rune stones remain to mark the graves of the Vikings. In 1397 Margaret of Denmark united the three Scandinavian kingdoms at Kalmar Castle, on the coast opposite the island of Oland; but the Swedes were restive, and in 1523, Gustavus Vasa, who had driven out the Danes, was elected king. By the middle of the sixteenth century the throne had become hereditary; and what with the wise rule of the Vasa kings and the decline of the Hanseatic League—which permitted them to secure the lion's share of the Baltic trade— Sweden had two centuries of great power in Europe. Protestantism gradually gained a foothold.

Sweden's greatest king, Gustavus Adolphus, joined in the Thirty Years' War and made his country mistress of the Baltic and a dominant military power. His daughter Christina, a mere child when she came to the throne, made the Swedish court a centre of European culture. A generation later Charles XII fought desperately with Peter the Great of Russia, but was worsted, and during the next hundred years Sweden lost most of her foreign possessions. In 1810

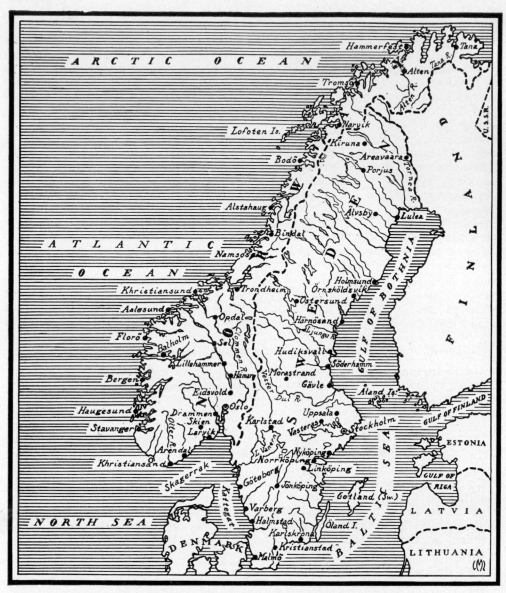

THE SCANDINAVIAN PENINSULA

the Swedish diet elected Bernadotte, one of Napoleon's generals, crown prince, and his line still rules in Sweden. Norway was joined to Sweden in 1814, but, in 1905, became independent. When the popular Gustavus V came to the throne in 1907 he dispensed with the coronation ceremony. Sweden was neutral in both world wars, though in the second war Germany occupied Norway and Denmark, and the three little states across the Baltic were taken by Russia.

As your steamer plies along the winding fjord to Stockholm you will see rising out of the quiet waters a granite city built on two groups of these rocky prominences, one in the Baltic, one in Lake Mälar. The waterfront is as clean as a boulevard, and on the rivers that flow deep within the heart of the city lie great steamers, little sail boat freighters laden with birch logs, and numbers of white passenger steamers. In winter the tourist will see long-distance skating races winding through the archipelago on silver ice, and in the harbor hilarious exhibitions of sail-skating. On one island stands the palace of the king, an impregnable looking structure built around a court; on another, hard by, is the red brick city hall with a roof of copper shingles green with weather-stain. Gleaming like the midnight sun on the tower of this building poises a great golden ball and above it the three golden crowns that are Sweden's coat-of-arms, symbol of the one-time joint sovereignty with Norway and Denmark. On other islands stand factories and lumber yards or schools and museums.

Stockholm is an uncommonly beautiful city by reason of its location, which has caused it to be termed the Venice of the North. Standing at the junction of Lake Mälar and the sea, it occupies all of the small islands that lie between their shores. Staden, the island that so nearly connects the two mainlands, was the nucleus

of the ancient city. To the north of this lies Norrström and to the south, Söderström. Norrmalm, at the heart of Norrström, is the part of the city that contains the finest buildings. Downtown you will like the government-operated phone booths on the street corners, the clean waterfront—so like a boulevard—and the opportunity of drinking coffee, in summer, at little green painted tables on the sidewalks beneath the drooping elms.

The fashionable suburb, where lives the royal family, is Ulriksdal. At Upsala is the Temple where, thousands of years before Christ, sacrifices were made to Odin. It stands neighbor to the University of Upsala, founded five centuries ago.

In visiting another suburb, Södermalm, one is taken up the cliff in two great iron elevators called the Maria and Katarina lifts. The Stor Kyrka, which also is worth a visit, dates back to Stockholm's thirteenth-century founder, Bürger

© E. N. A.

BUSY SPINNING-WHEEL IN THE HOME OF A SWEDISH YEOMAN

The yeomen, or peasant farmers, of Sweden are well known for their sturdy independence and industrious habits, and at the same time they cling to old traditions. Their homes are filled with good, solid furniture, often richly carved, and such old-fashioned articles as the above three-legged caldron and the spinning-wheel are in daily use.

ONE ROOM SERVES MANY PURPOSES IN THE HOMES OF THE STURDY DALE FOLK

©E.N.A.

Though many of the cottages in Dalecarlia are lit by electric light, as is this one, the kitchen, dining-room and bedroom may all be one room. In one corner we can see the stove and cooking pots, and across the room, in another corner, are the beds. These are rather like cupboards, and curtains are drawn across them during the day. A ladder is used by the person sleeping in the top berth when he wants to go to bed. Strips of brightly colored carpet are laid upon the floor, and help to give the room a bright, clean, homely air.

TWO LITTLE MAIDS OF MORA IN THEIR RUSTIC COSTUMES

On the northwest shore of beautiful Lake Siljan, in Dalarne, lies the village of Mora. It is a haunt of artists desirous of painting pictures of the beautiful costumes of the natives. The belfry tower, in front of which these girls stand, adjoins the curious old church of Mora, and, like many other such church towers in Swedish villages, is made of wood.

SWEDISH TRAVEL BUREAU

CHRISTMAS COMES IN SWEDEN

In Sweden, when Christmas time rolls around, charming angels in various attitudes, animals of all kinds and unique decorative designs in straw are in popular demand. Here skilled workers are fashioning a straw goat with impossibly long horns. The woman and girl have donned the colorful old costume of their district, as part of the holiday fun.

GLASSWARE OF DISTINCTION

This expert is engraving a vase by means of a copper wheel fitted to a lathe. The scene is the Orrefors factory in Sweden, established in 1898. The factory produces household glass of graceful, delicate shape; but it is known abroad chiefly for its beautiful "fine arts" ware, designed by eminent artists. Today there is no modern glass anywhere that excels Orrefors.

31

Jarl. The turreted Stadium was built in 1912 for the Olympic games. Skansen, the island annex to the Northern Museum, is what the Swedes call a hill garden. It would repay a visit by reason of its reproduction of the rural districts, old wooden churches and farmhouses set in characteristic surroundings.

Next in size is Gothenburg (Goteborg), the chief seaport, which is at the western end of the Göta Canal. This canal—through whose fifty or sixty locks five thousand vessels annually pass—connects the chain of lakes before mentioned, Vener, Vetter, and many smaller ones.

A Bird's-eye View

If we were mounted, like the boy who rode the wild goose in Selma Lagerlof's Wonderful Adventures of Nils, while we made the thousand-mile journey from south to north, we would get a bird's-eye view of four well marked geographical zones. These correspond to the ancient divisions of Sweden, namely, Gothland, Svealand, Norrland and Lapland.

Gothland, sometimes called Scania, is a region of rich farmlands, lakes and meadows, the stronghold of the dairy farmer. Here and there we will spy an ancient castle, with its round towers, or a church in the substantial northern Gothic architecture.

A Living from Five Acres

When you see one of the stalwart red farmhouses, steep-roofed against the winter snows, white-shuttered against the summer sunshine, with its fences fragrant with drying hay and its clover-breathing meadow placid with grazing cattle, it will be easy to realize that the *bondar* or dweller, as the freeholder is called, can make a good living from even five acres of the rich black soil. Often he can trace the tenure of his land back for a thousand years, but you will find his dairy of the most modern construction. You will also find the dairyman a member of a co-operative association.

Now on to Svealand. It was in the peasants of Dalecarlia that Gustavus Vasa, the patriot king who rescued Sweden from the Danes, found his mainstay. These farmers received him as a homeless fugitive and by their courage placed him on the throne. They were also the troopers who. in the Thirty Years' War, enabled Gustavus Adolphus to maintain the Protestant cause in Northern Europe. In Dalecarlia, or Dalarne, where gleams Lake Siljan like a jewel of the forest, survive all the ancient manners and traditions of the Swedish race. Here may be seen the costumes that originated in the days when every housewife did her own spinning and weaving. Here people may still sometimes be seen going long distances to church in huge open church boats with their eight pairs of oars. Here also one will find that the old-time arts of weaving and lace-making, metal and cabinet work—now on exhibition in the Northern Museum at Stockholm and the open-air museum in Skansen Park—are being taught in the schools.

Now let us cross the central lake portion of Svealand on our way to Norrland. The rivers become wilder, the forests more unbroken, as the land rises to the snow-capped mountains of the Norwegian frontier. Steamers can navigate hundreds of miles up the broad Indals and Angerman rivers.

Forests Perpetually Renewed

Sweden's two most valuable industries have for centuries been lumbering and iron-working, and her wood-pulp and paper industry is becoming increasingly important to the United States. Fully half of Sweden is under forest, and careful legislation regulates its cutting and replanting that the forests may be perpetually renewed.

The centre of the timber industry is Sundsvall, far to the north of the farm country. The flaxen-haired giants of lumbermen spend the crisp, white winter felling and trimming the firs and spruces and hauling them to the skidways or platforms built out over the banks of the rivers. With the breaking up of the ice in spring, the waiting logs are rafted

GIRLS OF LEKSAND wear their old-fashioned, brightly colored dresses on gala days. Their beautifully embroidered aprons show that they live in Leksand, for in Dalarne the costumes of the peasant folk vary from parish to parish. In Mora, for example, women wear red ribbons in their hair, and in Floda they have roses stitched on their frocks.

McLeish

GUARDS OF THE KING OF SWEDEN IN THEIR OLD-TIME UNIFORM

The Swedes make good soldiers, and at one time they ranked among the best in Europe, owing to the victories that they won early in the eighteenth century under their ambitious king, Charles XII. The dress of Swedish soldiers during that period of military greatness is faithfully reproduced in the uniform worn by these lifeguards.

and sent floating swiftly down the Indals or the Angerman to Sundsvall, to a battery of thirty humming sawmills. Nor is any waste of the precious timber permitted. The largest match factory in the world is operated at Jonkoping. The Swedish match trust once controlled over half the world's output, and became a factor in international finance. Originally an export trust it expanded into a financing organization with branches in several countries. This collapsed with the death of the promoter, Ivar Kruger.

North even of Norrland lies Lapland, a bleak waste of dwarf white birch, creeping willow and boggy tundra where the rosy streamers of the aurora borealis tingle up from the black horizon of the winter night.

Solid Mountain of Iron Ore

Around the head of the Gulf of Bothnia, across from Finland, dwell perhaps thirty-five thousand Finns, whose ancestors migrated from the Ural Mountains before the time of Christ. Here, as in Norway, nomadic tribes of short, dusky Lapps follow their reindeer from pasture to pasture over the moorlands.

In this far North exist some of the richest beds of iron ore in the world. At Gellivara, and at Kiruna, are solid mountains of ore, millions of tons of which are yearly exported. Though Gellivara lies within the Arctic Circle, the winter cold is tempered by the west winds from the Gulf Stream drift which impart, even to the eastern slope of Sweden, a milder quality to the climate than is usual in so high a latitude.

To transport iron ore from Sulea, on an arm of the Baltic, to the port of Narvik in Norway, an electric railroad has been built. The power comes from Porjus Falls, where a mammoth dam and hydro-electric plant were constructed during the long winter dusk, the men working under a glare of electric light. The formation of ice at the dam was prevented by thrusting electric rods into the water. The tourist could journey luxuriously on the Lapland express, for a hundred miles beyond Polar Circle station, to Abisko, on Lake Torne Träsk, which was once regarded as the end of the habitable world.

Abundant Electric Power

While Sweden's industrial development has until of late years been retarded by the lack of coal, the development of her vast resources in electric power is rapidly bringing about an industrial growth, of which the one most important item is the application of electric power to the smelting of iron. The great rivers abound in rapids and waterfalls that can be harnessed for the generation of electricity. The power plant at the Falls of Trollhattan commands two thousand horse power for the turning of factory wheels, and one of Sweden's most notable industries is the manufacture of Diesel engines. Hernösand, on the Gulf of Bothnia, was the first European town to have electric lights, and to-day half the farms employ electrically driven farm and household machinery. The promise of the near future is that the whole of Sweden will be electrified. So much for the more practical side of life. Sweden is also a country in which the white winters have their unique pleasures.

Skiing a Necessity in Winter

It is only of late years that skiing (pronounced *shee-ing*) has become a sport in Sweden. Its importance for a thousand years and more lay in its necessity as a mode of transportation. It was a commonplace in Sweden when the authors of the sixth century described a far northern people, meaning the Lapps, as the "speedily-sliding hunting people," while the skiing of the Norwegians was mentioned in the Sagas. A skier with an arm bow is shown on a runestone of the eleventh century at a crossroads near Upsala. Certain it is that when the Swedes first settled in the northern part of their country, their farms would have been completely isolated the greater part of the year but for skis, nor could those first settlers have been so skillful at hunting but for this footgear.

The first ski races in Sweden were

FISHERMEN OF MÖLLE discuss the fishing season together on a rock overlooking the quiet little haven, to which one of them has just returned from the sea with a few pollack that he has caught on a hand-line. Mölle is the base for a small fishing-fleet. It is situated on the headland of Kullen, which juts out into the Kattegat, the strait that separates Sweden and Denmark. Fishing is not the important industry in Sweden that it is in Norway, but it is carried on, nevertheless, by the inhabitants of many of the sea-coast villages.

© E.N.A

SWEDISH PEASANT GIRLS in their quaint, old-fashioned clothes have a wonderful charm. Their aprons are of soft leather, with the bodices elaborately decorated. The short jackets, fringed with thick wool, and the be-ribboned bonnets, add greatly to the effect of the beautiful dress. We may occasionally see these costumes in the towns.

WATERWAYS AND BRIDGES OF STOCKHOLM, THE CAPITAL OF SWEDEN, SEEN FROM AN AEROPLANE

Sweden has in the Göta Canal a connection between the North and Baltic seas and her inland lakes. This all-important canal, at one point, rises to a level of over three hundred feet above the Baltic. Stockholm itself, the Venice of the North, is intersected by many canals. In the photograph we see the vast swimming-baths, and, beyond the first bridge, the round islet of Strömsborg. Beyond the second bridge is the National Bank, behind which are the Houses of Parliament. To the right of these is seen the huge royal palace.

FLOATING TIMBER DIVIDED BY ITS OWNERS INTO GROUPS

Lumbering is one of the chief industries of Sweden, and the swift rivers of the country are utilized for carrying logs down to the great sawmills on the Gulf of Bothnia. Here, on the River Angerman, below the town of Solleftea, we see the timber as it has been sorted and rafted into sections, paint-branded and bark-marked by its different owners.

those arranged for school boys in the late seventies. The first jumping competition was held in Stockholm in 1880 (and it was won by the Norwegian Guardsmen of the King). After the first international ski races, in 1892, local ski clubs began to be formed throughout Sweden. To-day government-supported courses in skiing are given to school boys, who invariably spend Easter week in the snow-covered mountains of northern Sweden.

Ski relay racing is also practiced. Whereas the Norwegians, with their mountainous country, excel in jumping and short races, the Swedes, by reason of their more nearly level territory, prefer long races in which endurance takes precedence over speed. In the army, skiing is held to be an essential branch

MC LEISH

THIS FIDDLER of Helsingland, a district in eastern Sweden, is a popular figure at every local festival. With his tasselled cap, his long coat with its bright lining carefully displayed, knee-breeches and square-toed shoes, he seems rather a character from history than a man of today, as does also the young man wearing a leather apron.

WEAVING RIBBON such as is worn by Swedish country girls on caps and dresses and as head-bands, this woman of Dalarne is kept busy at her hand-loom. Bright colors worked in beautiful designs upon the aprons, kerchiefs and bonnets of the women, and on the waistcoats and coat-linings of the men, are in high favor with the peasants of Sweden.

41

"THERE'S SOMETHING ABOUT A SOLDIER"

The changing of the guard is always a thrilling ceremony to witness. In the square of the royal palace in Stockholm, built in Italian Renaissance style, the guard presents arms to the stirring accompaniment of the military band in the center background. The palace holds, within its walls, some rare collections of art treasures, among them many fine Gobelin tapestries.

ROYAL OPERA HOUSE IN STOCKHOLM

This view of the Royal Opera House, built in 1898, makes clear the reason why Stockholm is often called the "Venice of the North." The city includes several small islands separated from the Swedish coast by the Skaltsjo, a channel leading to the sea beyond. The islands are connected with the mainland by a number of bridges including the Norrbro and the Vasabro.

of the service. The northern garrisons are, indeed, compelled to use skis for six months of the year. The Swedes love ski-touring, and when the tour extends to the northern mountains, they sleep either in ski huts, or where these are not found, in sleeping-bags laid on the snow. In 1906 members of the ski club of Great Britain came for their first competition. There is now an International Federation. The highest peak in Sweden, Kebnekaise, was climbed for the first time in winter in 1908 by a man on skis. Since that date, ski-mountaineering, as it is called, where rope and ax have to be carried, is a sport of growing popularity.

The Swedes are the tallest race in Europe, the fairest in coloring and the longest lived. There has been little mixture of foreign blood. The Gothic strain represented by the Scandinavian peoples has permeated the blood of many nations.

Thrifty, idealistic, independent, the Swedes are generally well-to-do, aristocratic in their ideals, and enormously efficient. As far back as can be traced, southern Sweden was the home of the Goths. The weapons and utensils of bronze and stone and the skeletons found in the grave mounds all attest to this fact. Sweden proper has a population smaller than that of New York City, but the United States has a quarter as many Swedes as dwell in their ancient homeland.

The people of this hearty Northern race eat five times a day, and as in Norway, begin dinner with a *smörgasbord* of pickled fish, sausages like mosaics, smoked reindeer meat, piquant cheese and black rye bread with sweet butter, or crisp knäckebrod (the ä pronounced like o), resembling thin oat cakes.

This small and homogeneous people of granite self-control and punctilious polite-

Swedish Travel Bureau

SKIING AND SLEDGING AT A SWEDISH HOLIDAY RESORT

Saltsjöbaden is filled with holiday-makers all the year round, since it is famous for its sea-bathing in summer and for all manner of sports on the snow and ice in winter. Swedish children learn to skate and to ski at an early age, and the winters are usually severe enough to give them plenty of chances of showing their skill in such pastimes.

FLOWER-GATHERERS from Leksand wander over the meadows, white and golden with marguerites, that lie along the shores of the Ostervik, an arm of Lake Siljan, in Dalecarlia. This district is considered one of the most beautiful in Sweden; and, as we see here, the natives wear costumes that in charm and color are in keeping with the natural love-liness of the hills and meadows. Dalecarlia, which has been called the Land of the Dales on account of its many valleys, is dotted with little villages and lonely farmhouses.

LAPP CHILDREN have no settled home, since the tribes to which they belong are always wandering from place to place in search of game or of fresh pastures for their reindeer. They live sometimes in rough tents such as this, and sometimes in huts of turf like those ordinarily occupied by Norwegian Lapps. Among them wealth is not reckoned in terms of money, but of reindeer. The man who has several thousand in his herd is accounted rich. Lapp boys wear caps topped with gaily colored woolen tufts, and the girls, hoods.

45

Owen

HOW A LAPP MOTHER OF SWEDEN GIVES HER BABY AN AIRING

In the bleak north of Sweden are wandering tribes of Lapps who live by hunting and by keeping great herds of reindeer, from which they obtain hides for making clothing and an important part of their food in the shape of meat and milk. This baby's cradle, which can be hung from the ceiling when the mother is busy at home, is of reindeer hide.

ness is given to idealism. In 1914 Stockholm adopted a system of liquor control whereby sales are confined to licensed companies. Indeed, the Swedes have become moderate drinkers since the inauguration of the Bratt system, whereby applicants for liquor are investigated and the amounts they may purchase carefully regulated according to their means and personal habits. Divorce is freely obtainable upon mutual consent. This is due in part to the influence of Ellen Key, who advocated marriage for love only. Both men and women over 21 years of age are entitled to vote.

The Swedes, universally well educated, fond of all their arts, are also quick to adopt scientific inventions. They are becoming world-famed for their invention, manufacture and use of intricate electrical appliances, such as their lighthouses regulated by clockwork which need to

be attended only once in three months. Around Stockholm they are also making experiments in the growing of vegetables out of season in soil electrically heated. Since 1911 they have adopted a national trade mark displaying the three crowns on a blue and yellow ground.

There are several fine airports, and aviation, as in most countries, has rapidly developed. Regular passenger and mail service links the cities of Sweden with London and with most of the large cities on the continent.

The traveler will find illuminated maps in the Swedish railway stations, and at Stockholm he may see the native costumes on the cash-girls of the big department stores. Whatever else he does, he should visit the Scandinavian Northern Museum, located out of doors on the Djurgärd, before he leaves the picturesque Swedish capital.

SWEDEN: FACTS AND FIGURES

THE COUNTRY

Boundaries: Finland on the northeast, the Gulf of Bothnia and the Baltic Sea on the east, the Skagerak and Cattegat on the southwest and Norway on the west. Over half the country is covered by forests of pine, birch and spruce, while in the south are oak and beech forests. Total area, 173,403 square miles; population (est. 1948), 6,924,888.

GOVERNMENT

King wields executive power in conjunction with Council of State of about twelve ministers at whose head is the Prime Minister. The Parliament, or Diet, is composed of First and Second Chambers. Members of the former number 150, who are elected by members of the Landstings, or provincial representations, and by electors from six towns outside the Landstings. The Second Chamber has about 230 members elected by universal suffrage for four years. Both sexes over 21 have the right to vote.

COMMERCE AND INDUSTRIES

Agriculture is the principal occupation of the people. The chief crops are hay, fodderroots, potatoes, sugar-beets, oats, rye, wheat and barley. Mineral resources include iron, zinc, sulphur pyrites, copper and coal. Sawmilling, the making of pig iron and steel and the manu-

facture of cream separators, lighthouse apparatus, telephone supplies, motors and electrical machinery, porcelain and glass are among the chief industrial activities. Important exports are wood-pulp and paper manufactures, timber, metal goods and machinery, minerals, glass and earthenware and animal products. The imports include coal, raw textile materials, animal products, corn and flour.

COMMUNICATIONS

There are over 10,346 miles of railway, of which about two-fifths are owned by the state. Telegraph wires aggregate more than 79,338 miles, state telephone lines about 2,156,154 miles. Highway mileage totals 55,940. Post offices number more than 4,635.

RELIGION AND EDUCATION

The Lutheran Protestant Church is recognized as the state religion, but other creeds are permitted.

Public elementary education is compulsory and free. There are secondary schools and special schools of all kinds and two universities (Uppsala and Lund).

CHIEF TOWNS

Population, 1949: Stockholm, capital, 725,714; Göteborg (Gothenburg), 343,983; Malmö, 185-947; Norrköping, 83,279; Hälsingborg, 70,729.

THE FINNISH PEASANTS have high cheek bones, with gray or blue eyes, surprising in their dark faces. Vigorous, hard working, they are tenacious of purpose and serious of mind. This shows the kind of apron, tight bodice and kerchief and the fondness for a touch of red displayed by the women of that land of white birches and white winters.

48

THE LAND OF A THOUSAND LAKES

Finland and Its Progressive People

When one reads of the achievements of the Finns, naturally one expects them to be associated with a large and prosperous people. As a matter of fact the Finns are a small nation (three and a half millions) of Mongoloid origin, like the Hungarians, with whose language the Finnish has some elements in common. The coast of Finland is island-fringed and no country of Europe has an equal area of land that contains so many lakes. Forest covers nearly three-quarters of the land and the abundant waterways provide routes by which lumber and its products may reach the sea. Though under Swedish domination for centuries the Finns had been under Russian control for the hundred years before 1917 when they declared their independence. Swedish is the dominant language in the fringe of Swedish settlements along the Baltic and among the educated Finns. One of the best atlases in the world is that of Finland, and a Finn, Nurmi, proved himself the fastest runner in the world.

AMONG the first people to cross the Ural Mountains from Asia, the Mongol Finns were driven, about 800 A.D. from the Volga to a far northern region of glacier-gouged lakes and fir woods. What we know to-day as the Finnish peninsula presents, at its Arctic end, a granitic bridge of land between Russia and Sweden. Of the early Finns, little is known save that they were piratical sea rovers, until 1157, when Eric IX, King of Sweden, conquered them and brought them with him to Bishop Henry of Upsala to convert them to Christianity.

For the next five centuries Finland was incorporated as an integral part of Sweden. Thus it was that the Western ideals and the Lutheran faith were inculcated to survive even the later period of Russian dominance. In 1710 Peter the Great of Russia entered into a bitter struggle with Charles XII of Sweden in which his troops over-ran the whole of Finland. Sweden made repeated efforts to win back her lost province, and did keep the western part. Russia took over all of Finland in 1809, and Tsar Alexander entered into an agreement for the union of Finland and Russia on the basis that the Finnish constitution should be guaranteed. His successors did not keep the pledge, but attempted to make the country Russian. The Finns resisted stoutly. An oft-quoted saying ran, "We have ceased to be Swedes; we cannot become Russians: we must be Finns." The Declaration of Independence of December 6, 1917, was the outcome. But the Finns had to fight the Red armies of the new Russian state to make good their freedom, and it was not until 1919 that the Finnish republic was set up. Twenty-one years later, Russian troops marched again into Finland, as we shall see later in this chapter. Events seesawed from 1940 to 1945; but after the war the Finns had to cede some of their territory, and also special privileges, to the Soviet Union.

In this land of dense fir and pine woods, lumbering is a leading industry. Fully fifty per cent of the exports are timber, and nearly thirty per cent pulp and paper. Only a little over six per cent of the marshy land is cultivated. Clearings are made in the forest for pasturage and the growing of a few potatoes, flax, and the hardy cereals like rye. There are, however, over 385,000 farms on which three-fifths of the people live.

The parts of the country that are not forested contain many swamps, shallow lakes and rapid rivers. Indeed, the Finnish name for the country is *Suomi,* the swamp-land. To complete the picture, there is probably no part of the earth's surface more dotted with islands than the sea between the Åland Islands and Åbo, the ancient capital.

The rivers, filled with rapids, are excellent for generating electric power.

Cowl

RIVER KEMI SWEEPING PAST ROVANIEMI ON ITS COURSE TO THE GULF OF BOTHNIA

The River Kemi, rising in Lapland, flows in a southerly direction toward the Gulf of Bothnia, three hundred miles away. In the photograph we can see the little town of Rovaniemi. This place is just outside the Arctic Circle, and during the last fortnight in June the Midnight Sun can be seen from a hill close to the town. Northern Finland is not so attractive scenically as the southern portion; much of it is barren and uncultivable and the population is correspondingly small. Indeed, nearly three-quarters of the land is all but uninhabited.

BRIDGE OF TIMBER SPANNING ONE OF THE MANY STREAMS IN THE REPUBLIC OF FINLAND

Streams are so commonly encountered when traveling in Finland, and the amount of traffic over some of the roads is so slight that only the simplest wooden bridges have been thrown over many of the smaller waterways. The footway of this bridge is made of logs—and there is no hand rail to guide one in the dark. The woman riding astride despite her skirts seems to be quite at home in her crude saddle. Parts of Finland are so far from railways that the peasants have to make weary journeys afoot or on horseback.

51

LAKE PAIJANNE, SECOND LARGEST OF FINLAND'S 60,000 LAKES

OLAVINLINNA CASTLE IN THE RESORT TOWN OF SAVONLINNA

But one, the Ulea, is navigable for any great length. Boats of considerable size can traverse its whole length.

The extraordinary system of lakes is connected with the Gulf of Finland by canals that provide about 2,700 miles of navigable inland waterways for ships. Of these canals, the most important is the sluiced canal connecting Lake Saima with the Gulf of Finland. It permits ships from the Baltic to penetrate 270 miles inland. Lake Ladoga, which is cut by the Russian border, is the largest lake.

The three main lake basins are sepa-rated first by low flat hills which finally slope to the Gulf of Bothnia. Narrow moraines of earth and stone left by the ice-sheet run across Finland from north-west to southeast, rising as forested ridges from thirty to a hundred feet or more above the surrounding country.

This labyrinth of lakes, connected by short rapid streams, covers southern Finland. To the north, nearly uninhabited tracts of hill country, the Keel (Kjölen) Mountains, stretch into a land of dark winters where the days are only a few hours long. At the headwaters of the

52

Tornea, Finland reaches a finger into the highlands of Lapland, where flat-topped summits or *fjälls* rise from three to four thousand feet above sea level, and deep-sunk river basins make a dreary waste.

The Karelians, the people of the north and east, nearest Russia, are good musicians and accompany their singing on the national instrument, a kind of zither called the *kantele*. The Finns of the south and west, nearest Sweden, and Tavast-landers, who show that there has been some intermingling of Teutonic stock, are more serious minded and less inclined to play. The Lapps in the extreme north of Finland (as in northern Sweden and Norway) follow their reindeer herds.

The tar industry is an important one.

Portions of the bark are peeled from the pine trees, a little at a time, until the bare trunks are covered with a thick yellow substance. The trees are then felled and placed in a slow kiln shaped like a goblet with a hollow stem. Down the inside of this stem the tar runs into barrels.

The tar boats which take the barrels along the waterways to Uleaborg are specially built to shoot the rapids of the Oulu River, which occur on the last stage of the journey. Only professional pilots are then allowed to take charge of these boats, for the slightest mistake on the part of the helmsman would cause the boat to be dashed to pieces.

In summer Finland is a riot of wild flowers and wild berries, particularly strawberries and raspberries. The moun-

Courtesy, Finnish Travel Information Bureau

HOTEL AT ROVANIEMI, THREE MILES FROM THE ARCTIC CIRCLE

Much of the extensive territory in the far north of Europe, known as Lapland, belongs to Russia, but a part is divided between Sweden, Norway and Finland. In Finnish Lapland, it is estimated that there are about 2,000 Laplanders. Since the building of Petsamo Road to the Arctic Ocean and the completion of Rovaniemi, the capital, with a modern hotel, many tourists have been attracted to Lapland during the summer months.

PART OF THE GREAT BELT OF CONIFEROUS FOREST ON WHICH FINLAND'S CHIEF INDUSTRY DEPENDS

This photograph shows a group of lumbermen standing on a float with hooked poles collecting the logs as they come down stream, and distributing them into proper formation. These logs will be converted into building timber, wood pulp and paper, resin and turpentine. The pine forests, which grow in a belt from Sweden to the Amur lowlands, cover half the country. Finland has, in her forests, a source of livelihood for large numbers of her people. Lumbering is her main industry, and the crown forests cover a third of her area.

Photo by Burton Holmes, from Ewing Galloway

IMATRA RAPIDS, AN IMPORTANT SOURCE OF FINLAND'S ABUNDANT ELECTRIC POWER

The mighty rapids shown above, which are formed by the Vuoksen through which Lake Saima drains into Lake Ladoga, are estimated to be equal to 140,000 horse power. Finland lacks coal but possesses, in the rapid streams which connect her labyrinth of lakes, the abundance of water power which—used directly or transmitted in the form of electricity—makes possible the operation of her many sawmills and such other industries as the conversion of her timber into paper and wood-pulp and of her flax into linen. It also supplies electric current for lighting.

A COUNTRY OF SMALL FARMS

A large percentage of Finnish people live in rural areas. This scene in Somerniemi, in southern Finland, is typical. Agriculture is the country's chief occupation, accounting for the employment of about a million men and women. However, cultivated farm land comprises only a small part of the country's land surface, and it is divided into many small holdings.

56

tain ash is abundant and in autumn its brilliant scarlet berries add to the beauty of the countryside.

Bears and wolves, which were once found all over the country, have now almost disappeared. The elk has been saved by the game laws. Reindeer are found only in Lapland. In winter, Lapps come into Torneå with sledge loads of reindeer flesh, horns and skins.

Finnish life has to be arranged to suit the climate, which is characterized by a short, hot summer when everything grows quickly, followed by six months of winter. Torneå, at the head of the Gulf of Bothnia, has then only three hours of daylight, and the whole country is covered with snow. The lakes, rivers and canals are frozen for months.

Finnish hospitality always includes a good cup of coffee. The coffee-pot is kept on the back of the stove in constant readiness. With it one eats rye bread, smoked herring, sardines, dried reindeer meat, curdled milk, and the most excellent milk, butter, and potatoes.

The Finnish steam-bath is a peculiarly national affair. Every village and every farmstead throughout the country possesses a bathhouse. This is a large room with tree trunks fixed against the wall to form rough seats. On the floor is a heap of stones which have been heated in an oven or by a wood-fire. A pail of water is thrown on the stones, and this causes the room to be filled with steam. The bathers sit on the lowest seats at first and mount to the higher ones as they get used to the steam, meanwhile beating each other with thin birch twigs. The bath ends with a plunge into a cold stream, or sometimes with a roll in the snow.

For centuries Finland has excelled in the art of making beautiful rugs, and in olden days these rugs were part of a bride's dowry. They were used as bedspreads and as wall-hangings.

Finnish Legation

SEAL HUNTER SIGHTING HIS QUARRY FAR OUT ON THE ICE

In winter, when men shoot seals, they creep up to their quarry by lying flat on sledges propelled over the frozen sea by their feet. Their approach is concealed behind a piece of white material in which they have loopholes for their rifles. Or they may dispense with the sledge and creep over the ice camouflaged in white attire.

In November the Folk High Schools are opened. These institutions are found all over Finland, and now the young people who have worked on the farms all summer go on with their education.

The state offers instruction in dairy farming, navigation and other matters of practical interest, there are free libraries and lectures, and a number of co-operative agricultural societies. The University of Helsinki is an excellent climax to the public school system, and Finland is the home of several scientific societies of wide repute.

Politically and economically women have almost complete equality: they may enter any occupation and any profession save that of the Church and the Army. There are women lawyers, architects, government employees, and bank cashiers. Every girl is brought up to earn her own living, and women do not, usually, give up their work when they marry. As one consequence of woman's economic independence, divorce is easily secured. After a year of separation the marriage may be dissolved by mutual consent, without publicity.

Ancient Runes and Ballads

The Finns of pagan times had deified the forces of nature, and the country festivals still bear the stamp of these early beliefs. During the long summer twilights, they still clasp hands and sing the ancient runes and ballads which tell of the days when there was magic in the land. Superstition dictates many quaint customs. Thus, when a Finn enters a house in a remote region, he always says, "Good-day to all here," even if he is about to enter an empty farmhouse, for who knows that the *tomatar* (brownie) of the place might not otherwise be offended and work a mischief! It is a bad sign to hear a water-keppie shrieking from a pool. But then if you lose your way in the forest or on the sea, there is the Twilight Maiden who, if properly invoked, will spin a thread of gold to lead you home.

Wood-smoke and the fragrant odor of pine-trees, with the ax of the logger ringing on the wintry air—that is Finland in winter. The farmhouses are often of logs chinked closely with clay, with the roof at a steep slant to throw off the snow. Within, the huge wood stove as large as a furnace keeps everything snug.

The Spring Log Drive

In spring when the ice breaks out of the rivers, the loggers raft their winter's cut of logs to go downstream over the falls and rapids. The short, hot summer is a time of planting and harvesting such crops as have time to ripen, and often the grain has to be cured in the fall by artificial heat.

Thousands of tons of paper are exported every year. Electricity is generated from the waterfalls. The farmer in Finland finds it as lucky to have a water fall on his lands as the farmer in America finds it to discover an oil well. In addition, there is iron in the lakes, and in Finland's four thousand factories, iron-working is second to wood-working.

At Imatra, the finest falls in Finland are scenically so beautiful that every tourist visits them as a matter of course. These falls, rushing down a precipitous gorge, have been harnessed by the Imatra power plant (capacity, 216,000 horse power) which was put in operation in 1929. Tampere is built around a cataract that provides power for its cotton mills, and the falls go thundering down the main square—a foaming staircase.

Falls Turning Factory Wheels

Owing to the absence of coal, manufactures depend on water power or the electricity generated from water power. Such raw materials as logs and flax are converted into lumber, pulp and paper, linen and linseed oil respectively. The dairy farms yield butter for export. Finnish barley is a source of beer.

The peasants no longer wear a distinctive dress. The men generally prefer rough tweeds and high boots in the winter, and linen blouses secured around their waists by leather belts during the summer. The women wear bodices and

Finnish Legation

TAR BOAT WHICH SHOOTS THE RAPIDS IN FINLAND

Rapids are frequently encountered on the rivers of Finland, and the Finns have devised a special type of long, narrow boat for the purpose of shooting them. In the south the peasants go to church by boat, because the many shallow lakes would make a journey by land many times as long. These community owned boats will often accommodate a hundred people on the labyrinth of waterways that complicate travel in South Finland.

E. Young

FINNISH FARMER ON HIS WHEELLESS HAY WAIN

The crude hay wagon, made and used by farmers in Finland reminds one of the pony drag of the horse Indians of the Pacific Northwest, although the curved poles of the hay cart, so like the runners of a sleigh, do come nearer to taking the place of wheels than does the Cayuse contrivance. The horse is harnessed in the Russian manner.

aprons, the latter often being neatly embroidered. A colored handkerchief is the favorite headdress.

Helsinki (Helsingfors), which became the capital in 1821, has a unique architecture. Its stone and brick buildings are frequently ornamented with swans or frogs. It is a city of many bookshops, and one ought not to omit mention of the Kalevala, an epic volume containing the folk songs dating from the remotest times. These were handed down in metrical form in peasant households from one generation to another. The city is built on a rock and has one of the finest harbors in the world. The entrance to it is so narrow that large ships can enter only one at a time through a cleft in the rocky barrier. Helsinki was once protected by the fortress of Sveaborg, but this is now only an historical monument.

Within the harbor are numerous islands, one of which is occupied by Zoological Gardens and another by a park, with buildings for the meeting of various societies. Hogholm is a lovely island where, in summer, people come in hundreds to dine under the trees.

Nation-wide Prohibition

The republic should be of special interest to the United States because the two countries introduced, and after trial repealed nation-wide prohibition. It is interesting to recall, in this connection, that Finland was (with Norway) the first of the nations of Europe to accord full suffrage to women, and the women were practically unanimous in their support of the dry programme. The country districts seemed to favor prohibition at first as the law allowed them ample supplies of strong beverages for weddings and christenings, Christmas and St. John's Day. Remember also that Finland is a country—most of the year—of gray skies and a fierce struggle with nature for the means of human existence, of strong men who can stand amazing quantities of strong drink. Remember especially that the Finns (barring the Swedes within their borders) are of Mongol rather than of Nordic extraction. They are highly educated and liberal in their views. Public opinion, fruit of innumerable temperance societies, was ripe for prohibition at the time the Tsar of Russia imposed it as a war emergency measure. Later, when Finland elected to be independent, she continued prohibition. It was found that the law could not be enforced and in 1931 prohibition was replaced by government monopoly.

Russia Attacks Finland

Several months after the beginning of World War II, the Russians discovered that the Finnish border was too near Leningrad for Russia's safety. They demanded that the Finns give up considerable territory and lease the port of Hanko for a naval base. Finland refused, and on November 30, 1939, the Russians attacked. Despite brave resistance, the Finns were forced to yield, after 105 days of fighting. They had to give up 16,173 miles of territory, including the port of Hanko.

When the Germans attacked Russia in June, 1941, the Finns entered the war on Germany's side. With German aid they succeeded in regaining practically all of the territory ceded to Russia. After the war they were forced to make even greater concessions to Russia.

Ice Automobile Races

The short twilight of the winter day in Helsinki finds the streets white lanes of silence, save as the jingle of the *droshky* bells enlivens the crisp air. People huddle by in deep fur coats, their breath smoking, save on bright Sundays when they appear on skis, the girls in knickers and gay sweaters. The frozen harbor becomes the scene of ice hockey and of hair-raising automobile races. The better streets are cleaned by a device invented in Finland—a log-burning machine which melts successive hopperfuls of snow; and each merchant is obliged by law to keep the snow removed from his half of the highway.

The summers present an extreme contrast, with their long evenings, magical with sunset colors, and their restaurants

A WEDDING CUSTOM STILL OBSERVED BY THE PEASANTS

At one time many curious ceremonies were observed at weddings in Finland. One of the strangest was that of lecturing the bride until she cried. In the photograph we see the guests at the wedding feast witnessing the removal of the bridal veil. Unfortunately for the tourist, it is only in the country districts that these old customs survive to-day.

Apollo

EVERY PEASANT HOME HAS A COSY CORNER BY THE STOVE

In the peasants' cottages we shall always find a big white stove, about which the family sits during the long, cold winter. The wide hearth is raised several feet above the floor, and a flat projection at one side of the stove makes a warm bed. The cottages may be only one story wooden structures scantily furnished, but the stove provides cheer and comfort.

FINLAND—TIMBERLAND

Seventy-five per cent of Finland's land surface, or more than 60,000,000 acres, is heavily wooded with fir, spruce and birch.   More than 40,000,000 acres are cultivated forest lands whose crops keep the country's sawmills humming constantly.   The logs we see are floating to their mill through a series of lakes connected by canals.   This is Lake Lohja, in the southern part of Finland.

ARE THESE LOAVES DATED?

Although these women appear to be hanging up moccasins, they are actually suspending dozens of flat loaves of sour rye bread from the kitchen rafters. The bread is baked in huge quantities and hung up to dry. One baking will provide a family with bread for many months to come. The people of Finland are used to working hard and for long hours on end.

rhythmic with dance music. People perform marvelous feats of swimming and sail boating, large numbers retire to their villas on neighboring islands, commuting to the city on small steamers, and the market place is scoured daily by women with brooms and men with capacious hose.

Åbo, the ancient capital, was burned in 1827, and its library almost destroyed. Here three wonderful ice-breakers are used to keep open a channel to Åbo (now called Turku) throughout the winter.

Viipuri has had over six centuries of eventful history. Its castle, built by a Swedish nobleman, is romantically situated on a small island. In the center of the market place is a massive round tower, a remnant of the old fortifications which goes by the name of Fat Katarina. Viipuri has seen much warfare.

Borga is a place of steep, cobbled streets twisting up and down hill, and of wooden houses, red, yellow and green, clustered about a gray, old cathedral rich in wood-carvings, old brass, wall sconces and crystal chandeliers. It is probably the quaintest town in Finland.

The Åland Islands belong to Finland.

NEW RAILWAY STATION IN TAMPERE, FINLAND'S INDUSTRIAL CENTRE

Courtesy, Finnish Travel Information Bureau

CROWDED MORNING MARKET BY THE SOUTHERN HARBOR, HELSINKI

Helsinki, which is situated on a peninsula, possesses two harbors. In Southern Harbor, steamers come to anchor alongside the market place (the Salu Tors) where loads of produce from the surrounding district are brought for sale.

HELSINKI'S FAMOUS RAILWAY
STATION

RED-ROOFED CATHEDRAL IN
TAMPERE

COURTESY, FINNISH TRAVEL INFORMATION BUREAU

PARLIAMENT BUILDING IN HELSINKI, COMPLETED IN 1931

MONUMENT TO SPORTS

The huge stadium at Helsinki, dominated by its tall, modernistic tower, is a monument to the Finnish love of sports. In 1938, Helsinki was selected by the International Olympics Committee as the site of the 1940 games, which never materialized because of World War II. The stadium, completed in 1940, fulfilled its purpose when the Olympics came to Helsinki in 1952.

FINLAND: FACTS AND FIGURES

THE COUNTRY

Bounded on the north by Norway, on the west by Sweden and the Gulf of Bothnia, on the south by the Gulf of Finland, and on the east by Russia; 10% of the area is covered by lakes which are mostly in the southern part. Area, 130,165 square miles including 12,190 square miles of inland waters. According to 1944 armistice with Russia, Finland agreed to cede to Russia the Petsamo area and to lease to Russia for 50 years the Parkala headland. Population, (1950 est.) 4,028,910.

GOVERNMENT

Republic since 1919. President elected for six years and House of Representatives of 200 members for three years. Sixteen electoral districts with proportional representation. Universal suffrage at age of twenty-one. Voting system devised towards proportional representation.

COMMERCE AND INDUSTRIES

Agriculture is the chief occupation of the people, although only 6.6% of the land is cultivated. The principal crops are hay, oats, barley, rye and potatoes. Lumbering and fishing are important industries and dairy-farming is increasing. The chief exports are timber, paper and pulp, and butter, and the imports are textiles, cereals, metals and machinery.

COMMUNICATIONS

Railway mileage, 3,105, largely state-owned. Lakes connected with each other and with Gulf of Finland by canals. There are 28,704 miles of telegraph and 253,620 miles of telephone wires partly owned by the state (1948).

RELIGION AND EDUCATION

The national church is the Evangelical Lutheran with liberty of conscience guaranteed. Education is well developed. There are 11 training schools for elementary teachers and 3 universities (a state university at Helsinki, and a Finnish and a Swedish university at Turku). In addition there are numerous special schools.

CHIEF TOWNS

Population, 1950: Helsinki (Helsingfors), capital, 363,834; Tampere (Tammerfors), 103,-043; Turku, 101,239; Pori, 43,137; Vaasa, 34,-516; Oulu, 37,449; Lahti, 44,759; Kuopio, 32,-261; Jyvaskyla, 30,143; and Kotka, 24,138.

ISLANDS OF FIRE AND ICE

Iceland's Norsemen and the Eskimos of Greenland

Iceland, so-called because the Norsemen who landed there in the ninth century found ice in one of the fjords, is rather a land of fire than of ice. The island is composed entirely of volcanic matter and more than one hundred volcanoes still exist, while there are scores of hot springs and lakes of boiling mud. The folk of Iceland are the descendants of Norsemen as well as early Irish and others. They have developed into hard-working farmers and fishermen. Greenland, a vast island the interior of which is covered by an ice-cap that breaks off in huge bergs, was colonized by Eric the Red, who sailed over from Iceland. To-day a colony of Denmark, this land—green only in midsummer along a narrow coastal area—is inhabited chiefly by Eskimos who live on fish and seal meat.

ALTHOUGH Carthaginian mariners left fragmentary records of voyages into northern waters. Iceland was little known to Europe until adventurous Norsemen landed on the east coast about 850. They found a small colony of Irish already there and more Irish as well as Norsemen came later. The story of the early times is set down in the famous "Landnamabok" which may be translated "Book of Settlements." By 930 they had established good government, with an Althing or General Court of Parliament. Though largely employed in fishing and sheep-herding, they wrote sagas in the twelfth century which Icelandic children of to-day can read in the original twelfth-century Norse. In the thirteenth century Iceland established a personal union with Norway, retaining her ancient rights and laws; but in the fourteenth century passed with Norway under the rule of Denmark. In time Lutheranism was imposed by Danish battleships, a trade monopoly was likewise established by the stronger nation, and by the eighteenth century the handful of Icelanders had no outward independence left. By 1845, however, they were able to re-establish their Althing, and soon after a really great statesman came forward in the person of Jon Sigurdsson. In 1854, by throwing the trade of Iceland open to the world, he laid the foundation for the national prosperity of to-day, and in 1874 he achieved a constitution. In 1903 the Danish Minister to Iceland was displaced by an Icelandic Prime Minister, and in 1918 an Act of Union as between two independent nations was signed. In 1941, Iceland declared its complete independence.

Iceland is one of the most completely volcanic countries in the world. Indeed, in 1783, volcanic eruptions destroyed nearly nine thousand lives—an all but overwhelming disaster. The largest volcano, Hekla, in south Iceland, has made the surrounding country a desert, owing to the dust and boiling lava that it hurls out from time to time. Its last great eruption occurred in 1845. In the tableland of the interior, geysers and hot springs occur, often high in the unweathered lava of the mountain peaks amid ice and snow. The Great Geyser has a crater sixteen feet in diameter and intermittently spouts a column of boiling water over a hundred feet in height.

An island lying a little under six hundred miles to the northwest of the European mainland, it is possible that in recent geologic times Iceland was formed by volcanic eruptions along a crack in the earth's crust running through the Faroes toward Ireland. Though Iceland touches the Arctic Circle on the north, its southwestern portion is laved by the milder, fog-breeding waters of the North Atlantic drift. Of the ice-fields, Vatna. the largest, which in places rises to six thousand feet. is in the south.

Around the rugged coasts there are many islands, and on one group, called the Vestmanna Islands, the chief means of support of the inhabitants are the count-

GREENLAND: A COLONY OF DENMARK

less sea birds which have made their homes in the cliffs. These cliffs are the property of the government and are hired out to the islanders, who are experts in scaling the precipitous heights. They catch one variety of bird, the puffin, in a huge net not unlike that used by butterfly collectors.

The eider ducks, from which we get the eider down used for stuffing quilts, are also found in Iceland, and the birds are so tame that they will allow the islanders to stroke them while they are seated on their nests. The ducks pluck the down from their breasts to line their nests, and it is then collected and exported. The poor birds replace the down.

Reykjavik, on Faxa Fiord, is a trade center to which once a year the outlying farmers come with their trains of laden ponies to sell their wool. The town has a cathedral and a university, a state hospital, telephones and a radio station, and to the modern harbor come the half-dozen mail steamers of Iceland's steam-

ship company. Young people are taught English and Danish. One of the world's greatest sculptors, Einar Jónsson, was born at Reykjavik. During World War II the United States established an operations base here.

At Framnes and elsewhere on the northwest peninsula there are various whaling stations. The whaling vessels shoot their harpoons from cannon. On shore, the blubber is cut up by rotary machines and is then steamed to extract the oil, while the bones and refuse are converted into manure products for shipment to other countries.

The fishing, which is one of the most important industries, is conducted by means of steam trawlers and motor cutters. Quantities of split codfish are exported, chiefly to Spain, as is some herring and a little fish oil.

Dairying and sheep raising are important. Coal, petroleum, machinery and textiles have to be imported. There is a little gold in the country, but it has not been exploited. One interesting small export is Iceland spar, a refracting crystal used in optical instruments. In the waterfalls of the turbulent rivers, all of which flow northward except the Thorsa, there is great potential electric power and some of it has already been generated for lighting the larger towns. A much more extensive development is under way.

THE REPUBLIC OF ICELAND

GREENLAND HUNTERS CUTTING UP SEAL-MEAT

Seals are plentiful in the waters around Greenland. From these creatures the natives obtain food, clothing, lamp-oil and (from the dried membranes) window-panes. The sledge in the picture, on which the meat is to be taken home, is camouflaged with a square of linen to make it appear to the prospective quarry like a block of ice.

Iceland's small population is increasing. Somewhat more than half lives either in Reykjavik, the capital, or in smaller towns and villages. There is a public school system, prohibition has been in force since 1912 (save as Spain has induced Iceland to import Spanish wines), half a hundred savings banks exist and practically everyone contributes to an Old Age Pension Fund. Though several woolen factories have been established, they are looked upon chiefly as a possibility of the near future.

The real life of Iceland is not to be seen in the towns but among the little farms that are scattered over the roadless wastes. The typical Icelandic farm has a roof of turf and is surrounded by sheds and barns built of turf and bowlders. The windows are usually fastened shut for the winter, though a small opening which can be closed as required affords ventilation. Kerosene is the usual lamp fuel and peat the cooking fuel.

The entire family sleeps in a large room in the upper story, where bunks filled with dried seaweed and feathers serve as beds. No one could be more hospitable than these Icelandic farmers. They give of their best. Skyr is a favorite dish—a clotted milk eaten with sugar. There is also river salmon. When

Danish Legation

OFF THE COAST OF GREENLAND: ESKIMO WOMEN IN AN UMIAK, OR WOMEN'S BOAT

The umiaks used by the women are flat-bottomed boats made of sealskin stretched over wooden frames. These roomy vessels, stouter than the kayaks chiefly favored by the men, have flat bottoms and can carry heavy loads. They are used for moving the tribe and its belongings from one fishing-station to another, and are usually guided by one old man at the stern. The west coast is ice-bound in winter but open water prevails during most of the summer. Notice the elaborate beaded collars of several of the girls.

A MODERN HOSPITAL ON GREENLAND'S BLEAK SHORE

Few people live in Greenland, and those who do lead hazardous lives, fishing and hunting in icy waters or over treacherous fields of snow. This fine modern hospital is at Umanak, a hamlet of about 1,400 people on the coast of western Greenland. All the settlements on the island are along the coast, the only part that is ever even briefly green.

a visitor has finished his meal, with which delicious coffee is always served, he rises and says: "Thanks for the meal." The answer is always: "May it do you good." Their speech is the old Norse spoken a thousand years ago by the Scandinavian peoples, and their frames are tall and virile.

The farmer makes the most of the poor soil, growing turnips, potatoes, and hay. His chief occupation is the breeding of sheep and ponies. The flocks near the coast sometimes eat seaweed if grass is scarce, but a large proportion of the productive land is devoted to grass, and much hay is raised for the cattle as well as root crops.

The ponies play an important part on the farms. The roads in Iceland are few and bad, and horses are the chief means of transport. Indeed, there is one pony to every two persons. Sleighs are used in winter where the roads permit. In southern Iceland, however, good roads and bridges are being built and motorcars are becoming common.

We may often meet a girl leading a string of ponies each of which carries two cans of milk. They must go slowly to avoid churning the milk into butter.

These ponies are small and sturdy, their coats are long and their tails are thicker than those of horses. During a storm they turn their backs to the wind and their tails spread over their flanks, forming a natural protection. The ponies

PROUD OWNER

This Greenland lad's greatest treasures are his three husky-dog pups with which he is delighted to pose. The population of the island is composed of a few hundred Europeans, mostly Danes, and of non-Europeans who are called Greenlanders. Some in the less populous districts are pureblooded Eskimos, but most of the natives are of mixed European and Eskimo origin.

72

GREENLANDERS STUDY GEOGRAPHY

The schools of Greenland are largely under church tutelage. The Danish Minister of Public Worship appoints and pays the salaries of Danish and Moravian missionaries, who foster education. Instruction in the schools is in the native, or Eskimo, language. The display board at the right shows a model of a kayak, a sixteen-foot-long canoe that is usually made of sealskins.

HOT OFF THE PRESS!

A Greenlandic newspaper, printed in the Eskimo language, is being prepared for distribution. Since 1861 there have been several monthly periodicals appearing somewhat irregularly. Textbooks, pamphlets, official circulars and books are also printed at this office. A really native literature is evolving, covering religious subjects, biographies and books of popular interest.

are sure footed and carry their loads across fields of lava with a certainty that even a mule might envy. When a visitor calls at a farm he never lets his ponies graze near the buildings. The farmer would regard it as discourteous, for every blade of grass is precious.

Some Eskimo Stories

Now let us turn to the neighboring Greenland chiefly inhabited by Eskimos, though there are a few hundred whites and more of mixed blood. The Eskimos are interesting, and so are their dogs which are harnessed like the ribs of a fan in Greenland though they are driven tandem in Canada, or in pairs in Alaska. In fact Eskimos differ widely in different regions.

During the winter nights, the Eskimos occupy themselves with various handicrafts, making their clothing and their weapons from the materials at hand. As they work, they tell one another stories. A favorite tale runs thus: One day an old woman was scraping a wolfskin to cleanse it. By and by a strange man came and asked her what skin she was scraping. When she replied that it was a wolfskin he uttered a prolonged howl and ran off on all fours, for he was a wolf-man. Next day the old woman saw a great gathering of wolves, foxes and bears outside her hut, all growling savagely. "Ah!" she cried, "come in, all of you. I am boiling berries to make a pudding. You shall taste it if you will come into my hut."

She deceived them, however. First she put a pot of water on the fire to boil. Then she laid wet wood on the fire and stopped up the smokehole so that the hut was full of smoke. As the animals coughed and choked, and felt for the door to escape, she seized her husband's harpoon and slew them all. Thus she obtained their skins, which were of great value.

The Sun Swings Around the Sky

Greenland is a vast, inhospitable island, a waste of glaciers and snow-clad plateaus, the population of which (chiefly Eskimo) is over sixteen thousand. An island eight hundred miles wide by seventeen hundred long, this region is separated on the northwest by a narrow strait from Grant Land, Grinnell Land and Ellesmere Land.

In winter, when the Arctic night has settled down over the north, Greenland is a land of silence, save for the beating of the winds across the bitter wastes and the rustle of the hard flakes, when the snow shuts out the stars. But in the swift two months of summer even the treeless tundras brighten into mats of wild flowers —the seeds of which may have been brought by birds. In all frankness, myriads of mosquitoes also breed in the pools of melting snow. The sun swings around the sky, never once dipping clear beneath the horizon for a hundred and thirty nights as seen from Northern Greenland.

Half-way down the west coast, off the Nugsuak Peninsula, the tourist approaching by steamer is charmed by a scene of high blue mountains rising abruptly from the sea, while the cliffs of the shoreline gleam pink, with streaks of gray-green lichen in their seams, and eider ducks and Arctic tern in summer residence along their tops. Beneath, in the sounding sea, mountains of ice that have broken off from the interior ice-cap float green-blue and sparkling, with all but their peaks submerged. At times they float together with reverberating booms, startling the gulls into grating cries. Seals, peering about with sleek puppy-like heads, hump themselves over the water-darkened rocks or dive as some kayak, manned by a Mongol-faced Eskimo with spear upraised, comes darting toward them.

Flowers Fringe the Ice-Cap

Only along the southern coast are there treelike growths. There, in summer, the mean temperature is 46 degrees above zero, and the ground is not frozen for several feet beneath the surface; the dwarf birches and willow bushes spread out into lush green mats and the pale yellow of Arctic poppies embroiders the mossy tundra, clear to the eternal ice-cap that gleams a few miles inland.

Curiously enough, the northwest coast from Peary Land to Washington Land presents a broad stretch of water nearly free, in summer, of floating ice. The water off the eastern coast, however, is so distraught by opposing currents that the warring ice-cakes prevent ships from approaching.

The better part of Greenland consists of some of the most ancient rocks on earth. Throughout geologic time, invasions of the sea have left deposits of sediment on the submerged edge of the ancient plateau. From these sands and muds of various ages now hardened into rocks, we have a record of times past.

The glaciers break off when they reach the coast and form the icebergs so dreaded by sailors. Large bergs may rise as much as four hundred feet, though only one-ninth above water. In the sunshine they appear like huge ships of cut glass, but as they drift down to the Banks of Newfoundland they gradually vanish under the melting influence of the warmer seas.

The Eskimos of Greenland are chiefly found on the coast. A merry, friendly Mongoloid people whose menfolk stand little over five feet in height, they dress in furs, harpoon fish and seals, and love to eat the nourishing whale blubber when they can get this delicacy. But they have fallen an easy prey to diseases introduced by the white man.

The life of the Eskimos is one continual struggle to obtain food. They can live only where there is game, and when

THE COOKING DEVICE IN AN ESKIMO HOME OF GREENLAND

Moss probably forms the wick that dips into the seal oil and heats the container hung from the wooden frame. Now and again the cook pokes the wick with a sharp bone to brighten the flame. Dinner will probably consist of stewed seal meat. Notice the woman's Mongoloid hair and features and her heavy fur coat that serves as protection from the severe cold.

they have killed all the game in one district they move elsewhere. In the spring the tribes voyage from place to place, hunting the seal, walrus, reindeer, bears and eider ducks, and with the coming of the Arctic winter return to their villages. Their houses are usually built of stone, and the walls are covered with sealskins. A stone bench is used as a bed, dried grass forms the mattress and skins the bed clothes. Material for the windows is made from the dried membrane of seals.

The Eskimo boats are of two kinds, both made of sealskin stretched over a framework of wood. The hunter's boat is the kayak, a graceful craft propelled by a double paddle. The umiak, the women's boat, is used to transport the household goods during the spring migration. It must be greased with fat every other day to keep it water-tight.

The Eskimos depend upon seals for many things and hunt them cleverly. When the winter ice forms on the sea,

the seals make breathing-holes in it. An Eskimo, having found such a hole, takes his spear and waits patiently for the seal to come up to breathe. He may wait for hours, because the seal may have many such holes scattered over a large area; but sooner or later it will come to the fatal hole, and the sound of its breathing is the signal for the patient hunter to thrust his harpoon.

In the short Arctic spring this method is not practicable, because the seals crawl on to the ice to sleep in the sun. They are so afraid of polar bears, however, that they will bob up and down in the water for a long while before coming out to enjoy their sleep. Now is the Eskimo's chance. He lies down and, concealing his spear, commences to creep toward his prey. At once the seal raises its head suspiciously and moves a little nearer the water. The hunter instantly begins to imitate the actions of a seal crawling on the ice, and, if the imitation is good, he

MONKMEYER

TRANSPORTATION, INCORPORATED

These Iceland ponies are a well-known breed, of Celtic strain, similar to those formerly to be found in the north of Ireland and in the Hebrides. They are small and sturdy, usually of a dull yellowish color. Wide use is made of them in transporting goods and equipment from the coast to the interior, and they are a most common means of transportation throughout the island.

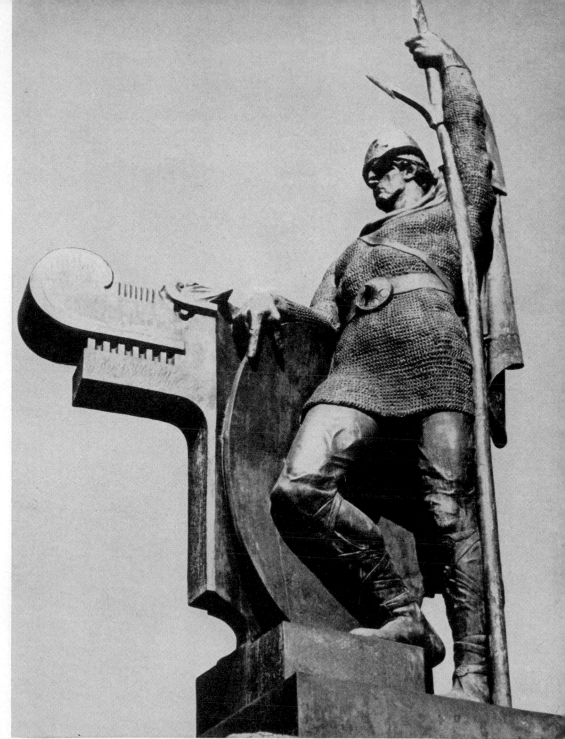

VIGOROUS STATUE OF A HARDY NORSEMAN

In Reykjavik, capital of Iceland, stands a huge statue of Leif Ericson, explorer and mariner. He was the son of Eric the Red. Leif is believed to have landed somewhere on the North American continent in the eleventh century. Here he established a community, which he called Vinland because of the profusion of vines that he found growing in the region.

77

NO RED HERRING IN THIS SHIPMENT

Fishing is a major industry in Iceland, where a large percentage of the people depend on it for support. Cod and herring are the chief catch, and herring oil is produced in great quantities. The Icelanders manufacture fishing equipment and crates in which the fish products are exported. The barrels on the wharf above contain herring, packed and ready for shipment.

HOT HOUSES OPERATED BY NATURAL STEAM

Volcanic activity plays an important part in Iceland's history and progress. Geysers and hot springs dot the island. Although much of Iceland's water power, roughly 2,500,000 horsepower, is still unharnessed, hot houses like those above are heated by the underground waters. Flowers, fruit and vegetables, once unknown in this northern area, can be raised in this way.

THE BRIDE KEEPS HER NAME

The wedding dress of this Icelandic bride is exquisitely embroidered in gold, which harmonizes with her linked belt and jeweled bracelet. The veil is of fine lace. The bride will not assume her husband's surname as is customary in most countries. In fact, surnames are less important here than elsewhere, and even telephone directories are arranged according to given names.

will be able to deceive his quarry. Gradually he approaches nearer and nearer, until he gets within range and can plunge his spear into the creature.

The clothes of the Eskimos are made of the skins of various animals. The women, like the men, wear sealskin trousers, and over these pull the native boots, or kamiker. The skins from which the boots are made are first chewed by the women to soften them, a practice which rapidly wears down the teeth. In the more civilized districts the women wear a long blouse of imported cloth, and their coarse black hair is adorned with ribbons. The unmarried women wear blue ribbons and the widows black. The women ornament their costumes either with beads, colored leather or feathers. They carry their babies in hoods which hang down the backs of their tunics.

The Plague of Mosquitoes

The great plague of Greenland in summer is not wolves or bears. It is the mosquitoes, that rise in clouds from the swamps and make life a misery to man and beast. Once the howls of a bear attracted the notice of some hunters. It was found that the animal had been so terribly bitten about the nose, eyes and ears that it was forced to open its mouth to breathe. The mosquitoes then bit its tongue and throat so severely that they, too, swelled, and the bear was suffocated. White people cover their heads with nets of fine gauze which keep these pests at bay.

Greenland was discovered perhaps as early as 900, and its parliament began about 1000. When the Norseman, Eric the Red, sailing over from Iceland, discovered its brief summer verdure he induced a band of his countrymen to come with sheep and cattle and colonize, in 985 or 986. (The ruins of that colony, which lasted for four hundred years, may still be seen.) In 1261 the Republic of Greenland voluntarily became a part of the then powerful Kingdom of Norway, but the original Norse colonists perished. The hardy Norsemen had built several towns, and at Harjolfsnes, one of the

larger settlements, there were a cathedral and several monasteries. The settlements maintained a flourishing trade with Europe, and it is recorded that they contributed a large quantity of walrus ivory to assist the Crusaders.

The Norse in Greenland

About 1300, some think that there may have been climatic changes in Greenland. It became colder, and the coast grew more and more ice-bound. At this time, too, the Norwegian shipping was suffering a decline. Early in the fifteenth century, the settlements were left to their fate. The Eskimos were coming southward, following the seals, and many encounters between the newcomers and the Norsemen are mentioned before all records cease.

Much medieval clothing was found in the tombs at Harjolfsnes, none dating later than the fifteenth century, a fact which would seem to show that this period saw the end of the Norse colonies in Greenland. Of the manner of their passing we know nothing, but, in view of known facts, it may be surmised that the enfeebled settlements were gradually overwhelmed.

Relations with Denmark

In 1721, a Danish missionary, Hans Egede, brought a Danish colony to Greenland which made several west coast settlements and established a trade with Denmark. It is now the only colonial possession of Denmark. The first data from which the north coastline was mapped were supplied by a Danish explorer, Knud Rasmussen, and by Admiral R. E. Peary of the U. S. Navy. In 1888 Fridtjof Nansen crossed the interior ice-cap on snowshoes, the first of a number of explorers to negotiate it successfully. To-day aviators can secure a bird's-eye view of a region in which inland travel was formerly a matter of snowshoes and sledges drawn by husky dogs. But the land is an unfriendly one and the largest settlement, Sydproven, has under a thousand inhabitants.

Various scientific expeditions have been

ESKIMO CHILDREN look forward eagerly to the spring, for then the ice breaks up and flat pieces come drifting to the shore; the boys stand on these and use them as rafts. They must balance themselves carefully or else the ice will overturn and throw them into the bitterly cold water in which they have never learned to swim.

81

CAPITAL ON TOP OF THE WORLD

The coastal city of Reykjavik, capital of Iceland, is situated on the Faxafloi. Although close to the Arctic Circle, Reykjavik has a mean temperature of about 40° F. Large numbers of volcanic springs make up for Iceland's lack of fuel. The boiling hot water is carried by aqueducts to the city to heat homes, offices, and hot houses that grow fruit, vegetables and flowers.

NOT PAVING STONES, BUT FISH!

This drying and salting field on the outskirts of Reykjavik is just one of many. Codfishing is a major industry of Iceland, providing employment for a large percentage of the people. The men catch and the women cure the fish. They split, clean and salt the cod and spread them in the sun to dry. At night they collect and cover the fish and respread them in the morning.

CROSSROADS FOR THREE GENERATIONS

This little square in Reykjavik presents a study in contrasts. The quaintness of the costume in the foreground is typical of a generation several times removed. It is pointed up by the informal attire of the young woman on the curb. More than one-third of the entire population of Iceland lives in Reykjavik, which was settled by Norsemen as early as the year 877.

TOWERING CLIFFS hem in the Umanak Fjord, opposite the village of Umanak, which is situated on an island off the Nugsuak peninsula. The Umanak Fjord is on the west coast of Greenland, and at its head is a glacier that sometimes advances as much as fifty feet in a day. Icebergs are continually breaking from this glacier, so that the waters are never free from masses of ice. Greenland, a colonial possession of Denmark, has a total population of about eighteen thousand, while its largest settlement, Godthaab, has about 1,300 persons.

WATERFALLS. Many small rivers made by the melting glaciers in the interior of Iceland have to leap great cliffs to reach the sea; the Seljalandsfoss, at the base of which this horseman stands, is in the district of South Land. The Norse word "foss" means a waterfall—the same word is found in Yorkshire, for Norsemen settled in both England and Iceland.

THE LITTLE TOWN OF SEYDISFJORDUR STRAGGLING ALONG THE SHORE OF THE FROZEN FJORD

Seydisfjordur, situated at the head of a fjord, in the northeast of Iceland, is an important place, though it has less than a thousand inhabitants, for it occupies a district where the population averages but 1.7 persons per square mile. The houses have leak-proof corrugated iron roofs, for the most northerly point of the island touches the Arctic Circle, and the white winters are usually severe. In summer there is continuous daylight for three months, and there is an equally long night in the winter. For weeks deep snow stops travel, save that by rough sledges.

made to Greenland. The Lady Franklin Bay Expedition starved at Cape Sabine the spring of 1884 because its relief ship was crushed in the drift ice. The Macmillan Arctic Expedition of 1923-24 placed a memorial to their memory.

The Dane, L. Mylius-Erichsen, explored eight hundred miles of coast in 1907, reaching Northeast Foreland, thence pressed westward to what is now Denmark Fjord, and on through the channel that makes Peary Land an island. But faced by darkness and starvation, he perished after marching 160 miles back across the ice toward his ship, as his records, found later, plainly show.

Greenland becomes increasingly important as the nations bordering on the North Atlantic prepare for the possibility of future global war. The shortest air route between New York and northern Europe is over the vast island. The fiords of Greenland—those that are free of ice—serve as excellent harbors for emergency sea patrols. During World War II the United States sent troops to Greenland. Some were there to meet any possible attack, others to search the ice wastes for downed airplane crews. The Allies also set up weather stations, airfields and a naval refueling base.

Under the terms of the treaty signed by Denmark and the United States in 1941, Denmark regained her colony at the end of the war. In 1951 the two countries signed a new agreement. The bases built by the Allies are now under Danish control, but any member of the North Atlantic Pact may man these bases or build new ones when the need arises.

Fog and menacing icebergs no longer keep ships and planes from the shores of either Greenland or its rocky neighbor, Iceland. They have both become way stations for travel between two worlds and vital sentries in North Atlantic defense.

ICELAND AND GREENLAND: FACTS AND FIGURES

ICELAND

An island in the North Atlantic Ocean, is one of the most volcanic regions on earth. It is 298 miles in length and 194 miles in breadth, with a total coastline of 3,730 miles. The area is 39,709 square miles and the population in 1948 was 138,502. By an Act of Union of 1918, Denmark acknowledged the island a free sovereign state with which they were united only in the person of the king. In 1944 all ties with Denmark were severed by a referendum. On June 17, 1944, the republic was formally proclaimed. Iceland has a Council of Ministers and Althing, or parliament. The Althing, more than one thousand years old, is the oldest parliamentary assembly in the world. There is universal suffrage and men and women over 21 years of age may vote.

About six-sevenths of Iceland is unproductive and less than one-quarter per cent is under cultivation. Hay, potatoes and turnips are the chief agricultural products. Fishing is the chief industry, with cod and herring representing the greatest catch. Spinning and weaving is a widespread industry. The exports of Iceland are livestock, salt, wool, fish products (cod, train-oil, herring and salmon), eiderdown and woolen wear, and their imports are cereals and flour, coffee, sugar, ale, wines, tobacco, manufactured wares, iron and metal wares, timber, salt and coal. There are no railways, but there are 2,734 miles of carriage roads. Telephone and telegraph lines in 1947 had a length of 9,700 miles. The Evangelical Lutheran Church is the national church. Elementary education is compulsory from 7 to 15 years. Besides several special schools, there is one university at Reykjavik. Population: Reykjavik, the capital, 53,384; Akureyri, 6,761; Hafnarfjordur, 4,699; Vestmannaevir, 3,501.

GREENLAND

Greenland is a colonial possession of Denmark, lying almost wholly within the Arctic Circle. Its area is 708,000 square miles, but most of it is under an ice-sheet and only 132,000 square miles are ice-free. In 1945 the population numbered 21,412, mostly Eskimos. It is divided into two inspectorates, each of which is responsible to the director of a board in Copenhagen. The trade of the country is a monopoly of Denmark. The principal exports are whale oil, cod-liver oil, seal, fox and reindeer skins, eiderdown and walrus ivory. Travel is by dog sled. The chief settlement and capital is Godthaab, population, 1,313.

WARM CLOTHING is necessary in Greenland, which is white most of the year. These children, it can be seen, wear sweaters and sealskin boots pulled up over their knees. As this ornate footgear is made with the fur inside, it is warm in the Arctic winter. According to the native custom, the father's cast-off clothing is cut down for the eldest son, who, when he outgrows it, passes it on to the brother next in size. It is fortunate that garments of sealskin are uncommonly durable, and that people do not mind looking bulky. The sweaters are European.

SOME GREENLANDERS dress like Eskimos and are so-called, but many of them are as European in type as this mother and child. Some of their white blood comes, no doubt, from Norse women as well as men, and dates from eight or nine centuries back, the period following the first Icelandic colonization of Greenland under Eric the Red in the year 986 A. D.

"FAIR WEATHER FRIEND"

A bronze figure of the modern Danish girl with her indispensable bicycle faces the Town Hall of Copenhagen on fair days.   When it rains she is replaced by a twin sister with an umbrella.

EUROPE'S OLDEST KINGDOM

Denmark and Its People

Denmark is one of the most highly developed countries of the Old World. Scientifically improved agriculture is the base of its wealth. However, due to its position by the sea, over which products of all kinds may be transported cheaply, Denmark has also developed a strong industry although it is almost devoid of raw materials. The Danes are one of the most enlightened nations in the world and they are proud of their advanced social legislation. This is, as a patriotic song puts it, a country "where few have too much and fewer too little."

DENMARK is the gentlest and most idyllic of all the Scandinavian countries. Its green pastures are dotted with brown and speckled cows, red or white farmhouses and whitewashed churches; and its quaint gardens and wind-caressed groves next to blue inlets and sandy beaches breathe a fairy-tale atmosphere of charm and undisturbed harmony. Perhaps it was not by chance that one of the world's great writers of fairy tales, Hans Christian Andersen, was a Dane.

Denmark's smiling and friendly landscape seems to invite the stranger to prolong his stay. It must have done so for thousands of years. Numerous finds and excavations indicate that Denmark has been inhabited for at least four thousand to five thousand years and possibly much longer. It is quite possible that the earliest settlers were the ancestors of today's Danes, because no relics have been found of peoples of different stock. The country's position at the entrance to the Baltic Sea, one of Europe's oldest trading routes going back to prehistoric times, favored early settlement here. At any rate, Denmark is the oldest existing state in Europe and was mentioned as united under one king as early as the eighth century A.D.

Denmark consists of one peninsula and 493 islands and islets; but only about a hundred isles are inhabited. The Danish peninsula, called Jylland by the Danes and Jutland by English-speaking people, is bigger than all the islands together. The whole of Denmark is flat. The highest elevations, one of them ambitiously called Mount Sky (Himmelbjaerget), are less than six hundred feet above sea level. The sea, of course, is the natural link between the different parts of the country, and so the Danes became a seafaring nation quite early in history. They roamed the neighboring seas and conquered neighboring lands. The Angles who colonized England, together with the Saxons, and gave that country its name, came originally from Angeln in what then was the southernmost corner of Denmark. The very name of Norway means the "way toward the north," implying that its earliest settlers came from the next-door neighbor to the south, Denmark. Centuries later, Danish Vikings founded the Danelaw in eastern England and conquered even distant Normandy (the name means "land of the men from the north"). Several Danish kings—Canute the Great among them—ruled over all England and Norway in addition to Denmark. Later in the Middle Ages, the chief area around which the Danes spread was the commercially important Baltic. This sea was practically a Danish lake in the thirteenth century. However, soon after, Danish sea power was contested first by the German cities of the Hanseatic League and later by the Dutch and by the Swedes. The struggle with Sweden for leadership of Scandinavia and domination of the Baltic lasted intermittently through many centuries. It led to the permanent loss of Denmark's foothold on the Scandinavian Peninsula, the provinces of Skaane, Halland and Blekinge, which today constitute the southern tip of Sweden but were part of Denmark until 1658.

Denmark is no longer a naval power,

DANISH CHILDREN are healthy little mortals, well cared for, well fed and well brought up. These children, flaxen-haired, blue-eyed and rosy, are wearing five forms of the Danish national dress, which is now, unfortunately, not often seen. We cannot tell from their appearance whether they are the children of well-to-do folk, peasants or artisans for there are virtually no class distinctions in Denmark and no great extremes of poverty and wealth. Though Denmark has a king, the country has had a democratic form of government for more than a hundred years.

THESE PEASANTS' COSTUMES of olden days still have their place in historical museums. They show that every district of Denmark once had its own characteristic dress. The headgear, especially, exhibited a marked variation of style. The woman on the left, for instance, dwelt among the sand dunes of the low coast of Jutland; she wore a face cloth for protection against sharp grains of sand blown by the wind. The flower-garlanded girl standing beside her was a bride from Fanö Island. Most of the dresses had tight bodices with kerchiefs.

THE KINGDOM OF DENMARK

but the Danes are still a seafaring people. The Danish straits are among the most trafficked waterways in the world, although the Germans siphoned off part of the Baltic trade by constructing the Kiel Canal through Holstein in the 1890's. In 1938 some 40,000 vessels with a total of 35,000,000 deadweight tons passed through Oresund (the Sound) alone. On the average, this is one quarter more than passes through the Suez Canal and almost twice as much traffic as passes through the Panama Canal. About half of the vital foreign trade of Denmark, which is the greatest foreign trade in relation to population of any country in the world, is carried in Danish bottoms. Most of the traffic between the different parts of Denmark and with near-by countries is carried by steamers and motor vessels and train-carrying ferries, but Denmark also has a dense railroad and highway network. The national vehicle is the bicycle, which means to Denmark what the automobile means to the United States and Canada. But there are more automobiles in Denmark

per capita than in any other European countries except Britain and France. Denmark has two of the longest bridges in the world—one 10,-534 feet long, between Zealand and Falster; the other, 3,860 feet, spanning the Little Belt (a strait) and connecting Jutland and the island of Funen.

Most foreigners coming to Denmark arrive in Copenhagen either by boat, by plane or by train and ferry. Copenhagen, the capital of Denmark, is the biggest city of Scandinavia. Due to its sheltered site on a small sound between the islands of Zealand (Sjaelland in Danish) and Amager, it early became the most important shipping center of the whole Baltic region. Not for nothing does its name (Kobenhavn in Danish) mean "merchants' haven." While the main part of the city is situated on Denmark's largest island, Zealand, the southern part of Copenhagen lies on Amager. On Amager is Copenhagen's Kastrup Airport. This is one of Europe's largest airports and has become the busiest air junction of the whole Continent. The Danish Air Lines, today an affiliate of the Scandinavian Airlines System, is the world's oldest commercial air line (established 1918).

The Danes call their capital "the city of beautiful towers." But the many gracious steeples in Dutch Renaissance and later styles are not its only mark of beauty. Copenhagen is an unusually appealing city. It is like a museum of exquisite samples of various styles of architecture, from the unique Stock Exchange, built 1619-40, with its grotesque spire formed by the entwined tails of four dragons standing on their heads, to the serene, unadorned loveliness of the modern Radio House. The old town has many narrow alleys and picturesque canals, but on the outskirts there are fine examples of twentieth-century

COPENHAGEN, "MERCHANTS' HAVEN"

The free port of Copenhagen is the distribution and assembly center for northern Europe. Domestic and foreign firms have plants here, and can export and import materials duty-free.

housing developments and town planning. Copenhagen is a city of many parks, and each park is used as a permanent exposition ground for sculpture. One of the most noteworthy statues is Eriksen's Little Mermaid. The figure is that of the character from Andersen's fairy tale. In the park of Langelinje, she watches the ships from a big boulder at the water's edge.

Copenhagen is often called the Paris of the North, and it is undoubtedly the gayest city of Scandinavia. Visitors from all over the neighboring countries are drawn to its opera, its world-famous ballet, its concerts and many plays and, last but not least, to Tivoli, an amusement park with old-fashioned charm and a fairy-tale atmosphere in the very middle of the city. The Danes have a gift for enjoying themselves, and in Copenhagen one can watch them give themselves to an art they thoroughly understand—how to spend hours of leisure within well-defined limitations of decorum. Here are also innumerable opportunities for indulging oneself in the culinary specialties for which Denmark is famous, the open sandwiches, or *smorrebrod*, which entice the eye as much as the palate and of which one well-known restaurant features not less than 172 varieties.

Founded in the twelfth century, Copenhagen has been the royal residence and national capital for more than five hundred years. It is also the largest industrial city of Scandinavia, with 43 per cent

WEALTHY DRAGONS

The Stock Exchange (Borsen) on a Copenhagen canal lifts a spire of twisted dragons' tails.

95

ON STROMO ISLAND, the largest of the Faroe group, a Danish possession far out in the North Atlantic, there is this stone memorial to Niels Finsen, a famous scientist and Nobel Prize winner in medicine, who was born on Stromo. The islanders are of Norse descent and speak a language much like the old Norse. These costumes are no longer worn.

of its productive population employed in industries and handicrafts. The main industries are iron and machinery, shipbuilding, textile and clothing manufacture and food processing. These industries not only supply more than two-thirds of the products needed at home but also provide Denmark with articles for export, using imported raw materials and semifinished goods. The flourishing Danish export business is due partly to the high quality of Danish products and partly to the city's excellent port facilities. These are larger and more modern than those of any other harbor of the Scandinavian and Baltic region and include a free port of twenty-one and a half acres in Copenhagen. This was Denmark's answer to Germany's construction of the Kiel Canal.

After World War II, Danish industry made a spectacularly fast recovery, thanks to the fact that the German surrender came before the Germans had time to carry out plans to destroy Danish plants. As soon as foreign raw materials were available again, the wheels of the Danish factories began turning. Within eight months industrial production rose from 23 per cent of the prewar level, in May 1945, to 100 per cent, in January 1946, and to 168 per cent in October 1951.

Elsinore's Haunted Castle

Although Copenhagen is the only large city, there are many quaint and picturesque towns on the island of Zealand. Best known abroad is Elsinore (Helsingör in Danish) of Shakespearean fame. Here, on the real site of HAMLET, the tragedy about the melancholy Danish prince is produced every year by a different foreign theater group. The open-air performances take place within the very walls of Kronborg Castle that the ghost of Hamlet's father is supposed to haunt. Today, this jewel of a castle in Dutch Renaissance architecture is only a museum of Denmark's glorious past. But through four centuries, from 1425 to 1855, this was the place where the Danes collected the Sound tolls from passing ships. The narrows are hardly broader than a wide river at this point, and originally the toll was collected

for passage through Danish territorial water in accordance with the international traditions of those days. But when the eastern shores of the Sound became Swedish in 1658, the straits became half Danish and half Swedish. Nevertheless, the Danes continued to collect what was the largest revenue item of the Danish crown for another two hundred years. Finally, American shipowners proclaimed that they would no longer stand for this antiquated interference with the freedom of the seas, and the tolls were abolished by international agreement once and for all.

Going west from Zealand, one passes another of the Danish straits. Large ferryboats carry the express trains from Copenhagen to Jutland and the rest of the Continent across the Great Belt (Storebaelt in Danish) in less than seventy-five minutes. After leaving Zealand, one

SCULPTURED SERENITY

From her rock at Copenhagen, the Little Mermaid of Andersen's fairy tale gazes out to sea.

crosses the island of Funen (Fyn in Danish), which is even more fairylike than the rest of the country. There are medieval castles and Renaissance manors, dreamlike towns and villages with one-story frame houses, whitewashed cottages with stork nests on the straw-thatched roofs and crooked cobblestoned alleys. Here, on Funen, Hans Christian Andersen was born in picturesque Odense. The house he lived in is preserved intact as a museum and is one of the country's main tourist attractions. The name indicates that

Odense already existed in pagan times with a shrine consecrated to Odin. Today, it is Denmark's third largest city, while still preserving many of its quaint characteristics of by-gone times. Its development is due largely to the growth of a large shipbuilding industry. Though the city is landlocked, it is connected with the sea by a fifteen-mile-long canal.

The third strait, the Little Belt (Lillebaelt), scarcely broader than a medium-sized river, separates this "garden of Denmark" from the fairly rugged Danish

FRESH FISH TODAY!

Copenhagen, once just a fishing village, retains some of its original atmosphere in the fish market along the Gammel Strand. The tower of St. Nikolaj Church is in the background.

HOME OF "THE MELANCHOLY DANE"

Kronborg Castle, setting for scenes in Shakespeare's *Hamlet*, is located at Elsinore, a seaport on the Danish island of Zealand. The Dutch Renaissance edifice dates back to 1580.

peninsula. Jutland is, in a way, the backbone of the nation, jutting out into the sea like a tremendous natural breakwater and protecting the fair and idyllic islands against the harsh western winds and the unruly waves of the North Sea.

Jutland, too, has quaint old towns, such as Aebeltoft and Ribe (birthplace of New York's social pioneer Jacob Riis), where nothing seems to have happened for centuries. More indicative of the stern Jutlanders' tenacious endurance, however, is the modern city of Esbjerg, Denmark's newest. Esbjerg, the only harbor on the peninsula's inhospitable west coast, was built after the duchies of Schleswig and Holstein were lost to Germany in 1864 and the southern North Sea port of Husum had become foreign territory. Today, with four miles of piers, Esbjerg is Denmark's foremost export center. Here, the butter, bacon, eggs and cheeses from Jutland's thriving farms are stowed into freighters that carry Danish products to England, France and overseas markets. Esbjerg is also the center of Denmark's deep-sea fishing fleet, which supplies, by means of highway trucks, the large cities of northern Germany with fresh fish.

The friendlier and more typically Danish east coast of Jutland harbors Denmark's second and third ports Aarhus and Aalborg. Both of them are busy commercial and industrial centers that have, nevertheless, preserved touch with their historic past in architecture and tradition. Aarhus is Denmark's second largest city. It has a unique open-air museum, the so-called "Old Town," with picturesque ancient buildings. Some still stand on their original sites and others have been transferred to Aarhus from all parts of the country and reconstructed in such a way that the atmosphere of an old urban community is preserved. In Lyngby, near Copenhagen, there is a similar museum of old farmhouses.

Near Aalborg is a national park of special interest for Americans. Here, in the heather-covered hills of Rebild, Danish-Americans bought an extensive tract of the heath that formerly covered a large part of Jutland and set it aside as a shrine of Danish-American co-operation and friendship. A so-called "Lincoln Log Cabin" made out of logs and shingles from all parts of the United States was set up, and each Fourth of July scores of thou-

OLD KILNS STILL USED FOR FIRING DANISH PORCELAIN

No product of Denmark is so widely known abroad as the exquisite porcelain, valued by all those who appreciate fine china. It has been developed by generations of craftsmen, working with loving care. The Royal Porcelain Factory was founded in 1775. Some of the loveliest pieces have a fluted effect with a delicate blue and creamy white underglaze.

THICK "WHEELS" OF CHEESE STORED FOR RIPENING

For its size Denmark is one of the greatest dairying countries on earth, and the production of milk each year is tremendous. A vast quantity of butter is made and is one of Denmark's chief exports. Cheese is also made although not so much of it is shipped abroad. The Danes themselves are fond of cheese and use it in a variety of dishes.

sands of Danes with kinsfolk in America meet here to celebrate the American Independence Day.

As time goes by, this national park will one day probably be all there is left of the famous Jutland heath. In the early 1950's there were still some 500,000 acres left of the original 2,000,000 after one of the most spectacular reclamation projects ever undertaken.

Like many other regions of the world, Jutland had suffered reckless deforestation during the Middle Ages when the Danish kings needed large wooden fleets to maintain naval supremacy in the Baltic. Slowly, but irresistibly, the majestic oak forests gave way to the encroaching heather, as the persistent western winds blew the denuded topsoil away. By the nineteenth century, the all-engulfing heather had become a major threat to cultivated areas and towns. After the rich farmlands of Schleswig-Holstein were lost in 1864, the slogan of E. Dalgas— "Recover at home what was lost abroad!" —finally caught on. After 1866 a large-scale attempt was made to stop the spreading of the wastelands and to turn unpro-

ductive areas into woods and arable land. It was a truly Herculean task for a small nation, because this was long before steam-shovels, power drills and bulldozers were ever heard of. Every effort to penetrate the stony hardpan had to be made by hand. But the effort was successful. More than one and a half million acres were reclaimed and converted, first into woodland, and later, when new topsoil had formed, into pastures and fields.

Here and elsewhere, Denmark has laid under the plow poorer soil than most other countries have; but within a few generations it has managed to lay on this poor soil the foundations of one of the most successful agricultures in all history.

This development started in the winter of 1881–82. A group of farmers were sitting together in the Olgod Inn, twenty miles north of Esbjerg, discussing their plight. Until some ten years earlier they had been making good money sending quantities of grain to England after the repeal of the English Corn Laws in 1846. But with improved transportation facilities by land and by sea, such as railroads and steamships, overseas countries like the

BIRTHPLACE OF IMMORTALITY

Odense is famous as the birthplace of Hans Christian Andersen, immortalized in his delightful fairy tales. The house in which he was born (below) is now a museum containing his effects.

"WHEN GRANDMOTHER WAS YOUNG"

At the open-air museum of Lyngby, near Copenhagen, these two gracious young ladies pose for visitors. They are wearing the picturesque costumes of an earlier era in Danish history.

United States, Argentina and Russia started dumping huge quantities of wheat into the British granaries. The bottom dropped out of the market, and Danish agriculture, which slowly had become a one-crop system, was threatened with utter ruin.

That winter day in the Olgod Inn, a young man spoke up and the farmers listened. This young dairy assistant had an idea. If it was no longer profitable to sell grain to the British, why not try something else, say, butter? He had figured out a way to go about the venture—a way

that smaller farmers, without the dairy facilities of the wealthy ones, might take. Suppose they all got together and dumped their individual batches of butter into big casks to be marketed as a unit? Another fellow had an even better idea. Instead of collecting the butter on the various farms, it would be easier just to collect the milk and have the churning done in one place, as was done in the dairies on some of the big estates. Only, this particular dairy should belong to all the participating farmers together. The principle was "one for all and all for one," similar

103

"TOWN OF THE STORKS"

Ribe, in southwest Jutland, is the oldest town in Denmark and probably in all Scandinavia. Storks, beloved birds of Denmark, seem to prefer roof-tops in this town for their nesting.

to the idea behind the consumers' co-operative societies that had begun to spread. The rich and the poor, the man with thirty cows and the little fellow with only one, would all have an equal voice in running the affair. The profits would be distributed according to the contributions of each.

In this way, Denmark got its first co-operative dairy. It was a tremendous success, and the idea spread like wildfire. Five years later, there were already 350 co-operative dairies in Denmark. Today, there are almost 1,500, and they are processing more than 90 per cent of all Danish milk.

One particular advantage of this system was that the skim milk was returned to the farmers who fed it to their pigs. This gave birth to another grand idea. The

farmers also got together in regard to establishing co-operative slaughter-houses. Here, pigs raised by individual farmers—but to standard size, age and weight on a standard diet—could be slaughtered and transformed into bacon and ham for English breakfast tables. This, too, was a roaring success, and today 61 co-operative packing houses handle 85 per cent of the Danish pigs. The first was established in 1887, only five years after the first co-operative dairy.

Later came co-operative egg-collecting societies. The Danish farmers left it to their overseas competitors to supply the British with bread, but they undertook to furnish everything else that belonged on the English breakfast table. The short distance to the market gave them an advantage that was hard to beat, until modern refrigeration enabled the farmers of New Zealand and other Commonwealth countries to ship their products to London in fresh condition. But in the meantime the Danes had won a reputation for unchanging standards of excellence in quality, and this reputation is the very foundation of the country's wealth. The quality of the Danish products is supervised strictly by the Government, and there

The Folk High Schools are nonvocational institutes of advanced education for farm boys and girls. They admit students at least eighteen years old who have left primary school at fourteen or fifteen and have had several years' practical experience in agriculture. They are boarding schools and try to build up a strong community feeling in the students by stressing good citizenship and community activities. The main subjects taught are his-

SLEEK DAIRY CATTLE BOUND FOR PASTURE

Typical of what appeals to visitors in Denmark is this peaceful little village in the central part of Jutland, with one of the quaint windmills that are all too rapidly disappearing from the scene.

are scientific check-ups to prevent any inferior goods from being shipped abroad.

Peasants are usually a cautious folk and hard to win for costly and uncertain experiments. An idea like the co-operative scheme might never have caught on had Denmark not had, for those days, an unusually enlightened and progressive farm population. It did not take the Danish farmers a long time to figure out on which side their bread was buttered. This was mainly due to the development of a peculiar Danish institution, the so-called Folk High Schools.

tory, philosophy, religion, civics and literature. At the same time, they offer courses that will help the student improve his farming, such as—animal husbandry, truck gardening, chemical soil analysis, and use of fertilizers, and accounting. Oral instruction—that is, lectures—and free-for-all discussions are the main teaching methods. Tests and examinations are banned and no diplomas are given. The first school was opened in Rodding in the duchy of Schleswig in 1844, but the movement caught on only after the loss of Schleswig and Holstein twenty years later. There are now fifty-eight government-supported Folk High Schools training over six thousand students yearly at nominal cost (about $20 a month, including board and tuition). It is estimated that about one-third of the rural population has at one time or another attended the schools.

Like the other Scandinavian nations,

carried out after 1930 under the sponsorship of Labor governments but with the active support of most other political parties. One of the most unusual features is the so-called Danish People's Holiday. This co-operative association offers, at nominal cost, recreation facilities that enable the worker and his family to get the maximum benefit from his twelve days'

WORKSHOP OF MASTER CRAFTSMEN

In the Georg Jensen workshop, the exquisite Jensen silverware is fashioned. Originals of the sauceboat at the left and the jug at the right are in Copenhagen's Industrial Art Museum.

Denmark is one of the world's most advanced countries in social legislation. Scandinavians quite generally subscribe to the idea of the welfare state. Denmark was the first country to abolish slave trade (1798), to institute free and compulsory elementary school education (1814) and to introduce a free old-age pension system (1891). Spectacular social reforms were

annual paid vacation. Such a vacation is guaranteed every Dane by law, regardless of how often he changes his employment. This venture is supported financially by the Government, the trade unions and the employers' associations.

Other outstanding features of Danish social legislation are extensive free maternity care and a municipal nurse and

RURAL CONSUMERS' CO-OPERATIVE

Denmark has co-operative societies for purchasing, marketing, production, insurance and banking. From ten to twelve per cent of the country's total retail trade is handled by co-operatives.

servant service to help with the household chores during a housewife's illness. By medical standards, Denmark ranks as one of the most advanced countries in the world, largely due to its excellent medical facilities which are accessible to anybody at negligible charges. Denmark is leading the world in the fight against tuberculosis and has played an important part in the extensive campaign to control the disease in war-ravaged Europe.

Ever since the eighteenth century, Denmark has tried to keep out of foreign wars, but not always with success. In Napoleonic times, Copenhagen was bombarded and the Danish fleet was captured by the British; Norway was lost to Sweden. In 1864, the duchies of Schleswig, Holstein and Lauenburg were ceded to Prussia and Austria, but the northern part of Schleswig (Nordslesvig in Danish) became Danish again in 1920 after a plebiscite. During World War I, Denmark managed to remain neutral, but its traditional neutrality broke down in World War II. Denmark proper was invaded by the Germans on April 9, 1940, and its possessions, the Faeroe Islands and Greenland, were occupied by the British and American

troops to forestall German landings. Because of the underground resistance of the Danes, Denmark was recognized as a belligerent and an ally by the Western powers. It became a member of the United Nations after the liberation in the spring of 1945.

"ONE FOR GOOD MEASURE"

Butter is being weighed from the churn in one of Denmark's numerous co-operative dairies.

In 1918, Denmark recognized its former possession Iceland as a free and independent nation connected with Denmark by a common king, but this last tie was severed in 1944 when the Icelanders proclaimed their country a republic. During World War II, Denmark escaped actual warfare, but was impoverished by German exploitation of its resources. However, recovery was greatly speeded up by Marshall Plan aid from the United States to the tune of $266,000,000. During the cold war, Denmark felt exposed at the entrance to a sea that the Russians would like to make a Soviet lake. In view of the Russian interest in the "northern Dardanelles," through which the large Soviet submarine fleet would have to pass in case of another major war, the Danes discarded their traditional neutrality for good and joined the North Atlantic Treaty Organization. Denmark is a stanch member of the Atlantic community.

BY GUNNAR LEISTIKOW

DENMARK: FACTS AND FIGURES

THE COUNTRY

The total area of Denmark is 16,576 square miles, and the population is 4,279,000. To Denmark belong also the Faeroe Islands (540 sq. mi., 30,000 pop.) north of the Shetland Islands between Norway and Iceland; and Greenland (84,000 sq. mi., 21,000 pop.). The Faeroe Islands, inhabited by descendants of Norwegian Vikings, are self-governing, with their own legislature. Greenland, according to the findings of a French expedition in 1951, is not one tremendous island but an archipelago of at least three islands. Its inhabitants are mostly of Eskimo stock. A sweeping administrative reform was carried out in 1951 in order to give the Greenlanders a greater say in their own affairs.

The Danes are, like the Swedes, Norwegians and Icelanders, of Germanic stock and speak a Scandinavian language. In North Slesvig there is a minority of less than 40,000 Germans. The Danes are soft-spoken and friendly, tolerant and averse to all extremes. They are very down-to-earth and display what has been called an "uncommon common sense."

GOVERNMENT

Denmark is a kingdom with a democratic constitution since 1849 (amended in 1915 and 1920) with greatly reduced royal powers. The legislative power is jointly vested in the king and the two-house Parliament, called the Rigsdagen. The executive branch, under a prime minister, must have the confidence of the lower house (Folketinget). In this respect it is similar to the British system. The lower house has 151 members elected by equal and direct ballot. The upper house (Landstinget) has 76 members elected indirectly by voters over 35 years of age. The King, Frederick IX, acceded to the throne in 1947.

COMMERCE AND INDUSTRIES

The most important occupation is agriculture, but more people are employed in crafts and industries. Sweeping land reforms laid the foundation for a wealthy class of freeholders as early as 1788. The typical Danish farm is seldom bigger than 40 acres and specializes in scientific dairy farming, pig raising and egg production, all for export. Denmark raises about four times as much food as the Danes eat themselves. Although Denmark's exports are mainly farm products, industrial goods account for more than 25 per cent. Main items are ships, Diesel motors (42 per cent of all Diesel motors in ocean-going vessels of all nations were Danish-built in 1939), agricultural machinery, canned foods, beer and fruit beverages, and cement. Famous export products are also objects of industrial art, such as pottery from the Royal Copenhagen Porcelain works and others, and silverware (Georg Jensen).

COMMUNICATIONS

Railroads, 2,665 miles (1,500 state-owned). Telegraph lines, 202,473 miles. Telephone lines, 1,681,175 miles; 542,000 telephones.

RELIGION AND EDUCATION

The established church is Lutheran, to which the king must belong. There is religious freedom. Elementary education is compulsory for the ages 7 through 14. There are two universities, in Copenhagen and Aarhus, with about 6,100 and 1,200 students respectively. There is also a Technological Institute and an Agricultural College in Copenhagen. Standards of education, science, arts and literature are high. So is literacy. In 1938, Denmark published 15 times as many books per capita as the United States. Danish men of letters have won more Nobel Prizes in proportion to population than those of any other nation.

CHIEF CITIES

Copenhagen, the capital, 1,163,000 pop.; Aarhus, 150,000; Odense, 113,000; Aalborg, 87,000; Randers, 51,000; Esbjerg, 50,000; Horsens, 38,000; Kolding, 31,000 (1950 estimates).

THE GERMAN HOMELAND

Slowly Recovering from the Shock of Defeat

Once a country of highly developed industries, big and beautiful modern cities, fertile and well cared for fields of rye, wheat and sugar-beets, Germany is now a defeated and divided country, her future unsettled and unpredictable. Less than thirty years after her defeat in World War I, Germany began anew a war of conquest, involving almost every country of the world. Reconstruction after World War I was speeded up by the establishment of a military dictatorship under Adolf Hitler, determined upon the expansion of German power at any cost. But Germany's second gamble for world power in World War II was an even greater and more final failure than the first, despite early successes. Her cities were bombed unceasingly, her industries and transport system virtually destroyed; her countryside devastated. The reconstruction of Germany after this second defeat is proceeding at a slow pace, and the Allied powers responsible for her defeat are careful to protect themselves against a future outbreak of violent militarism in Germany.

IN the year 101-02 B.C. a strange army of savage men from Central Europe, the Cimbri and Teutons, planned an invasion of northern Italy. The men of this army were fair-haired, blue-eyed muscular Teutons who were seeking new lands. So fierce and brave were these skin-clad warriors—these "barbarians" as the Romans called them—that for a time they withstood the trained legions of Rome. After much fighting, however, the Romans vanquished and utterly routed them and drove them back into Central Europe. There they settled in places where the richest pastures were to be found.

The deep, rich forests east of the Rhine had been the haunt of the red deer and of the wolves that preyed upon them. When Julius Cæsar was conquering Gaul he heard of many tribes living across the great river. The Gauls called them Germans but they seem to have called themselves Teutons; if you have read Cæsar's Gallic War you will remember the names of many of them. Some of those prominent in later times were the Suebi, the Langobardi (Lombards), the Angles, Saxons, Goths and Burgundians. Possibly they originated in the northern grasslands of Central Asia. These rude Germanic tribes, the ancestors of many of the white people of Europe and North America, were, when the Romans first knew them, almost as primitive as the Iroquois Indians at the time of Columbus. Each tribe lived its separate way, making itself shelters of logs and subsisting largely on the game and wild fruit of the woodlands and the cattle it had brought.

Toward the end of the fourth century A.D. the Goths, tribes living along the Danube, were set upon by fierce nomad Mongolians from Central Asia, the Huns —ugly bow-legged yellow men on horseback. The Goths were forced to flee across the great boundary river into Roman territory. There followed the Battle of Adrianople (378 A.D.) which first showed the Germans that they could overcome the Romans. (In time this discovery led to the break-up of the Roman Empire in Western Europe.)

The Huns, meanwhile, were not affected by the hardships of warfare, for they even slept and ate on horseback. They swept over the country like a scourge, burning and destroying every thing with which they came in contact, scattering tribes and altering the very face of Europe. Upon the death of their leader, Attila, in 453, the menace of the Huns came to an end, and soon the German tribes—Alemanni, Saxons, Franks, Vandals, Goths, Frisians and others— were settled peacefully once more.

It was under Charles the Great, better known as Charlemagne, who reigned from 768 to 814, that the German peoples became powerful. Though he styled himself emperor and ruler of the Roman Em-

GERMANY DIVIDED, WITH TWO CAPITALS, BONN AND BERLIN

FRANKFORT-ON-MAIN, AN IMPORTANT COMMERCIAL CENTRE, AS IT LOOKED BEFORE THE WAR

Frankfort (or Frankfurt) on the Main has long been important in commerce and industry. The river Main, which joins the Rhine only twenty-four miles away, is abustle with boats and barges carrying goods to and from the interior. The city is a great railroad centre, with lines raying out in all directions; and before the war it was also a banking town of world renown. During the war munitions were made here, and were routed through here to the front; so it was a bombing target for the Allies. Great damage was done to buildings and to bridges.

111

BEAUTIFUL VIEW OVER BADENWEILER AND ITS ENVIRONS ON THE OUTSKIRTS OF THE BLACK FOREST

The Black Forest in mountainous southern Germany, so named because of its thick-set hemlocks, firs and spruces which admit no sunlight, is largely state-owned and is kept in a thriving condition by a body of highly skilled foresters. That there is as much woodland to-day as there was, say, a hundred years ago, is due to the fact that no one is permitted to cut down a tree, even on his own land, without planting another in its place. Here are still found the red deer and the fox, the pheasant and the woodcock, and here bands of students and tourists love to explore.

WITHIN THE WALLS OF A FINE OLD CASTLE IN THURINGIA

In the Thuringian Forest is a peak crowned by a castle known as the Wartburg, built about 1100. After Martin Luther was outlawed, in 1521, by Emperor Charles V, he was brought here for a time, ostensibly a prisoner, by his friend the Elector Frederick III, and here Luther translated the New Testament into German. His desk may still be seen.

113

PEASANTS OF THE NÖRDLINGEN DISTRICT OF BAVARIA IN THE COSTUME THAT ONCE WAS COMMON

Everyone likes to dress up in the costumes of olden times; and these Bavarian farm folk, in costumes of long ago, are cheerfully showing us the way their grandparents used to look. Most of them here are in holiday attire. The man at the left is wearing a denim work-smock. Notice the odd baskets carried by the three women on the right; these baskets have been shaped to fit against the sides of the bearers. Bavaria is a lofty section, bounded on the south by spurs of the Alps Mountains, containing several peaks more than 8,ooo feet high.

GIRLS OF SANKT GEORGEN **IN** THEIR OLD-FASHIONED DRESSES

Sankt Georgen is a little village in the Black Forest, and if we visit it on Sunday we shall
see the people of the neighborhood in their distinctive costumes. These young girls look
extremely prim and sedate in their neat attire, and, indeed, the folk of Sankt Georgen are less
high-spirited than are the peasants of many other districts.

McLeish

BEAUTIFUL TIMBERED HOUSES IN A VILLAGE OF THE RHINE

Farmhouses in Germany are typically arranged in farm villages varying from half a dozen to several hundred dwellings. Each is a centre of community life, with a clean cobbled market place flanked by a church and a town hall. Cows and oxen are used more commonly than horses for draft animals. The architecture reminds one of Grimm's Fairy Tales.

116

EVERY MEMBER OF A FARM FAMILY WORKS IN GERMANY

These peasants of Würtemberg have gathered the flax-harvest and are now preparing the fibre for the market. The man is carrying out the process known as "scutching," in which the stems are pressed and then beaten in order to separate the fibres from the wood. The fibres are then tied into bundles. Modern methods are now generally employed.

WOMAN OF RÜGEN ISLAND READY TO WEAVE AT HER LOOM

Rügen, the largest German island in the Baltic Sea, separated from the mainland by the Strait of Strelosund, is a land of long winters, though the wooded east coast is scenically lovely. The women of the island still do their own weaving, while the men put in their spare time at wood-carving. Many such home industries evolve into little country factories.

McLeish

FACING COBLENZ THE FORTRESS OF EHRENBREITSTEIN OVERLOOKS THE RHINE AND THE MOSELLE

The fortress for which the town of Ehrenbreitstein is famous was, until 1918, one of the strongest fortresses in all Germany. It was built in a nearly impregnable situation on a rock 385 feet above the Rhine. The present fortress replaces an older one that was captured by the French in 1631, by the Imperialists in 1637 and again by the French in 1799. On two of these occasions the garrison was forced to surrender through famine. The fortress is joined to Coblenz by a bridge. Here the Rhine flows within Germany, in Rhenish Prussia.

THE TOWERING LORELEI JUTTING OUT INTO THE RHINE

This cliff, known as the Lorelei, towers for over four hundred feet above the river on the right bank near St. Goarshausen. According to ancient legend, the cliff is haunted by a siren who by her singing entices admiring boatmen into the dangerous rapids at its foot. To-day the cliff is pierced by a railway tunnel at this point where the Rhine is narrowest.

pire, Charlemagne was really only the suzerain of many independent princes.

The change to feudalism was important. At the time of the Crusades the German nobles raised walled towns, built churches and founded universities. The Hanseatic League was formed when over eighty cities, led by Lübeck, Hamburg and Bremen, banded together for the control of trade in the Baltic and elsewhere. The League had to fend off the lawlessness of the robber knights.

All through the Middle Ages no one spoke of Germany, but of the Germanies. The so-called Holy Roman Empire which followed, after a time, the empire of Charlemagne, was a collection of two to three hundred separate states, some small, some larger, over which the emperor had little real power. If he were a strong man, who had also inherited great possessions, he might be able to keep his unruly dukes and counts in order. The emperor,

however, did not pass the title to his son. Seven great princes chose the emperor, and they usually chose a man who was too weak to make them much trouble. Generally they chose a member of the House of Hapsburg.

The Empire did not, however, include all of modern Germany. Prussia was never a member, but on the other hand, Austria was included. These states of the Empire were ruled by kings, archdukes, dukes, counts and knights. Many "free cities" were members of the Empire. A "free city" was one which had no other overlord except the emperor. In fact, Hamburg, Lübeck and Bremen were members of the later German Empire and since, have become members of the Reich.

The story of the old Empire (which came to an end during the Napoleonic Wars) and of the new German Empire which arose in 1870, is too long to tell.

Haeckel

RUINS OF AN ANCIENT CASTLE IN THE GIANT MOUNTAINS

The Riesengebirge, or Giant Mountains, twenty-three miles in length, separate Bohemia from Prussian Silesia. The lower slopes of the hills are covered with woods of silver pine, larch and beech. On a craggy point above the village of Hermsdorf are the ruins of a castle destroyed by lightning in 1675, as the picture shows.

Just at the end of World War I Emperor Wilhelm abdicated, and the rulers of the separate states either abdicated or were deposed, and a republic was set up. The twenty-six states were reduced to eighteen and later to seventeen.

By the peace treaties Germany lost both area and population. The country was exhausted by four years of war, and was compelled to pay war damages to the Allies. Food was scarce and there was much unemployment. The people were embittered and resentful. Many wished to restore the monarchy, while others wished a more radical government. The moderates favoring the republic had difficulty in maintaining the government.

Meanwhile a new party founded by

Adolf Hitler, called the Nazi, gained many followers. By 1933 it had control of the Reichstag and began to remake the government. President Hindenburg died in 1934, and Hitler was made supreme head of the state with the title of *Fuehrer* or "Leader."

Severe persecution of the Jews followed. They were charged with all the misfortunes of Germany. Professors were expelled from the universities; judges and officials lost their positions; doctors were driven from the hospitals; lawyers were not allowed to practice; the people were forbidden to buy from Jewish merchants; no Jew might be a banker; property was confiscated; thousands were sent to concentration camps. The Reich also attempted to control the churches, both Protestant and Catholic, in spite of all resistance.

Germany Begins to Arm

When the Nazis came to power they at once began to arm, and Germany had very strong military and air forces, armed with the most powerful weapons of destruction. The naval force was smaller, though there were many submarines.

The old dream of a Germany controlling all of Middle Europe was revived, and it was announced that all Germans should be brought under the Reich. In 1938 Austria was incorporated into Germany. The industrial portion of Czechoslovakia was inhabited chiefly by Germans, and strong Nazi sentiment developed among the Sudetens, so called from the Sudeten Mountains in this region. Hitler took up their cause, and, in spite of the protests of France and Great Britain, annexed the districts late in 1938. Poland and Hungary also took over parts of Slovakia.

Slovakia had always been jealous of Czech influence and early in 1939 declared herself an independent state under German protection. Bohemia and Moravia were declared protectorates of the Reich in March 1939, and the gallant little state of Czechoslovakia was laid prostrate. At almost the same time the city of Memel and the surrounding district were taken from Lithuania. The city had formerly been German, but had been given to Lithuania when that state was revived after the first World War.

The Demand for Danzig

Though Hitler had declared that German territorial demands were now satisfied it was only a few months until demands for Danzig and a highway across the Polish Corridor were made. In the Middle Ages Danzig was a free city, but fell to Prussia in 1793. After World War I it was again made a free city in order to give Poland a port, and the Corridor led up to it, thus separating East Prussia from the remainder of Germany. Nazi sentiment had become strong in Danzig, and probably most of the people wished annexation. Poland refused the German demands, as she feared that she would soon be left an inland state with no access to the ocean.

Great Britain and France announced that they would support Poland. Knowing that immediate aid could not be sent, the Germans on September 1, 1939, invaded Poland at several points with infantry, cavalry, artillery, mechanized battalions and bombing planes. Though the Poles fought desperately, they were outnumbered, inferior in weapons of warfare, and apparently not well led.

Hitler had boasted that it would be a Blitzkrieg or "lightning war." Warsaw surrendered, September 27. Meanwhile a pact had been made with Russia, and Russian troops marched in and occupied more than half of Poland. When resistance ceased, an agreement was made dividing the country between Germany and Russia. Meanwhile Great Britain and France declared war, though little fighting took place on the Western front for some months. The Allies contented themselves with blockading Germany's ports. For her part Germany loosed her submarines and a certain number of surface raiders against Allied shipping.

In April, 1940, Germany suddenly struck. She occupied Denmark and invaded Norway, claiming that the British had designs on these two countries. The Norwegians,

KNOX

THE OLD MARKUSTURM in Rothenburg, Bavaria, is a relic of the walled towns of the Middle Ages. This town, gable-roofed against the winter snows, is mentioned in a document of 942 A. D. By the time of the Crusades the German nobles had built many walled towns. Rothenburg was bombed during World War II and the clock tower was damaged.

MC LEISH

AT WORMS, northwest of Heidelberg, on the Rhine, a fine cathedral, a massive Romanesque building in the Byzantine style, rises hard by the market-place. In this ancient town, called by the Merovingians Wormatia, Martin Luther was tried in 1521.

123

ONCE AGAIN DRESDEN IS IN RUINS

Dresden was laid waste by the fire of 1685. The Seven Years' War put an end to the growth of the city and the bombardment of 1760 destroyed many of its buildings. During the Napoleonic wars Dresden suffered considerably. In World War II air raids caused the greatest destruction Dresden ever endured.

OLD TOWN HALL OF ULM WITH ITS FAMOUS FRESCOED FACADE

The town hall at Ulm, an old fortified town of Würtemberg, on the Danube, is a sixteenth-century building the style of which shows the transition from late Gothic to Renaissance. Study the frescoes on its façade, which were, however, retouched in 1925. German Ulm lies on the left bank of the Danube opposite New Ulm in Bavaria, on the right bank.

125

BAVARIAN HIGHLAND PEASANTS who live among the hills no longer wear these costly medieval costumes, though doubtless many are stored away. The much-befringed, flower-topped headgear of the man needs must be balanced by securely tying the ribbon in a firm under-the-chin bow. His appearance seems more unique than the women's attire.

HAECKEL

BRIDAL CLOAKS of heavily brocaded ribbon topped by stiffly starched embroidered ruffs were once worn by every Bückeburg bride. The floral headdress was an integral part of the ceremonial costume. Bückeburg, thirty miles southwest of Hanover, was the capital of Schaumburg-Lippe, a former principality of Germany.

THE GRAF ZEPPELIN OVER FRIEDRICHSHAFEN, GERMANY

This was one of the most famous airships developed by Germany during the 1920's. It made a record for such aircraft in 1929, when it flew around the world in a little more than twenty-one days. Though other countries followed Germany's lead in building airships, for a time, they met with so many disasters that building these huge ships has been given up as impractical. The emphasis in aviation today is on heavier-than-air craft.

aided by the British, resisted, but in vain. Within two months the Nazis had completed their conquest of the country.

In May the Germans invaded neutral Holland and Belgium. Holland was conquered in a few days; the Belgians, with French and British aid, held firm for several weeks. At last little Belgium gave up the fight. The Germans turned their attention to France and that country was brought to her knees in June.

In July the Germans launched a series of terrible air raids on England. The English were not daunted. The Germans never gained control of the skies over Britain; they had to give up any idea they might have had of invading that country. They contented themselves for a time with organizing their European conquests.

In April, 1941, Germany turned to the southeast. In a series of lightning thrusts she overwhelmed Yugoslavia, where a pro-Ally government had come into power. Then she invaded Greece, which had held off an Italian attack. That brave little country was soon overrun.

War's End and Occupation

Overconfident with victories in surrounding countries, Hitler sought to spread his conquests. Nevertheless, Goering's air war against Britain failed to set the stage for invasion. Goaded by impatience and convinced that the Red Army was weak, Hitler ordered the invasion of Russia in June 1941—in spite of the treaty of friendship that had been signed with Russia only two years before.

At first the Germans were successful and drove to within a few miles of Moscow. However, in the winter of 1942-43, after their long siege of Stalingrad was broken, the Germans began a long retreat. In the west, North Africa was lost and, in 1944, the Western Allies landed in France. They and the Russians now squeezed all Germany between their giant pincers, and the whole nazi state collapsed in May 1945.

At Potsdam, the following summer, the victorious Allies began a long period of German disarmament and reconstruction, setting up four zones of occupation with a military command of each. In her zone

Russia has used every possible means to keep all Germans from going along with Western policy. Russia has wanted a unified Germany that might fall into the Soviet sphere of influence. The Western Powers united their occupational zones and later helped set up a republic at Bonn. This new Government steadily gained political independence for the people of Western Germany. The Russians have built what they call a police force in their zone. In West Germany, plans to arm and place German troops in a North Atlantic Pact army have met with opposition from all sides. Germans are wary of taking sides openly against Russia. Russia opposes such plans with threats of war, and some Western nations fear the rebirth of a German army of any kind.

Canals and Waterways

Germany, a green forest land, is picturesquely sub-alpine on the Bavarian highlands south of the Danube. North Germany is a great plain, central and southern Germany are mountainous. The rivers all flow north. The Rhine with its splendid system of canals permits the entry of big ships to many of the industrial towns. The Kiel Canal which cuts across from the North Sea to the Baltic saves a voyage around Denmark. The Danube is Germany's outlet to Eastern Europe. The rivers, canals and the railways, to say nothing of the air lines, furnish easy transportation of freight and passengers.

With the exception of an area of large farms on the plains of northern Prussia, where rye is the best grain to withstand the severe winters, the typical farm throughout Germany is that of ten to twenty acres laid out in a long strip and intensively cultivated. The typical farmer lives sociably in a farm village and belongs to a co-operative credit association, though he seldom buys or sells co-operatively. If he lives on a sheltered slope in the Rhineland or the Bavarian highlands he raises grapes and hops in addition to his fruits and vegetables and his few farm animals. He can always get that important fertilizer, potash salts, from Prussia, though he also feeds his land

BOWERS

NEAR ST. GOARSHAUSEN, in South Germany, is some of the loveliest scenery in the famous Rhine gorge. Vineyards cover the hillsides and many of the heights are crowned by castles, from which the robber-barons of the olden days levied toll upon the river traffic. The little village of St. Goarshausen is commanded by just such a stronghold, which is called Katz Castle. The original building was erected in 1393, but it was destroyed by the French in 1806, and the present one was erected upon its foundations.

130

THE ROOFS OF SPALT, a village near Nuremberg, shelter attics suitable for drying hops. Another place where the character of the country has determined the character of the farmhouse is in the Black Forest of Baden. Here a farmer builds a commodious house up the slope of the mountain, with a roomy loft for hay, which can be dropped through a chute, and balconies under five-foot eaves for fire-wood, bees and poultry. His cattle he shelters by housing them between the mountainside and the warm kitchen-living-room.

LEIBNITZ'S HOUSE IN HANOVER

The philosopher Leibnitz's seventeenth-century dwelling, with its sandstone façade and rich plastic ornamentation, has become a museum. It is located on a corner of the Kaiserstrasse in Hanover, an important city of Prussia.

©E.N.A.

on the seventh day does one see their historic gala costumes as they go picnicking in the woods.

The government is strict in preserving the game in the splendid natural forests. Deer, wild boars and game birds are to be found in abundance.

The farm-villages are usually a little off the railroad and some of their red tiled roofs are centuries old. The kitchen–living-room on the ground floor is flanked by a barn and stable under the same sheltering roof, high-pitched against the weight of winter snows. The wooden frame that is left exposed over the concrete house walls, or their stone foundations, is often made homelike by the training of vines over trellises. The men cut the winter fuel in the forest and the women and children drive the ox or cow-team for the load. Small surpluses of fresh produce are taken to market, often by these same women with toy-like hand-carts or pack-baskets. Those of the family who work in one of the many small country factories usually prefer to live at home and work in their garden evenings. The incredibly low-priced commutation tickets on the work-trains enable them to avoid living in the cities and creating slums.

from the manure pile in front of his stable door. His farm is remarkably self-sufficient. Baden, Bavaria and Würtemberg, the last named lying along the Swiss border, are the best farm regions. There one finds farmers who conserve and enrich their land, which may have been in the family for generations. Many of these farmers who are enterprising have been adding farm improvements, even to such domestic luxuries as plumbing and electric lights. It is their pleasure to work from sun to sun, and only

As for these little country factories, the small group of workmen are on friendly terms with the owner, and those who do not live at home are housed by him. Each community may have its own village butcher who slaughters and packs for his own community. These factories are one step beyond the home industries which are still, in places, carried on during the winter months. Despite the existence of a number of really large manu-

© E. N. A.

TWIN TOWERS OF COLOGNE'S MAGNIFICENT GOTHIC CATHEDRAL

Cologne Cathedral, which is dedicated to St. Peter, is one of the finest examples of Gothic architecture in the world. It was founded in 1248, but was not completed until 1880. The twin towers are over five hundred feet in height. Cologne, important also as an industrial city, was heavily bombed by air in World War II and much damage was done.

BAVARIAN BRIDES sometimes receive cows for wedding presents. Bavaria is an agricultural country tenacious of old customs. A third of the state is deeply forested, and the mountains are almost as delightful as Switzerland. The self-sufficient small farms raise vines on the sheltered slopes, many cattle and some grain. Bavaria is five-sevenths Catholic.

HAECKEL

WENDISH GIRLS seldom wear their old-time costumes which included elaborate headdresses. The Wendish peasants, often called Sorbs, live in the upper Spree Valley from Bautzen to north of Kottbus. Many of the young peasant girls now work in the neighboring towns; pedaling back and forth on their bicycles.

135

© Aerofilms

EXTENSIVE DOCKS AND QUAYS LINING THE BANKS OF THE RIVER ELBE AT HAMBURG

Hamburg, the most important seaport in Germany, was once a member of the Hanseatic League. In 1815, it joined the German Confederation as one of the four free cities which it remained until 1935 when it became a part of the German Reich. Harbor facilities were, before 1941, the most complete in the world. A tunnel under the river gives easy access to the left bank where docks, engineering works and shipbuilding yards were established. Hamburg was the target of heavy bombing by the British in World War II.

factories in other districts, there were, before the second world war, more than a million industrial establishments to twelve million workers, an average of only twelve workers to a plant. During the war this was radically changed; huge factories with hundreds and even thousands of employes were operated under government supervision.

The Ruhr basin, with its rich coal mines and mammoth steel works, was Germany's arsenal in both world wars. After the second, it became part of the British zone of occupation. Future control of its factories and mines remained a problem, however. Though extremely important to the recovery of the whole Continent, how could they be managed so that they might never serve to make munitions again? Finally, at the end of 1948, the Western powers announced that they had agreed to set up an international authority in the Ruhr. It will weave the Ruhr industries into the economic recovery of Germany and of all Europe, and, at the same time, make certain that Germany can not use them for rearmament.

A Mighty Nation's Fall

True, many raw materials for German manufacturing had to be imported, including iron from the rich mines of Lorraine, wool and cotton and other products. Many raw materials had to be transported over long distances. All these difficulties and disadvantages the Germans had painstakingly overcome, and just before 1914 Germany was one of the three greatest commercial countries in the world. All this changed. Two wars and two defeats and two post-war depressions reduced the once-great nation to the position of a pensioner on the bounty of her conquerors. Yet with intelligence and determination Germany is attacking her problems. The problems are manifold. The flower of her young manhood was lost in the wars. Factories, shipyards, whole towns and cities were demolished. When the Nazi leaders fell, there were few men left equipped to govern, since —and this is perhaps the greatest of Germany's tragedies—the Nazi spell had been cast over the people so effectively that it has been difficult for them to "think themselves" in tune with the modern democratic world.

Love of Education

The chief characteristic of the Germans, both of the children and the grown-ups, is perhaps their love of education. There are no children who need less persuasion to go to school than German boys and girls. The German kindergarten has become so well known that the word has been absorbed into the English language.

Education is compulsory for children between six and fourteen. By a law of 1920, four years is required in the Foundation School; there is an elementary or Volkschule supported by the state in conjunction with the municipalities; a Middle School, and for those who work, evening classes in continuation schools; while the classical and scientific schools for boys and certain schools for girls prepare them for the universities.

The famous University of Heidelberg is picturesquely surrounded by forests and vineyards. Around the red roofed houses of the sleepy university town, with its quaint churches, flows the winding River Neckar. Here many tales are told of the favorite sport of the students—dueling with swords. This method of settling differences, while appearing to be very drastic, was, in reality, seldom dangerous, although slight cuts that healed into red scars, of which their owners were inordinately proud, were frequently inflicted. Jena and Göttingen are among other ancient university towns, where one pictures the student body as consuming stein after stein of beer with feast of reason and flow of soul.

Good Housewives in Germany

Nowhere in the world, perhaps, are there such economical cooks and efficient housekeepers as in Germany. Every girl has an elaborate training in the art of managing a house. When she gets married her parents give her a wedding present of bed and table linen.

Like most northern peoples, the Germans like rich, heat-producing foods—sausages, goose breast, highly ripe cheeses, washed down with quantities of light beer. Summer evenings they love to sit outside cafés drinking from tall tankards and puffing at long pipes.

German Food to be Sampled

The tourist will assuredly sample German beer with crisp salt pretzels, spicy frankfurters served with sauerkraut, and firm brown pumpernickel with the thinnest possible wafer of Limburger cheese; then at Christmas time the little squares of caraway-seed cake stamped perhaps with birds and flowers, and the frosted gingerbread men baked for the children. Pretzels were once made in the Black Forest—where they are still called *bretzeln*—to be eaten during Holy Week. The twinings represented the ropes of the Crucifixion.

So long as the country was in the hands of a military aristocracy, it was etiquette for women to step aside for soldiers as well as officers; and if one dropped so much as the flap of an envelope to the street, a policeman would be sure to make that one pick it up.

Everywhere the Germans impress us as being exceptionally formal. A German would not sit down in a restaurant in which strangers were already seated without first making a stiff bow; and etiquette among university students of certain societies required dueling according to a very strict code. When a German is introduced to anyone, he usually clicks his heels and makes a low bow.

Importance of the Theatre

The theatre has always occupied an important place in German life. Dresden, Munich, Berlin, etc., have particularly fine theatres, opera-houses and art galleries. The Germans regard the drama as an important educational force.

One hears the best music in Berlin, Leipzig, Dresden and Munich. Leipzig is a progressive town, most of it modern, though the older quarters are a maze of narrow streets. Here huge commercial fairs, attended by business men from every corner of Europe, are held. Munich is best visited at the time of its great music festival. In Hanover, the capital of the old kingdom of Hanover, buildings and customs have survived through centuries. This town is of particular interest as it was a king of Hanover who became George I of England. The three Georges who followed him and William IV were also kings of Hanover, as well as of Great Britain. Hanover has many crooked streets winding between fine old buildings that artists never tire of painting. From Hanover it is no great distance to Bückeburg, where some of the inhabitants still wear the quaint costumes of long ago.

District of the Spreewald

About two hours' journey from Berlin is the Spreewald, a low-lying district of about 160 square miles converted into islands by the tributaries of the Spree. Here the peasants wear their quaint national costumes and have retained many strange customs. The children go to school by boat, and even the cattle are taken to market in this way, for the streams are almost the only roads. A magnificent royal forest, full of wild life, adds to the natural beauty of this region, which is a part of Germany not easily forgotten.

The most impressive sight in the Spreewald is the funeral of a peasant. The hearse is a boat which glides slowly on its way carrying the coffin to its last resting-place. Behind it comes a procession of mourners in boats, the women wearing long white scarves which make them look like ghosts.

It is to the country, especially to the districts of the south and west, and to the smaller towns that we must go if we wish to see the old Germany. Here, in spite of war and revolution, we can almost imagine that we are back in the Middle Ages. After the well built towns of North Germany, with their elaborate public buildings and monuments, medieval Königsberg, Rothenburg and Greifswald are an extraordinary contrast.

Georg Haeckel

NEW TOWN HALL OF LEIPZIG, FIRST CITY IN SAXONY AND ONE OF GERMANY'S PRINCIPAL COMMERCIAL CENTRES

The new town hall of Leipzig, occupying the southwest corner of the inner town, is a handsome pile in the German Renaissance style, begun in 1899 and completed in 1905. It stands on the site of the Pleissenburg, the ancient citadel of which the only remaining relic is the carefully pre-served and reconstructed tower. Leipzig, a large industrial town in Saxony, birthplace of W. Richard Wagner, the dramatic composer, poet and essayist, is a musical centre, and the centre of German book publishing and selling, and contains one of Europe's most ancient universities.

In the River Neckar Valley

Up the valley of the River Neckar (beyond Heidelberg) is the district of Swabia. Here, among beautiful hills and valleys, we may see many old castles and fortresses. It is a land of woodsmen and quaintly garbed peasants, and has health-giving springs which have been visited by invalids from early Roman times. In the little town of Marbach the poet Schiller was born. Wienburg, Wimpfen and Heilbron are other places where we can see something of peasant life.

In the old German towns there is always a quaint market place, generally cobbled and surrounded by gabled houses. Here the peasants bring their wares from the surrounding countryside. The fairs and markets are like scenes from a fairy tale of the brothers Grimm. The stalls are shaded by bright umbrellas and some of the peasants still dress as their ancestors did hundreds of years ago.

Everyone has heard of the beauty of the valley of the Rhine, which is made even more romantic by the old castles crowning so many of the heights. The best part of this lovely district lies between Bingen and Bonn. There are numerous legends about the Rhine and the Rhineland. Wagner composed three world-famous operas based on them.

Cologne and Its Cathedral

The chief town on the banks of the River Rhine is Cologne. The port of Cologne was founded in 38 B.C. To-day it is a large metropolis and contains many historical treasures and monuments, and old buildings side by side with modern shops. It is called the holy city because of its many churches. Rising above all are the two spires of its famous cathedral.

Cologne is the fourth largest city of the Federal Republic; it is one of the Rhine's busiest ports, being a center of trade between Switzerland, southern Germany and the Low Countries. Dresden, capital of Saxony, in the East German Republic, is noted for many fine buildings.

Berlin is treated in another chapter.

Hamburg, a great port on the North Sea, at the mouth of the Elbe, was formerly one of the greatest ship-building centers in the world; but it was bombed again and again during the war. The shipyards, and much of the city, were destroyed. Hamburg came into being when Charlemagne built a fort on the spot. Bremen, Kiel, Stettin, Lübeck and Königsberg were also important ports. Königsberg is in the part of East Prussia taken by Russia after Germany's defeat; and Stettin, called Szczecin in Polish, was given to Poland.

Romantic Black Forest Region

The upper course of the Rhine River winds through the fabled Black Forest. Medieval castles, fit settings for fairy tales, still lie hidden in the deep wood. Here the winters are intensely cold, and not a great many years ago, wolves pursued travelers in the remoter fastnesses. To-day tourists go to the Black Forest for the winter sports—skiing, skating, sledding and just tramping through the pine-covered highlands and into splendid valleys, such as the Murgthal. Most of the Black Foresters herd cattle; few farm because the soil is so poor. The hills are very ancient. Not far below the topsoil is a hard crust of granite, some limestone and clay, and such minerals as silver, lead, copper, iron and cobalt. Some inhabitants fell the pine and form the timbers into rafts for shipment down the Rhine to Holland where the lumber is highly prized.

Other industries of the region are wood-carving, toy- and watchmaking and the manufacture of musical instruments. The healthful baths of Baden-Baden, also in the forest, are of world-wide fame.

Just before the outbreak of World War II Germany had the fifth largest merchant marine in the world, with a tonnage of well over 4,000,000. When war broke out, Allied naval power drove Germany's merchant ships from the seven seas. Some of her vessels were intercepted by Allied warships and either captured or else scuttled by their own crews. Others sought refuge in neutral harbors. Many of these were confiscated when erstwhile

ONE OF THE MANY CANALS IN THE OLD QUARTER OF HAMBURG

In the old portions of Hamburg, where it rains two days out of every three, many canals and inlets flow through the city. At certain times these waterways can be crossed dry-shod, but at times of very high water they may flood the lower buildings. At the end of the canal you can see the spire of St. Nicholas Church.

neutral nations, like Mexico and Brazil, entered the war on the side of the Allies. It will be a very long time before the country can hope to build up another merchant marine to compare with that of her prewar days, or be of any consequence in world trade.

German Aircraft

Germany's accomplishments in the air have been important. Count von Zeppelin built the first successful lighter-than-air passenger airship and thereafter the Germans kept in the lead with this type of craft. The most famous dirigible of all, perhaps, was the Graf Zeppelin, designed by Dr. Hugo Eckener. In 1928 this enormous craft crossed the ocean to Lakehurst, New Jersey. Next year it made a trip around the world by way of Tokyo, Los Angeles and Lakehurst. Later the Graf Zeppelin made regular trips between Germany and South America. In 1936 a still larger ship, the Hindenburg, made a number of transatlantic trips. It was destroyed in May, 1937, by a mysterious fire as it was about to land at Lakehurst, on its first trip of the year. After that time the Germans devoted comparatively little attention to the dirigible.

Germans contributed considerably to the development of heavier-than-air craft, and their planes have kept abreast of the latest developments in heavier-than-air manufacture. Before World War II the planes of the German company known as the Deutsche Lufthansa made regular trips between the principal cities not only of Germany but of Europe. This company also provided service to Africa and South America and set up a number of affiliated companies in various countries. Of course the Lufthansa did not survive Germany's defeat.

World Manufacturer of Drugs

Germany became a leader in the manufacture of drugs, dyes and other coaltar products. She learned how to make synthetic gasoline from lignite (brown coal) and in two world wars she was able to maintain the fuel supplies of her armies with this synthetic gasoline.

In the 1890's there was at Leverkusen, near Cologne, a dye and chemical plant laid out in blocks like city streets, surrounded by a model town for workers. At Leunawerk, near Merseburg, there was a plant that was a city in itself. In the words of one visitor: "At one corner stands an assemblage of huge gas tanks, at another a group of truncated balloons of ammonia liquor. Eleven monumental chimneys mark the largest steam-generating station in the world. Its shrieks and odors and its towering flame where waste gases are burned from a high stack make it seem an inferno. Hum of dynamos, rows of self-registering dials, machinery working at pressures and temperatures beyond human endurance, these too impress the visitor." The Leunawerk plant, which was started in 1916, was truly something to be remembered. It was originally designed to make explosives for the German armies of World War I. After the first world war it was returned to peacetime manufacturing.

Nitrogen-fixation for Farmlands

The huge Leunawerk plant was turned to the conversion of brown coal into synthetic gasoline and into gleaming white nitrogen fertilizer for Germany's farmlands. During World War II, explosives were again made at the plant.

The Krupp Works, originally a steel manufacturing plant, was founded at Essen in 1800 by Friedrich Krupp, a German ironmaster. The company turned in the course of time to the manufacture of munitions; the Krupp Works became a renowned munitions plant. It supplied the Central Powers with most of the munitions used by them in World War I.

After the war Krupp's turned to the fixation of nitrogen fertilizer from the air and the manufacture of synthetic gasoline from coal. Other products turned out at this time included turbines, cash registers and agricultural machinery. The Krupp Works engaged again in the manufacture of munitions after the Nazis came into power. The plant was heavily bombed many times in World War II by the British Royal Air Force.

V-E Day and V-J Day, both in 1945, marked the beginning of profound changes in the field of government all over the world. The end of the Third German Reich highlighted the many boundary and government shifts.

None of Germany's boundaries endure except as defined and approved by the Allies. In June, 1945, the Allies announced division of most of the land comprising pre-war Germany into four zones of occupation controlled by France, the United Kingdom, the United States and the Union of Soviet Socialist Republics.

The rise and ruin of Berlin as Germany's capital and a world metropolis have taken place within the last three-quarters of a century. The transport facilities of Berlin made her one of the chief bomb targets of the Allied forces.

GERMANY: FACTS AND FIGURES

THE COUNTRY

Germany occupies the great northern plain of Europe between the Alps and the North and Baltic seas and between the Rhine and Oder rivers. The Federal Republic (Western Germany), with its capital at Bonn, was formed from the British, French and U.S. zones of occupation; the Democratic Republic (Eastern Germany), with its capital at Berlin, was formed from the Soviet zone. Germany lost considerable territory at the end of World War II, especially on the east, to the Soviet Union and to Poland. Western Germany: area, 94,723 sq. mi.; population, 44,637,260. Eastern Germany: area, 41,369 sq. mi.; population, 17,313,734. Berlin, under the Allied Control Council: area, 343 sq. mi.; population, 3,199,938.

GOVERNMENT

The Federal Republic of Germany is a democratic federal state. It is governed under a "Basic Law," or constitution, which went into effect in May 1949. There is a Federal Diet; a Federal Council, consisting of provincial representatives; and a Federal Convention, consisting of the Diet and an equal number of representatives elected from the provincial legislatures. The Federal Convention elects both the president and the prime minister. The Cabinet is proposed by the prime minister. Eastern Germany: closely supervised by Soviet officials; a constitution enacted in October 1949 set up a parliament, premier and Cabinet.

COMMERCE AND INDUSTRIES

Small estates and peasant proprietorship prevail in the west and south German states while large estates prevailed in the northeast before World War II. Crops are potatoes, sugar beets, and rye. Forestry is an important industry and carried on under state control on scientific lines. There are coal and iron mines in Prussia, brown coal in Central Germany, copper and iron in the Harz, iron in the Westerwald and coal in Saxony. From the North Sea and the Baltic Sea there is a large yield of fish. The principal industries include iron and steel manufactures, electrical goods, chemicals, textiles, linen, cotton goods, woolens, beet-root sugar, potash, glass, porcelain and earthenware, clocks and wooden ware, tobacco products and beer.

The chief articles of export are iron and steel, chemicals, machinery, electrical parts, silk, sugar, woolens, cottons, leather, clothing, toys, furs, coal, paper, glassware, ceramics and chinaware, paints and hops. Imports are cotton, wool, wheat, oil seeds, cotton yarn, iron and steel, tobacco, lard, timber, meats, copper and automobiles.

COMMUNICATIONS

Pre-war railway length, 42,299 miles; 1949 (Bizone—British and American zones), 19,063 miles. Highway length (West German Federal Republic), 63,862 miles. Telephone sets (West Germany, 1949), 1,974,036; (East Germany) 250,000. Length of inland waterways, 3,183.

RELIGION AND EDUCATION

Council of the Evangelical Church annulled the constitution of the Hitler-sponsored state church in 1946. 62% of the total population is Protestant and 35% Catholic, according to census. Education from 6 to 14 compulsory and highly developed. Supplementary to the elementary schools is a system of secondary and continuation schools and gymnasia, which prepare pupils in a nine years' course for the universities and learned professions, and technical high schools, normal schools, agricultural high schools and commercial schools. There are 25 universities.

CHIEF TOWNS

Populations of principal cities (1946 census): Berlin, 3,199,938. *West Germany:* Bonn (capital), 94,000; Hamburg, 1,403,300; Munich, 751,-967; Essen, 524,728; Cologne, 491,380; Dortmund, 436,491; Frankfurt, 424,065; Düsseldorf, 420,909; Stuttgart, 414,072; Bremen, 385,266; Duisburg, 356,408; Hanover, 354,955; Wuppertal, 325,846; Nuremberg, 312,338; Gelsenkirchen, 265,793; Bochum, 246,477; Lübeck, 223,059; Kiel, 214,335; Mannheim, 211,614; Wiesbaden, 188,370; Brunswick, 181,375; Oberhausen, 174,-117; Karlsruhe, 172,343; Augsburg, 160,055; Krefeld-Uerdingen, 150,354; Solingen, 133,001; Mulheim-on-Ruhr, 132,370; Bielefeld, 132,276. *East Germany:* Leipzig, 607,655; Dresden, 467,-966; Chemnitz, 250,188; Magdeburg, 236,326; Halle, 222,505; Erfurt, 174,633.

BERLINERS TAKE TO THE COUNTRYSIDE

The bicycle is a popular form of transportation in Germany. Boys and girls cycle to school, and their elders cycle to work. On vacations the city-folk love to don a regional costume, pack a bundle of food and other provisions, and set off. They may go to the Hartz Mountains in central Germany, or south to Bavaria and the foothills of the Alps.

Berlin in Eclipse

Life Goes On Amid the Ruins

Berlin is not a dying city. Dusk has closed down upon the strange Nazi gods who ruled there for ten troubled years, but the people remain, and it is people that give life to a city. Berlin, like other cities which were crushed by the war, is slowly being rebuilt. For a few of the people, life begins to approach normal; for most the vista looks grim enough. The fact that Berlin is being ruled in sections, by powers of widely differing political philosophy, makes a confused situation. Yet today the visitor sees a city in the process of recovery and transition. In order to understand Berlin and its people, one must try to visualize the metropolis as it was before the war.

THE air route is the ideal approach to Berlin. By no other means can one grasp the size of the area that the city covers. Of course, many buildings were destroyed and streets torn up by bombs during the war, but people who knew Berlin in the old days can still recognize it even in its battered condition. Venerable, and in many cases, unbeautiful landmarks of the present and of a bygone day have been sacrificed to the demands of war. Railroad yards, factories and warehouses, governmental buildings, palaces and private dwellings, all lay in the path of destruction. To a person peering out of a plane, the most amazing thing is the number of landmarks that survive. For example, one can pick out from the cluttering buildings—like a tiny object seen through a microscope—the palace of the Reichstag, the chief administrative building of the German nation during the empire, the republic and the Nazi dictatorship.

Berlin is new as European towns go. As a great capital it is less than a hundred years old, and few of its notable buildings are much older. It has never been especially noted for architectural beauty or distinction, and it has none of relics of medieval times that distinguish Nuremburg, Paris, or even London.

It is spread out over a sandy plain in the bleak northeastern part of Germany. Through the city cuts the river Spree (pronounced "shpray"), a navigable stream, connected by a system of canals with the Oder and the Elbe. A tiny fishing village existed here as early as the thirteenth century. In 1448 it became the official residence of the Hohenzollern family, ruling house of the duchy of Brandenburg. Later, when the Hohenzollerns became kings of Prussia, and still later when William I and his great minister, Bismarck, united most of the independent German states into the German Empire, Berlin's importance as the Hohenzollern capital grew.

During the reigns of the kings of Prussia and under the empire, much of the building was done which set the style for the city as we have known it. The rulers of Berlin, from the time of Frederick the Great to the end of the first World War, were ardent admirers of French architecture and landscaping; especially of the period of Louis XIV. The native Prussian characteristics could not be completely overcome by French taste, however, so that most of the royally inspired and planned architecture of Berlin had a heaviness and stiffness that the French models escaped.

The central feature of Berlin, and the center of social and official life, was around Unter-den-Linden, a mile-long double avenue reaching from the old imperial palace to the Brandenburg Gate, at the entrance to the park called the *Tiergarten.* The avenue takes its name from the rows of lime trees (lindens) planted along its length.

No city so bristled with outdoor statuary and monuments as did Berlin. Most of these were testimonials to the military and other virtues of the Hohenzollerns.

GERMANS LOVE THE OUTDOOR LIFE

Berlin is fortunate in having a network of streams, lakes and woods in its suburbs. In the spring and summer, young and old love to escape from city life and relax in water sports and in the pleasures of the country-side. Grünewald and the Havel Lakes, Spandau and the Spreewald are favorite locales. In winter these waterways are often used for ice-skating.

The artistic merit of most of the statues was questioned, yet they were a source of deep pride to the patriotic residents of the capital. The war changed things considerably. Hardest hit of all Berlin's treasures were the thirty-two statues of historic German military leaders which stood on the Siegesallee in the Tiergarten.

Oddly enough, Berlin owed her magnificent airport, the Tempelhof, to Frederick the Great, who first created the flat, smooth area of land as a parade ground. In 1948 this airport became the terminal for the "airlift" of American and British planes bringing in food and other supplies to the blockaded city. The airlift, though costly, proved to be extraordinarily successful.

Unhappily, both for the city itself and for the world's hopes of peace, Berlin became the focal point of the "cold war" between the Western powers and the Soviet Union. Part of the trouble was a matter of location. After the war, Russia occupied the eastern part of Germany, which includes Berlin. Yet the city itself was occupied by all four powers, the United States, Britain, France and the Soviet, each of which controlled what came to be called a "sector." Rail and road transportation between the West and the Western sectors of the city, therefore, had to pass through the Soviet zone; and early in 1948 the Soviet began to restrict these lines, finally cutting these sectors off altogether, and putting the people there in danger of starvation. To relieve this desperate situation, the Western powers put the airlift into operation at the end of June 1948. Tons of food, medicine, even machinery, were flown into the blockaded sectors during the following months.

Berliners had elected a city government, but as friction grew worse between the Western sectors and the Soviet sector—adding to international tension—a Communist-dominated "government" was set up in the Soviet sector.

In Berlin, more than in other German cities, one may feel that boundless energy and ambition which have driven Germany to her greatest heights and deepest despairs. But not on Sunday. On Sunday the streets are deserted. At this same hour in Paris the Champs Elysées is thronged with a chattering, strolling mob; but every German who can do so spends Sunday in the country. Those who cannot, go to the city parks. So, if the visitor wishes to leave the bustling city and spend the day, or the weekend in the country he will find

he has plenty of company. By eight o'clock of a Saturday morn the canals and rivers are swarming with craft carrying families and groups of friends to the tree-girt lakes that are not too far from the city. Such a welter of happy confusion! Back to nature for a few hours. Make the utmost use of that precious leisure! The sun-flecked landscape is one of wistful, nostalgic beauty.

Rowboats trail along through the watery lanes, under gracefully arched bridges—of which Berlin has even more than Venice itself!

Stumble to the first propitious spot and sit on some verdant bank to watch the scene. Sailing craft and motor launches, rowboats and canoes dot the lake. Groups of swimmers plow sparkling ribbons through the blue. Children splash along

GERMAN CHILDREN AT SPORTS CARNIVAL

A love of sports, including every type of outdoor exercise, has long been characteristic of the German people. They enjoy camping and hiking, as well as games, such as football, track and swimming races. This enthusiasm, however, has been used by German political leaders as a means of organizing the people for war. Sport must be adapted to peaceful living.

GERMANS RETURN TO THE WORK OF PEACE

To feed the conquered nation, these former German soldiers are being sent out by the Allied authorities to help with the harvest. The girls, who will share in the work, join in songs as they march to the fields. Slowly, very slowly, peacetime conditions and activities are being revived; Germans are being encouraged to work in solving their own food problem.

the shore. Berlin is so far north that it enjoys from sixteen to eighteen hours of summer daylight. The holiday afternoons have a timeless quality.

A picnic supper is delicious, when eaten under the trees. Coffee bubbles with a hunger-teasing aroma, mixed with discussions of Goethe and Shakespeare, the morals of the younger generation, the high cost of living, the music of Wagner or Richard Strauss. Huddle at the water's edge and sing a song that will drift across the lake, when darkness falls. To crown a day of never-to-be-forgotten experiences, sleep in a flimsy tent, guarded, perhaps by an old, imposing castle.

If a longer excursion is not possible, Father takes the family walking in the park on clear Sundays. All give obedient heed to the *"Verboten"* signs on the grass.

Verboten (forbidden) is as potent as ever. Berliners have a deep sense of respect for law, for organization and the symbols of power.

Berlin city workers have easily accessible contact with the land that is so dear to the German heart. Here centers the odd-hour and the week-end life of a substantial number of families.

Screber was a famous physician in the days of 1860. A philanthropist honored the doctor by founding the so-called *Screber Garten* movement. This trend, which spread to most cities of Germany, promotes bodily fitness through exercise, and minimizes food cost. The land is public-owned, but implements and seed and use of the land is furnished to the gardeners at a nominal fee. Beside each garden is a wee tool-and-implement shed.

The city-dwelling youths of all the German towns have walking clubs. They make long marches over the country-side singing as they march. They may camp in the open at night; or they may spend the night at one of the simple youth hostels which have been provided for them.

Every true Berliner loves to sit and sip and talk; and there are in the city innumerable outdoor restaurants where a group may sit for hours in cheerful indolence. The tables are of plain deal; covered with bright checkered cotton cloths. The chairs or benches are hard. But there is a band playing gay or sentimental tunes and here and there a waiter bursts into song. In some of the more informal places, families even make their own coffee, the restaurant providing water and cups.

Less festive, perhaps, are the fashionable restaurants, where the coffee is flavored with the thrill of seeing and displaying the newest clothes. Ah, yes! Berliners crowd the sidewalk cafes to see and to be seen. If a visitor comes from a warmer clime he may find a social venture a chilly experience.

There was a time when far more beer than coffee was drunk in the restaurants, which were called, appropriately enough, beer gardens. Beer gardens are proud of their old names and their bustling respectability; yet judge of the amount habitually drunk by the best people in the olden days by a cellar rule of the Electorate of Bavaria in 1648: "Countesses and ladies of nobility are allowed four quarts for the day and three quarts for the night!"

In 1690 an ordinance was passed by the Elector Frederick III forbidding the burghers of the neighborhood to allow their hogs to root around on the public street, as they were injuring the trees!

Press Association, Inc.

BERLINERS SEARCH FOR THEIR HOMES

When the guns and the air raids had ceased, with the coming of peace, the people of Berlin piled their few possessions into carts and went to search for their former homes amid the ruins. Only a small proportion of the houses could be reoccupied. Makeshift quarters had to be found until the time might come when it would be possible to rebuild these dwellings.

Press Association, Inc.

DOWNFALL OF THE GERMAN CAPITAL

The numerous aerial bombardments of Berlin and the guns of the Russian artillery brought tremendous destruction to what had been the fourth largest city in the world. Many sections were almost completely wiped out. Years must pass before the city can wear any semblance of its former appearance. The same thing is true of Hamburg and many other German cities.

The concern which the Elector Frederick showed for the welfare of the city's trees has been characteristic of most Berliners in recent times. Before the war a census of trees standing in streets and squares—not counting those in parks— totaled half a million. Dorthea, wife of the Great Elector, herself planted the first linden tree in 1681. Perhaps it would have been fairer to have named the wide boulevard, Unter-den-Linden, after Dorthea, instead of after the tree she planted.

As recently as 1870 the city streets were largely unpaved, and housing, drainage and water supplies were very poor indeed. This state of affairs was not allowed to continue much longer, however, and in our own century Berlin has been noted for its well-kept streets and modern facilities.

When pavements were laid and pipes and conduits placed under the streets, some of the dignified old patriarchs were carefully dug up and transplanted in other, more hospitable, locations.

There are few trees left now; the scorching breath of war has withered them; but there can be no doubt that trees will again line the streets and squares of the city. Trees. Therein has always lain Berlin's greatest hold on the hearts of its people. Armies of trees in close formation stood in public parks, and through them were cut beguiling avenues and paths.

"Where'er you walk, cool gales shall
    fan the glade;
Trees where you sit shall crowd
    Into the shade."

Finding a husband continues to be the principal preoccupation of Berlin's young women. Keeping house for their husbands and children is the main business of Berlin's wives. Husbands in Germany have seldom had to suffer through experimental housekeeping, for Gretchen is already an experienced domestic artist when she marries. She has learned from her mother to cook well and to keep her household in spick-and-span order. She will in turn pass these domestic virtues on to her daughter. This combination of industry, frugality and inborn business acumen has produced a proud womanhood, and these qualities have been thoroughly tested by the difficulties of life under the Nazi regime and during the war. The women have borne up with dignity in making the best of any situation. This may be attributed to apathy or to icy resolution, but it is a fact. One may well wonder whether, in the years to come, the women of Berlin will reject the edict of Bismarck and later of Hitler, which limited her sphere to the four K's—*Kinder, Kleider, Küche, Kirche*

(children, clothes, kitchen and church).

Big, busy Berlin, like St. Louis or Chicago, sits at the center of a vast railroad net. Under normal conditions the rails race day and night with never-ending traffic linking all of Germany with all of Europe and even linking Berlin to distant Asia.

Today no portion of Germany is more than twelve hours from Berlin by rail. Through Berlin pass the lines connecting Paris with Warsaw and Moscow, the Scandinavian countries with Italy, and the North Sea ports with Odessa. From the point of view of land transportation, Germany's capital enjoys facilities unsurpassed by any other European city.

Because it is spread over so much territory, the Berlin tourist's casual eye overlooks the Spree's enormous water-borne traffic. But a glance at a big-scale city map shows how conveniently the capital is served by canals and rivers which connect it with inland cities.

Press Association, Inc.

POSTWAR POVERTY IN BERLIN

Three homeless families, sixteen people in all, occupy a single room fitted with wooden bunks in the style of soldiers' barracks. Here eleven of the occupants are shown waiting for a pot of soup to cook on the stove. These people were cared for by the Red Cross. Throughout Germany the destruction of cities left countless families without a home.

WAITING TO GO HOME

Displaced persons, old and young, were sent to their former homes from displaced persons camps run by the United Nations Relief and Rehabilitation Administration (UNRRA).

A large number of fruit barges come in from the provinces, bringing apples, pears, and peaches in their holds. In some cases these loads are marketed directly from the barges, which find mooring at advantageous points within the town.

Canals link the rivers to form the inland port. Constructed in most of the abandoned valleys carved by the glacial streams which ran along the front of the former ice-sheet, the canals make east-west crossroads. It is easy to see why Berlin, with its unusual facilities for land, air and water transport, became a great industrial and trade center as well as a governmental city. In all probability the reconstructed city will continue to be a great center.

Plans have already been projected for the creation of a new city out of the wreckage of the old. According to the *Festsetzungsplan* the new Berlin will comprise a theater city, a university city and a technological city. In the past the majority of Berliners have been apartment dwellers. The desire for a one-family house with a garden has become very general among the citizens. In the new city large open spaces, the *Dauerwalder,* will be reserved for playgrounds and sports grounds and allotment gardens. The great traffic arteries that connect Berlin with neighboring towns make easily accessible the attractive country on the outskirts of the city. The new Berlin, with the River Spree extended to three times its present width, is to be a "garden city." The general plan is intended to direct all these tendencies on the right lines. The *Stadtverordneteneuersammlung* or general assembly of town councillors will be the central body.

Not quite so apt today would be Mark Twain's delicious comment on German speech. He likened a German in the midst of a sentence to an underwater swimmer, except that he ultimately does end holding his verb in his mouth. The language, particularly the written language, is in a state of evolution. The tendency is American tempo—crisp, short sentences rather than the traditional long-winded style. So it is not only Berlin's physical aspect which is undergoing change today.

The city has been in a state of transition and recuperation. The pompous old architectural forms vanished. Native Berliners do not deplore this. In fact, they are happy to see a style of realistic beauty evolve in keeping with today's needs.

The day-to-day decisions of the occupying powers are helping to set some strange new patterns in this city which refused to die. We must follow the swiftly moving course of events as they are reported in our newspapers and over the radio if we wish to see Berlin-after-the-war. No one can safely predict the future, but it is reasonable to suppose that Berlin has had her hour as capital of a mighty state.

However, it is likely to remain a leading "character" on the world stage as long as the "iron curtain" divides its streets and its inhabitants, as well as the forces of occupation. To really recover in spirit, to build new homes and schools, to revive trade with the rest of Germany and of the world, Berlin must, some day, become a united whole again.

A State with a Glorious Past

How Poland Rose and Fell

Through the Middle Ages and the Renaissance, Poland was a great force in eastern Europe, but in the eighteenth century, Austria, Germany and Russia began whittling away at Poland's territory until there was no Poland left at all. At the end of World War I Poland emerged as a sovereign republic, only to be split up again between Germany and Russia when World War II began. In 1941 Germany opened its invasion of Russia and occupied all of Poland. When the Russian armies swept back the Germans, Poland's independence was again proclaimed. But since 1945 Poland has been closely drawn in as a satellite by Soviet Russia and independence is yet far away.

ONCE upon a time the kingdom of Poland stretched from the Baltic to the Black Sea. By the nineteenth century there was no Poland. Three great empires—the German, Russian and Austro-Hungarian—had gobbled her. Whenever Poles tried to recover their liberty, they were sent into exile, imprisoned or killed. Poles were forbidden for a time even to use their own language.

When Poland was restored in 1918 the people began to dream of making their country again a world power. It was the sixth largest state in Europe in both area and population, though only half the size of the old kingdom of Poland. The soil was rich and well-watered. The name Poland means Land of the Plains, which is descriptive of it. With the exception of that portion lying in the Carpathians in the south, the plains region presented to the traveler of yesteryear, sailing through the Bay of Danzig down the Vistula to Warsaw, the yellow of broad, ripening fields of grain, the rich earthy smell of level acres of potatoes and sugar beets. Over in the Black Country of Silesia the coveted lands still are level. The cities are less attractive, sombre with soft-coal smoke, though possessed of many buildings of historic interest.

In summer the mountain pastures of the Carpathians are musical with the tinkle of cattle-bells and the weird flute-playing of shepherds guarding their flocks. In winter the Carpathians take on a wild beauty—pines and junipers leaded with snow, the air biting, the sky at night spangled with stars. In peaceful times, it is a wonderful region for winter sports, skiing and tobogganing.

The Poles are hard workers who love the soil and till it diligently. They combine the qualities of many stocks, though they are largely of Slavic origin.

THE REPUBLIC OF POLAND

153

Polish Legation

TURNING PUSSY-WILLOWS INTO BASKETS ON THE POLISH PLAIN

Willows grow profusely along the rivers of the Polish plain. This natural resource is put to good use by the industrious peasants, for nothing is more suitable for basket-making than the pliant young osiers, as Europeans call them. Here we see a mother and father busy making hampers outside their thatched cottage while the five children watch the process, eager to learn this agreeable way of earning, possibly, shoes to wear to school.

They have produced some of the great artists and scientists. Copernicus, who wrote a famous book in which he suggested that the earth actually moves around the sun and not the sun around the earth, was a Pole; so was Chopin, the composer; and so was Paderewski, the pianist, who was chosen prime minister of the Polish republic. Madame Curie (Marie Sklo-dowska), discoverer of radium, was born at Warsaw. Poland is the land of Ladislas Reymont and the birthplace of Joseph Conrad, to name only a few of her great ones.

Five out of every ten people in Poland live on the land. A Polish farmer can do wonders with a small tract; however, some of the very large estates were

SKIERS ENJOY THE STEEP, SNOWY MOUNTAINS NEAR ZAKOPANE

In southern Poland, close to the border of Czechoslovakia, is the resort town of Zakopane. It is about three thousand feet above sea level in a section of the Carpathians called the High Tatra. The town was founded in the sixteenth century and in later years became a fun and health center, with sanitoria and hotels for convalescents, sportsmen and vacationers.

155

as large, in olden days, as little countries, and their owners ruled over them like princes. The size of some of the old estates can be imagined by the fact that the largest two were together as big as England. All the peasants were the serfs of the nobles. Although no longer serfs, Polish farmers have little freedom under the communist system of state control.

The Poles originated in the ancient pagan tribe of Slavs that made its way from the northern grasslands to the Vistula. Christianity came to Poland from Rome in 965 and the country has remained predominantly Catholic.

Boleslaus the Brave was the first King of Poland. He came to the throne in 1025 determined to withstand German aggression, but the Teutons gained a foothold two centuries later. In the thirteenth century Poland played an important role in preventing savage hordes of Mongolian Tatars from entering the green lands of Western Europe. On account of helplessness against the Germans, she became for a time united with Lithuania when her nobles persuaded Hedwiga to marry Jagiello, the Grand Prince of the more powerful country to the north. As King of Poland, he changed his name, in 1386, to Ladislas II, and together the two countries defeated the Knights on the field of Tannenberg (Grunewald) in 1410. In the sixteenth century Poland, under the leadership of John Sobieski, stopped the Turks on their way across Europe to make converts to Mohammed by the sword; and in 1683 came gloriously to the rescue when Austria was on the point of losing Vienna to the Turks.

Now came a time when the rulers of Poland's three most powerful neighbors were unusually covetous of Poland's mines and forests and her vast agricultural estates, which were held by a few nobles and worked by many serfs, with

PIX

TO MARKET, TO MARKET! TOWARD THE TOWN OF MINSK MAZOWIECKI

Not to be confused with the much larger city of Minsk in White Russia, Minsk Mazowiecki is not far from Warsaw. The hard-working peasants of this town see few automobiles. They carry their products to market in primitive wagons drawn by plodding horses. Once the majority of Poles were farmers, but the advance of industrialization is changing that.

THE CLOTH HALL IN THE MARKET PLACE OF KRAKOW

Planned and built in the thirteenth century, after the Tatars had laid waste nearly all of the old city, the famous Cloth Hall (Sukiennice) has been altered in some ways through the years; but it has retained its Moslem design. Krakow is a very ancient city, and this cobblestoned square still has an air of the Middle Ages about it.

LUSTY SON AND HEIR OF A POLISH PEASANT FAMILY

During the brief period of Poland's independence (twenty years, between wars) much was done to improve the condition of the peasants; and all arable land in the country was put under cultivation. Although, in this period, Poland made wonderful progress in mining and in industry, agriculture remained the chief pursuit of the people.

SUNDAY CLOTHING THAT BRIGHTENS THE STREETS OF ZYRARDÓW

Southwest of Warsaw lies Zyrardów, to which Philippe de Girard brought his newly invented flax-spinning machine in 1835. The town has since become an industrial center, famous for the gorgeously striped fabrics in which these girls are attired. Full skirt and apron are woven in all the hues of the rainbow. Such gaily colored national costumes are seldom seen nowadays.

no middle class whatever. Alarmed, Poland made the mistake of asking aid of non-Christian Turkey. Outraged Austria, Russia and Prussia sent troops into Poland and in 1772 divided a third of her territory among themselves.

Twenty-one years later Prussia and Russia again decided to help themselves to Poland. Within two years Poland was again divided, this time ceasing to exist as an independent state. Her national feeling persisted, however, despite laws forbidding even the reading of Polish literature. When World War I broke out, though entire regiments refused to fight and were shot down, other Poles were forced to fight in both the Russian and the German armies. Some Poles managed to escape to the Allies.

The Republic of Poland was proclaimed on November 9, 1918. In 1920 Bolshevik invaders burned the harvests, but their drive finally was repulsed. Poland had been fought over until fields were pitted deep with shell holes.

Negotiations at the Versailles peace conference granted Poland the provinces of Posen and West Prussia, with the exception of Danzig, which was set up as a free city. These territories were taken from Germany. From Russia and Austria, Poland received Vilna (eastern Lithuania), Galicia and part of Silesia.

A New Constitution

The government, based on the constitution of 1921, was democratic; there were two Houses of Parliament elected by all citizens over twenty-one years of age, and a president elected by Parliament.

Unfortunately the democratic constitution did not solve Poland's many difficulties. The German mark, which at that time was rapidly losing all value, was the standard national currency. The entire new republic suffered from the same inflation that was causing so much misery in her defeated neighbor to the west.

There were as many solutions to the financial ills of Poland as there were parties in Parliament, and these numbered from eight to ten. There were people favoring close co-operation with France.

Others looked to Russia for help in spite of the fact that the new rulers in Russia —the Communists—were known to encourage attacks on Poland's eastern border. Public feeling in Poland had always tended to regard Russia with hate and fear. The most powerful party at the time was that of Joseph Pilsudski, who had led an army that fought with Germany and Austria during World War I against Russia.

Dictatorship and Inflation

Although his ruthless methods alarmed many people, Pilsudski had followers among both rich and poor and was able to take over the government as dictator in 1926. In solving Poland's first problem, inflation, Pilsudski felt that it would be necessary to weaken the constitutional rights of other parties. He planned to strengthen Poland's currency by withdrawing German marks and backing up a new exchange with revenues from high taxes. It was also necessary to place merchants, farmers and manufacturers under the tight control of government.

For a time he succeeded in his plans. He balanced Poland's budget; he reduced the nation's indebtedness to other countries and to people within Poland. Indeed, for three years before 1930, his treasury showed a surplus, and Polish products found markets throughout the world. Profits from exports paid for needed improvements within the country. People were not so drastically affected by the seasonal ups and downs of farm life. In days of plenty Pilsudski stored food. In days of scarcity he dipped into storehouses and distributed food to the needy. During this time of stability the dictator's opponents were seldom heard outside the halls of Parliament. But, because Poland depended on the stability of France and the other nations with which she traded, her prosperity was short-lived. She went down to ruin with France in the depression that swept the world in 1930. Pilsudski's government went deeply into debt. The former surplus was used up.

Another cause of unrest was Pilsudski's inability to get along with other nations.

THE CHIMNEY SWEEP ON HIS TRADITIONAL ROUND IN KATOWICE

Katowice on the Rawa River, where ancient practice and modern ways go hand in hand, is one of Poland's large cities. It is a manufacturing center situated in the vital coal-producing region of Silesia. Poland is richly endowed with coal deposits. The marked increase in coal mined in recent years has been an important factor in her industrial advance.

McLeish

BAREFOOT TOWNSFOLK OF ZYRARDÓW GATHER TOGETHER IN A COBBLED STREET OF THEIR TOWN

The garb of these townspeople tells its own tale of poverty. The woman on the left carries her shoes to save them; the water-carrier in the foreground wears unabashed breeches made of a colored bedspread; and the kerchiefs of all of the women, their shawls and aprons, suggest a certain independence of current styles. On Sundays, however, they all have church attire of the brilliant stripes and plaids, and boots with colored laces, so dear to their peasant hearts. One can readily see in the above photograph that their physical type inclines toward the short and stalwart.

He knew that Germany would never give up all control of Danzig, and that Lithuania would never allow a Polish corridor through that land. Yet he needed both Danzig and a port on the Baltic in Lithuania. He bargained at gunpoint and across the diplomatic council table to gain both ends. He failed; and as a result, his control of Poland was weakened. After his death in 1935, the nation was torn by violent strife and diplomatic indecision.

A Troubled Horizon

Each political party wanted to steer Poland in a different direction, at a time when a settled course was of the most vital concern. Hitler had gained control in Germany. He had forces massed on Poland's border, threatening to move in and capture Danzig.

Poland's eastern provinces, Galicia especially, were peopled by Ukrainians and White Russians—people who were never happy under Polish rule. Russia threatened to take up the cause of these peoples and annex a third of Poland. With Russia and Germany crowding her from east and west, Poland was doomed.

Hitler attacked in September of 1939 and shared the unhappy land with Russia, which moved in at the same time from the east. The Cabinet of Poland escaped first to Rumania and then went on to Paris and finally London. During World War II, the Cabinet organized those Poles who, like the members of the Government, had fled to France and England. It set up a fighting force to help defeat Germany and thus bring nearer the return of Poland's freedom. The Government-in-Exile also negotiated with Russia, once that nation had been invaded by Germany, to have Polish troops fight alongside the Red Army.

During the war, whether living in that part of their country controlled by Germany or by Russia, the Poles who remained at home had a hard time of it. Many were conscripted into the German army, most Jews and underground fighters were killed in purges, and many Poles were taken to work in German war plants. Those who escaped these terrors watched their property destroyed and lived in constant fear.

Poland was scarred deeply by the war. Her means of producing coal and iron and steel were completely ruined. Without the products of heavy industry she could not rebuild her cities and trade with other nations for the money that was needed to farm her rich but gutted land.

At the Yalta conference, Allied leaders granted the country the southern portion of East Prussia and the free city of Danzig, and took from her the troublesome lands bordering White Russia and the Ukraine. The western boundary was to be fixed when a peace treaty with Germany should be made. Awaiting that treaty, Poland was given the rights to all German territory east of a line formed by the Oder and Neisse rivers, including the important Baltic port, Stettin, which the Poles now call Szczecin. Actually, as a result of postwar arrangements, Poland has moved several hundred miles to the west. In the move she has gained the plentiful coal fields of Silesia, and a broad coastal front on the Baltic.

The postwar Government was set up by Communists and Socialists who either had stayed at home or had worked and fought with Russia. Following the usual communist policy, the Government has encouraged industry, somewhat to the neglect of agriculture. Most of Poland's money goes to building up the coal and iron and steel industries. This emphasis has resulted in a large movement of people from the farms to big cities.

Government Ownership

The Government, being thoroughly communistic, followed its model, the Soviet Government in Russia, and planned, at first, to bring all agriculture under its control. It intended to do away with private ownership of farms, placing all small holdings under collective management. This program has gone forward, but at a halting pace. Peasants have resisted the Government at almost every turn. And they resist because the one-party system that has kept the Government in power leaves them with no voice in Parliament.

163

many new factories. Yet he still dons the traditional, bright-hued costume for Sunday strolls or for festival days in the village square. In winter evenings the peasant women weave strips of colored cloth, orange and blue, or perhaps green and purple, then join the strips into coats of many colors.

Old-time merrymaking is still a part of harvest time in Poland; a corn-shucking or a barn-raising is the occasion for a feast and square dance, perhaps outdoors round a bonfire. The mazurka and polka, favorite Polish dance tunes, send couples whirling with a zest that is by no means confined to the young folks.

Of all the many holidays observed by the people of Poland, the most joyous

The parties that once represented the interests of the peasant class in Warsaw no longer exist. Any member of these once powerful groups, as well as members of even the Communist party who refused to follow the orders sent out from the Russian Government, were liquidated —sent to prison, exiled, or silenced in some other way.

Though the war, Communist rule generally, and the build-up of industry in particular have virtually turned life in Poland upside down, many of the customs of country life have not changed.

Working in the fields, the peasant wears denims and tough leather shoes made by the thousands in Poland's

Fanshawe

MOUNTAINEER MUSICIANS OF SOUTH POLAND

The mountaineers of the Tatras are born musicians and on every feast day and holiday fill the forest aisles with their haunting melodies. The upper of these figures is that of an aged piper. These gaily decked men are all Gorals.

A VILLAGE BAND AND CHOIR THROUGH WHICH THE POLISH LOVE OF MUSIC FINDS EXPRESSION

The Poles are very musical. Polish music, which we know through the compositions of Chopin, Hofmann and Paderewski, harks back to ancient times. The church music and carols are extraordinarily beautiful, the folk-songs and dance music romantic and spirited. Every village has its band, frequently assisted by a choir of girls, to render its patriotic national airs. The familiar Polonaise is the dance of Great Poland, the Cracovienne that of Lesser Poland, the Mazurka of Mazovia, and the Kujawiak of Kujawia. Every province has its own dance and folk song.

THE ORNATE TOWN HALL OF POZNAN

Both outside and in, the Town Hall is rich with reminders of the past. The structure was begun at the end of the thirteenth century, but in the years 1550–60 it acquired a late Renaissance appearance at the hands of John Baptist Quadro, an Italian architect. It contains one of Poland's most valuable collections of historic objects.

ASSEMBLING TRACTOR ENGINES IN A FACTORY NEAR WARSAW

Manufacturing plants like this have increased Poland's production in recent years. Out-of-date methods of peasant farmers are gradually giving way to modern machinery.

A QUIET MOMENT ALONGSIDE A PIER AT SZCZECIN

Formerly the German Stettin, Szczecin is one of Poland's main ports on the Baltic Sea. It lies at the head of the Oder River and is connected with Berlin by ship canal.

© E.N.A.

STATELY MUNICIPAL BUILDINGS IN WHICH POLAND'S FINANCIAL ADMINISTRATION WAS HOUSED

Warsaw once possessed buildings worthy of its position as capital of the Polish Republic—beautiful old palaces and historical houses, many of them belonging to the Polish nobility and dating from the glorious days of Poland's former independence. Not a few were converted into municipal buildings. The many-columned edifice seen above was used for the offices of the Ministry of Finance. Warsaw was bombed heavily by the Germans when they invaded the country in 1939 and, unfortunately, most of the buildings were badly damaged or in many cases completely in ruins.

Polish Research and Information Service

LEARNING THE ART OF WEAVING

This girl is acquiring a highly useful skill in a trade school in Warsaw. The loom is a rather old-fashioned one but it requires a higher degree of craftsmanship from the worker than would a more modern type. The Polish Government is bending every effort to industrialize the country and sets high value on the skills needed in factories.

feast is on Christmas Eve, starting sometimes at four in the afternoon, sometimes a little later. Beforehand, the mother will have made a little manger in an outbuilding, with perhaps a beautifully dressed doll in it, to show where Christ was born. At the feast a little wisp of hay is put under each person's dish as a symbol.

St. John's Eve was celebrated in old days by the country folk to drive away

the evil spirits. Nowadays great bonfires are lit, and the young people gather around them, dressed in their brightest, to dance and sing. After a time the dancing becomes more and more rapid, the young men jump over the bonfire, to show how brave they are, and they pick up buckets of water and try to throw them over the girls, who run away.

All Poles love sport. The Polish countryman is a born horseman. The

169

McLeish

PALACE OF THE OLD POLISH KINGS IN THE HEART OF WARSAW

This statue of Sigismund Vasa stood for over three hundred years in Castle Square. "When the sword of Sigismund points downwards," ran a legend, "Poland will be free." The sword was displaced during World War I, and for the following twenty-one years Poland was a free country. The Germans bombed Warsaw mercilessly when they took Poland in 1939.

EVERYDAY LIFE GOES ON MID WARSAW'S RUINS

A clothing "shop" has been set up in the doorway of a blasted building on Poznenska Street; and customers stop to buy the garments quite as if it were an ordinary store. Slowly, however, the scars of war on the face of the once beautiful city are being erased. Rebuilding is not new in Warsaw; parts have been rebuilt many times during the city's long history.

Uhlans, the famous German cavalry, were originally Poles, and Napoleon's Polish Lancers were well known.

There were large forests in parts of Poland in which once the lynx and beaver were to be found. A few bison are still seen, but the elk and wild goat have gone farther north. Sometimes brown bears are met, game birds there are in plenty, and wolves lurk in lonely woods, keeping out of sight unless they are driven by cold and hunger into the villages, to steal what animals they can. Wild boars are still brought in by huntsmen. Most of the country folk fear the wolves. Peasant women will whisper tales of how wolves came down to a village one bad winter and attacked and ate children; men will warn a stranger not to wander out alone at night without his shotgun; they will tell how packs have overwhelmed sleighs going through the forests, and have eaten first the horses and then the people. A favorite sport in northern Poland is to entice the wolves out of their hiding-places to kill them. A party of men starts out in a cart, the men concealing themselves as well as they can under hay. They hang a young pig in a sack from the rear of the cart, and its loud squeals attract the attention of the wolves which creep up to seize it and are then shot by the men.

The rivers play a big rôle in Polish life. Poland's greatest river, the Vistula, flows through the heart of the country from the Carpathian Mountain to the Baltic Sea. The Vistula and its tributaries drain the major portion of Poland and form its natural and historical pathway to the sea. The many tributaries of the Vistula keep the country fertile and enable the people to travel easily from one part to another. The rivers abound in fish; and in winter, when they may be frozen over for six months, they make fine roads for sledges.

To the south, in the foothills of the Carpathian Mountains, the flowing streams provide sources of water power. Before World War II, work on dams was begun, to use this power; and construction is going forward again. The center of this activity is where the San River flows into the Vistula. Around the junction of these two rivers, the Polish Government has started to build a vast industrial region that eventually will cover about 24,000 square miles.

POLAND: FACTS AND FIGURES

THE COUNTRY

This country of central Europe is bounded on the west and north by Germany, the Baltic Sea, Lithuania and Latvia, east by Russia, and south by Rumania, Hungary and Slovakia. It is drained by a number of important rivers, including the Vistula and the Dniester, while in the south the wooded range of the Carpathian Mountains forms a natural boundary. Total area is 121,131 square miles, compared to 150,470 in 1939. Total population is 23,929,757, compared to 34,775,698 in 1939. Poland is about one-fifth as large as it was in 1939, as it lost eastern Poland to Russia at the end of World War II.

GOVERNMENT

The Republic of Poland has been governed under a 32-article interim constitution, called "the little charter," since 1947. Power is divided between the president, executive (council of ministers), the Sjem (a one-house parliament) and the Council of State. The latter is composed of the president, three vice-presidents of Parliament, the chairman of the Supreme Control Board (financial) and three other members. The president is elected for a term of seven years by the Sjem.

COMMERCE AND INDUSTRIES

Chief occupations of the people are agriculture and, since World War II, industry. The main crops are potatoes, rye, sugar-beets, oats, wheat, barley, hemp, hops and chicory. The Polish state placed a limit on the size of holdings. Stock-raising is important also. Over one-fifth of the area is forest-covered. The minerals include coal, iron, salt, petroleum and potash. Other industries are manufactures of textiles and paper, chemicals, timber, iron, and oil-refining and sugar-refining. The principal exports are cereals, dairy produce, timber, sugar, flax, coal, iron, steel, petroleum, chemicals and textiles. Fertilizers, machinery, fish, cocoa and foodstuffs are imported.

COMMUNICATIONS

There are 16,080 miles of railway, state-owned; and there are 60,216 miles of road, 14,348 miles of telegraph wires, and 941,366 miles of telephone lines. There are also about 3,089 miles of navigable waterways.

RELIGION AND EDUCATION

No established church and ostensibly all creeds tolerated. Roman Catholicism is the religion of the majority. Education free and elementary education obligatory. There are 74 colleges for teachers and 764 professional and technical schools. There are 12 universities and 19 other institutions of university rank. In 1946, they had a total of 52,730 students.

CHIEF TOWNS

Warsaw, capital, 606,778; Lodz, 600,608; Cracow, 307,392; Poznan, 305,735; Breslau, 302,312; Gdansk (Danzig), 175,986; Szczecin (Stettin) 175,043; Katowice, 168,705; Bydgoszcz, 153,982; Chorzow, 138,313; Zabrze (Hindenburg), 127,577; Gliwice, 124,551; Bytom, 117,321; Czestochowa, 116,009. (Estimated 1949 population figures.)

IN THREE BALTIC COUNTRIES

People of Esthonia, Latvia and Lithuania

On the eastern shore of the Baltic Sea there are four countries which, until after World War I, were just provinces of Russia. The largest of them, Finland, we deal with elsewhere. Three—Esthonia (also spelled Estonia), Latvia and Lithuania—appear in this chapter. The people of these countries kept their ideas of freedom during the years of Russian rule; they became free at last as a result of World War I. They maintained their independence for a little more than twenty years. In 1939 Russia compelled them to allow their ports to be used as Russian naval bases. In 1940 she occupied them; they soon became sovietized in the Russian fashion. When the Germans attacked Russia in June, 1941, they invaded Esthonia, Latvia and Lithuania. After Germany's defeat, the three little republics again became members of the Soviet Union.

CENTURIES ago strange tribes from the northern grasslands of Asia came driving their flocks and herds before them and settled along the eastern border of the Baltic Sea. At that time Western Europe was still primeval forest, and these people long known as Letts, Esthonians (or Estonians), and Lithuanians, were sturdy fire and sun-worshipers. The Letto-Lithuanian languages were the oldest in Europe—older, even, than Latin—in fact, allied to the Sanskrit of ancient India. The Esthonians pastured their herds in the marshy, green lakelands between the Gulf of Finland and the Gulf of Riga; while the Lithuanians appear to have settled between the rivers Salis and Vistula, and the Letts between these two peoples. They did not voluntarily accept Christianity until near the end of the fourteenth century.

About the middle of the fifteenth century the federal state of Livonia was founded. It included the Esthonia and the Latvia of to-day. It is interesting to know in this connection that the word Livonian means sword-bearing and that the Livonian Knights of about 1200 formed the nucleus of the Teutonic Knights and in 1237 united with them, but separated in 1521. Russia, Poland and the Scandinavian countries contended for control of the region, and finally Lithuania was combined with Poland. With the partitions of Poland, all of the region fell to Russia. However, many of the great landowners were Germans, and in the cities the leading people were rich German tradesmen. The real rulers of the country were the German barons who, from their castles, kept the people serfs and almost slaves. Even when Russia declared that all serfs were free, the Germans managed to keep them in subjection, by propaganda in school and church.

In World War I, the German armies invaded the Baltic provinces, and there was much fighting, in the course of which many of the castles and estates of the old barons were destroyed, and many cities and villages burned. Not until the end of the war did the peasants obtain arms that enabled them to fight for their freedom. Driving out the Russians, in 1918 they declared their independence as three separate countries.

They succeeded in retaining their independence until World War II. In the year 1939 Russia had forced them to allow her to establish naval bases on their shores. In the following year the Russians occupied all three countries, claiming that their governments were decidedly unfriendly to Russia. In 1940, the three republics voted to become a part of the Soviet Union. From 1941 to 1945 German troops occupied the area; after the defeat of Germany Soviet Russia once more took possession of Esthonia, Latvia and Lithuania.

During the long period that they were under czarist rule they had not been allowed to learn their own languages in the schools. In Lithuania, for forty years the people had books printed abroad and smuggled across the border. Several thousand men were at one time sent to Siberia for using a prayer book which had been so smuggled. Once freed from Russia, each of the three countries revived its mother tongue. Their languages are, however, so difficult for foreigners to learn that nearly all of the townspeople have to be able to speak one or more of the languages of those with whom they have trade relations. A boy or girl in Riga learns to speak not only Latvian, but also Russian and perhaps English or German or French as well.

The three little countries were a great loss to Russia in the period between wars, for they lie along the Baltic Sea, Esthonia being the northern-

Sovfoto
A RADIO-ASSEMBLY SHOP IN LATVIA

most and Lithuania the southernmost, with Latvia between them. On the north, Esthonia is separated from the kindred republic of Finland by the Gulf of Finland. Russia and Poland bound the three states on the east, and East Prussia is Lithuania's neighbor on the south. The population of all three is less than six millions. Most of the people are either farmers, fishermen, lumbermen or wood-carvers.

Each country has a fine port, and their level reaches are now largely cleared for agriculture, though something under a quarter is still covered with pine and fir timber, which can be floated down the rivers at the time of the spring floods.

Rye is the grain best adapted to that northern climate, and potatoes grow so

well and form such a staple food of the peasantry that Esthonia for one has been called the Potato Republic. Be it mentioned, nearly every farm has its distillery for making alcohol from the vegetable. The natives are tall and blond, hard-working and eager for the education long denied them. At harvest time or during the spring log-drive or a sheep-shearing or a house-raising, groups of neighbors go from farm to farm, or from lumber camp to lumber camp, rendering free mutual aid.

While the timber is a source of wealth, wolves lurk in their dark fastnesses; and though they rarely attack people, when the hunger of a long, cold winter makes them desperate, they creep down the village streets at night killing and eating chickens and small animals, and it is never considered safe for children to go out alone after dark.

People keep warm by the aid of huge stoves that reach from floor to ceiling. In winter the water in the Gulf of Finland and the Baltic Sea freezes just enough to make it impossible to cross by boat yet not enough for sleighs. At certain ports, like Reval, a channel is kept open by ice-breakers that ships may go in and out; but in the old days a man who wanted to go from Reval to Helsinki in Finland—about forty miles across the gulf—would have to travel around by land, and the journey would take three or four days. Now, however, there are aeroplanes crossing the ice every day, and he can traverse the frozen sea in a few minutes.

Once, it was dangerous and lonely for the crews when the ships were frozen in and could not move, for no one knew where they were. They could not send for help, and sometimes they starved to death. Now when a ship is icebound, the crew send a wireless message; and if they are short of food, an aeroplane can bring it. The crew can also relieve the tedium of waiting by listening to the

CHRISTMAS PARTY STARTING OFF FOR A SLEIGH RIDE

The Baltic States have a variety of winter sports, and the abundance of snow provides them with a long sleighing season. Only those who have experienced it can understand the fascination of a country drive in winter, when the sleigh skims the crisp snow through the pine-scented woodlands, and there is no sound save sleigh bells and flying hoofs.

Latvian Govt.

HOW THE FORESTS ADD TO THE WEALTH OF LATVIA

Latvia is a flat country. Swamps and lakes are numerous; but there is enough timber for export in large quantities. Perhaps a quarter of the country is covered with forests. In them are found certain kinds of pine from which pitch, tar and turpentine are obtained. Here we see a little factory in a forest where the timber is received after it has been cut.

175

Latvian Govt.

BRINGING FUEL FOR THE WINTER INTO A VILLAGE OF THE REPUBLIC OF LATVIA

Latvia, on the whole, is a flat country and in some parts resembles the rolling prairies of North America. There are, however, many vast forests, from which the Letts, as the people of Latvia are called, obtain timber for their houses and supplies of fuel. In the country districts nearly all the buildings are of wood, though here and there houses of brick are to be seen. For a brief space of time, between the two world wars, Latvia was a free country. In 1940, however, the Soviet Union annexed the old Baltic provinces; and today the iron curtain hides Latvia.

176

RIGA'S SKYLINE FROM THE RIVER

Behind Riga's new embankment on the Dvina (Daugava) River rise the spires of her famous Gothic churches. Riga was a member of the Hanseatic League—a confederacy of cities in the Baltic area, Germany and Holland that flourished in the thirteenth and fourteenth centuries. Some of the old Hanseatic storehouses and granaries still stand in the old section of Riga.

PHOTOS, SOVFOTO

A COLLECTIVE FARM, LATVIA

Most of Latvia's individual farms have been thrown into large collectives and are managed according to the Soviet pattern. Agricultural implements move from farm to farm, from a central tractor station. Latvia is an agricultural country, raising barley, rye, wheat and other grains, flax and potatoes. The raising of livestock is important, and there is much timber.

wireless concerts broadcasted from different stations.

The Baltic sailors have always been renowned for their courage, and in olden times they were famed for something less creditable, for there were many pirates among them who raided coast towns and attacked lonely ships. One of the most terrible of these Baltic pirates and the last of them all was Baron Ungern Sternberg. He was the lord of an island, and from his house he would, on winter nights, hang out false lights to lure passing ships on to the rocks where they would be wrecked; whereupon he would kill their crews and seize their cargoes. His deeds were discussed the world over, and even in the streets around the London docks notices were posted as a warning to sailors, saying, "Beware of Ungern Sternberg the Sea Robber."

For years no one dared stop him, but at last he was seized; and when his house was examined, vast quantities of goods that had been taken from lost ships were found under the floor. He was put in

© E. N. A.

ESTHONIAN WOMEN WELL PROTECTED FROM THE BITING COLD

In Esthonia the winter is long and severe, even more so than in Latvia and Lithuania. It is possible that only the hardiest have survived. To keep out the cold, the peasant women wear large sheepskin coats with the fleece inside, and thick boots. As in Latvia, wood is the chief fuel, and the sawing of the daily supply of logs is a long and tiring job.

WOMEN HELP THE MEN IN THE FIELDS OF ESTHONIA

Fields blue with flax or fragrant with hay relieve the green of pine woods. On most of the large farms scientific methods are employed, and there are agricultural schools for training the young farmers. A sledge-like vehicle is used for carting the hay, and the sturdy women lend a capable hand at harvest time. The Esthonians are a vigorous Finnish race.

Esthonian Legation

FARM LABORERS EATING THEIR MIDDAY MEAL IN THE SHADE

Summer in Esthonia is a short season but hot, and the farm laborers are glad of a rest in the middle of the day, for they must work from dawn till dusk. Agriculture is one of the most important industries in Esthonia. Rye, oats, barley, flax and potatoes are cultivated. Potatoes are grown so extensively that it has been called The Potato Republic.

THATCHED AND ROUGHHEWN LITHUANIAN HOMESTEAD BUILT BY THE PEASANT OWNERS

The Lithuanian peasants are skilled with their hands and do all kinds of woodwork. They are even able to build their own houses. The women of the household spin and weave the linen underclothing and woolen outer garments, and the men make tables, chairs, beds, benches, wagons, and any other articles that are needed. As a tribute, it has been said that the Lithuanian rides on horseback into the forest and returns in a coach. Many of the peasant houses are provided with only one living-room, and usually the horses are sheltered under the same roof in winter.

ESTHONIAN LABORERS GATHERED ABOUT THE SAMOVAR

Like most inhabitants of cold countries these peasants eat and drink a great deal, but their tastes are not extravagant, and black bread and weak tea form for them a satisfying meal. They are, for the most part, endowed with a lively temperament and a keen sense of humor.

MEN LOADING A TRAIN WITH OIL-SHALE IN ESTHONIA

In the northern provinces of Esthonia there are quarries of shale from which a green oil can be obtained. It is used as a substitute for coal in gas works, steamships and locomotives. There is very little coal or iron in Esthonia, Latvia and Lithuania. As this hinders the development of industries, shale oil will be an element in Esthonia's future development.

Latvian Govt.

LETTS WEARING WREATHS OF OAK LEAVES ON ST. JOHN'S DAY

Ligo, as the Letts term St. John's Day, is one of the principal holidays in Latvia, and the peasants gather masses of foliage to decorate themselves and their houses. They like to use oak leaves for this purpose if they can. The festival is really a relic of certain celebrations which were formerly held when the religion of the Letts was a Nature worship.

ESTHONIAN FISHERMAN PLAYING UPON A STRANGE INSTRUMENT

The hardy fishermen of Esthonia are fond of the rather crude music produced by an instrument that might almost be a distant relative of the Scottish bagpipes. The Esthonians are a musical race and many of the small villages have music societies, while operas and concerts are frequently to be heard in the larger towns.

IN THE WARM CORNER OF A LITHUANIAN PEASANT'S HOME

In winter the family gathers around the large brick stove, and at night they sleep on top of it, defying the blizzards from between two fat feather-beds. The baby's cradle is suspended from the ceiling and can be gently swung from side to side. By the stove is a pot of potatoes, a part of the family meal.

prison, dressed as a peasant and brought to trial with chains around his hands and feet, for people still feared him. He was then sent into exile in Siberia, and his name was struck off the roll of the nobility.

In the old days, when there were few roads in the Baltic States and the peasants could not easily get from one place to another, they spent much of their time in winter carving beautiful furniture and embroidering fine apparel. Pictures show the Baltic people of other days with embroidered shoes, the women with embroidered white linen bodices, dark striped skirts and high hats of many colors. They had to wear short skirts in winter because the snow was so deep.

Value a Good Education

The villagers, even when they were serfs, valued schooling, and now that they are their own masters, these Baltic peoples mean to have their children well educated. Therefore these countries spend a proportionately generous amount on good schools and universities, some of which, like that of Dorpat, are hundreds of years old.

Black Rye Bread the Staple

Black rye bread is the mainstay of the peasants and a favorite even with wealthier people, as are strong cheeses. One Baltic specialty is an elaborate cake decorated with colored sugar. Fish from the rivers have ever formed an important article of diet, whether eaten fresh, smoked or pickled.

The long winter of the Baltic lands is so cold that most of the country folk wear valenka—high felt boots made in the Russian style. These are exceptionally warm, though not waterproof. Those who can afford to do so dress in furs; those who cannot have clothing padded with wool. In winter the people get from place to place by means of horse-drawn sleighs; and a sleigh ride over the snow, with the harness bells tinkling, is a jolly experience.

Spring sometimes brings disaster, because when the river ice begins to thaw, pieces float down stream and often get jammed together, forming dams. Then the rivers overflow, sometimes flooding whole villages. To prevent these floods the ice-dams are often blown up with charges of dynamite; but there is still the risk of the broken ice tearing down the river and perhaps sweeping away bridges and damaging buildings on the banks.

The port city of Reval, now called Tallinn, is the capital of Esthonia. It was originally a large castle, one of the biggest in Northern Europe. It was built upon a hill and surrounded by strong walls. The castle still stands and much of the walls remain. Just below them come ancient streets on which one sees horse-drawn droshkies, the drivers of which wear red sashes. There are almost no motor cars. There are houses with steep roofs of red tile and churches with round towers and narrow steeples. Around the market place one sees arched entrances and high-walled courtyards reminiscent of four hundred years ago.

Reval, a Walled City

Reval has had need of its castle and strong walls, for there has probably been as much fighting around this city as anywhere in Europe. For hundreds of years armies have fought for and tried to capture it. What is true of this fine city has been true of the country as a whole.

In our century it has changed masters many times. Before the first world war it was a part of the old Russian Empire. It was occupied by German troops during World War I; then it had about twenty years of freedom. Germany again occupied it during World War II. Esthonia became a member republic of the Union of Soviet Socialist Republics in 1940.

In Esthonia's great epic, Kálevi Poëg (The Son of Kálev), by Frederic Rheinhold Kreutzwald (1803-82), have been preserved no less than two thousand legends centring around a twelfth-century hero.

Riga, the capital of Latvia and the largest port of the Baltic States, is modern, but it has an old quarter where women sweep narrow, cobbled streets, deliver

THE ESTONIANS are related to the Magyars of Hungary. Their native dress is characterized by a durable long skirt and sleeveless woolen bodice worn over a launderable guimpe. The embroidered sleeve bands in bright colors, with cuffs, belts and hems to match, and the clean white aprons are not so individual as the heavy silver necklaces.

185

MEMEL—NOT-TOO-EASILY-FITTED PIECE IN THE BALTIC JIGSAW

Memel was founded in 1252 by the Livonian Order of Knights, who gave it to the Teutonic Knights. It was long a German city, but by the Treaty of Versailles which ended the first World War, Memel went to the newly-made independent state of Lithuania. Germany recaptured it in 1939; and it was returned to Lithuania (now part of Russia) in 1945. Memel exports timber, grain and fish, cattle and dairy products, hides and wool. Officially, the town is known by the Lithuanians as Klaipeda. Here we are alongside the river Dange in Memel.

cans of milk and shove wheelbarrows. The old city is a remnant of more prosperous days. Riga was once a member of the Hanseatic League. As such it thrived in the trade between the Scandinavian countries and the Byzantine Empire. During the nineteenth century, Riga grew to greatness. Under Russian rule, German traders and manufacturers built up the industry of the port. At the brink of World War I, it was the third largest city on the Baltic Sea, having more than a half-million residents. Only Stockholm and St. Petersburg (present-day Leningrad) then overshadowed Riga. Almost a quarter of the exports of tsarist Russia left its docks. After World War I, Riga flourished as the capital and industrial center of the new Latvia. As the hub of many railroads and as the terminus for the pine timber that floated down the western Dvina from the forests of the interior, Riga grew in industrial wealth. It produced fine radios and telephone sets. There were factories making electric railway engines and cars, and others producing electric parts for autos.

Riga is built on both banks of the Dvina, ten miles from the river's entry into the Gulf of Riga. Within the city limits, but at a considerable distance from the heart of the city, is a lovely stretch of sand spits on the gulf. In summer these beaches used to attract thousands of visitors.

Another important Latvian port is Liepaja (better known as Libau; and Libava, in Russian). Unlike Riga, which is clogged during cold months, Liepaja is usually free of ice throughout the year. It, too, belonged to the Hanseatic League. Lithuania, Poland, Sweden, Germany and Russia have all controlled the port at various times. Today it is one of Russia's naval bases.

Lithuania's Old Capital

Vilnius (or Wilno, or Vilna), the capital of Lithuania, is one of the oldest cities in the Baltic region. Today it is third in size after Riga, and Tallin, in Estonia. For many centuries Vilnius has been the center of northeastern Polish, western Russian and Lithuanian trade. A uni-

versity was established in the sixteenth century.

During 1920 in her drive against marauding Bolsheviks, Poland captured Vilnius. Lithuania demanded the return of its historic capital, but Poland refused to give it up even at the command of the League of Nations. An unwise treaty in 1923 granted the city to Poland. From then till 1939 Vilnius was a trouble spot. In 1939 Poland was invaded, defeated and divided by Russia and Germany. By the terms of the German-Russian non-aggression pact, which preceded the division of Poland, Russia occupied the Vilnius area and immediately returned the city to Lithuania. The Lithuanians hurriedly moved their capital from Kaunas, but they could not enjoy the gift for long. In 1940 Russia made Lithuania and its neighbors, Estonia and Latvia, a part of the Soviet Union of socialist states. Russian military leaders soon took control of both the Parliament and civil affairs in Vilnius and the other capitals.

The capital of Estonia is Tallinn (or Revel). It is also an important old city of the Baltic area. It has a fine harbor on the Gulf of Finland across the water from the Finnish capital, Helsinki, called Helsingfors in Swedish.

The Baltic People

The people of the Baltic states live in an area that awards mixed blessings. The ports and cities are crossroads of the important routes of north European trade. Except for the brief period of Lithuanian greatness in the Middle Ages, the Balts have never moved from their borders in order to strengthen the position at home. They have, instead, stayed within the frontiers to work, sometimes as slaves, for foreign overseers that have come to tap the wealth. The one opportunity—their twenty years of independence—to build and prosper was stopped short by the second World War. Today there is slim hope for a return of independence for many years to come.

A scattered barbarian population roamed over the lands of Latvia, Lithuania, Estonia and Russia during the first

FLORENCE FARMBOROUGH

OLD-TIME COSTUMES of the Letts are very rarely to be seen, save in the districts remote from the influence of the towns. A loose cloak, secured by a large, round metal brooch, is one of the most distinctive features of the national dress. The ornamentation varies according to the taste of the wearer and also according to the district.

THE WOMEN OF RUCAVA are especially noted, in Latvia, for their needlework. In this photograph we can see some of the beautiful embroideries and homespun clothing that they produce. The peasant women lead a hard life, for they start to work at the age of seven, and when they are fifteen they are supposed to undertake adult responsibilities.

millennium of the Christian Era. The Slavs pushed to the coast the relic peoples speaking primitive Indo-European tongues, who became Lithuanians and Latvians. They also drove westward into their respective territories the Estonians, Finns and Lapps from their northern Russian hunting grounds.

In old Russia the Baltic area was officially designated as the "Western Territory," which from Peter I onward served for commerce with the west. It comprised what became known as Peter's famous "window on Europe." Through a window, however, one can smile amiably at a neighbor, and also stick out a menacing rifle.

These windows now seem to be boarded up forever. Very little of what goes on behind them is known by the nations outside. Since 1940, when the republics became part of the Soviet Union, many natives of the unfortunate countries have wisely escaped westward.

Many who could not leave in time were sent from their homes to work in the interior of Russia. Large naval, air and army bases now fortify the Baltic coast.

ESTHONIA (ESTONIA), LATVIA AND LITHUANIA: FACTS AND FIGURES

ESTHONIA (ESTONIA)

The most northern of these three countries has Russia on the east, Latvia on the south, the Gulf of Riga and the Baltic Sea on the west and the Gulf of Finland on the north. The total area is 18,353 square miles and the population is 1,117,300. At the time of the Russian Revolution in 1917, Esthonia declared her independence of Russia and by the Treaty of Tartu in 1918, Soviet Russia recognized it as an independent country. In 1940, after ten months of Russian occupation, Esthonia's communist government voted to join the Soviet Union.

Agriculture and dairying occupy about 70% of the people. Potatoes, oats, barley, rye and wheat are the principal crops and the dairy factories, 87% of which are co-operative, produce a large amount of butter, which is the chief export. Forests cover 21.5% of the area and timber is also exported. The other industries are the making of textiles, paper, cement and oil-shale, matches, flax and leather. There is a total railway mileage of 1,329. Five-sixths of the population are Lutherans, the rest Greek Orthodox and Catholics. Elementary education is compulsory. There are universities at Tartu and Tallinn. Chief towns: Tallinn (Revel), capital, 146,500; Tartu (Dorpat), 60,000.

LATVIA

Bounded on the north by the Gulf of Riga and Esthonia, on the east by Russia, on the south by Lithuania and Poland, and on the west by the Baltic Sea. The total area is 25,200 square miles and the population 1,950,000. From 1918, when Latvia gained her independence from Russia, until 1940 a democratic republic. In July 1940, Latvia became a member of the U.S.S.R.

The people are occupied mainly with agriculture but industrial life is increasing. Rye, barley, oats, potatoes and flax are the principal crops. Stock-raising is carried on extensively. The industries consist of distilling, brewing, flax and sugar. Lumber is the chief export.

There are 1,863 miles of railway and 2,775 miles more of navigable inland waterways. Telegraph lines, 2,265 miles and telephone lines, 24,879 miles. Fifty-six per cent of the people are Protestant and twenty-four per cent Roman Catholic. There are 1,904 elementary schools, mostly supported by the state, and there is one university located at Riga. The chief towns are Riga, the capital, 393,211; Liepaja (Libau), 57,098; Daugavpils (Dvinsk), 45,160.

LITHUANIA

Bounded on the north by Latvia, on the east and south by Poland, on the southwest by East Prussia, and on the west by the Baltic Sea. Total area, 25,500 square miles; population, 2,-879,070. The independence of Lithuania was proclaimed in 1918 and was formally recognized in 1922. The constitution adopted that year was democratic, but in 1926 Parliament collapsed and a dictator controlled single-party elections and Parliament from then until 1939 when Russia occupied Lithuania. In July 1940 the new communist Parliament voted to join the Soviet Union.

Agriculture and industry are the chief occupations. Wheat, barley, oats, potatoes, peas, and flax are grown. Poultry-raising, goose-farming, stock-raising and bee-keeping are important. 16.3% of the land is forest-covered. Exports consist of timber, foodstuffs, flax and linseed; and the imports are textiles, food and agricultural machinery. There are 1,917 miles of railway and 397 miles of navigable waterways. The majority of the population is Roman Catholic, about 80 per cent. There are 4,032 elementary and secondary schools. The University of Kovno opened in 1922. The chief towns are Vilnius (Vilna), the capital, 209,400; Kaunas (Kovno), 154,100; Klaipeda (Memel), 38,900; Siaulai (Shavli), 31,600.

THE PEOPLES OF A TORN NATION

Czechoslovakia—The Heart of Europe

At the end of World War I, when the Austro-Hungarian Empire was broken up, several of its former territories, inhabited by Slavic peoples—chiefly Czechs and Slovaks—united to form the republic of Czechoslovakia. The new nation inherited the industrial heart of the old empire and prospered under a democratic government. However, the happy years ended with the Munich Pact of 1938, by which Hitler gained a western slice of Czechoslovakia and soon engulfed the country. After World War II, the nation's future again looked bright, but now trouble came from the east. In 1948, by a surprise move, Communists gained control of the government. Since then Czechoslovakia has become a satellite, hidden behind the iron curtain, of Russia.

AS TIME is measured among the nations of the earth, Czechoslovakia is new, though its peoples have a long and checkered history. Most of the ethnic groups that make up the present state—Czechs, Slovaks, Moravians and others —are Slavs whose tribal forebears, many centuries ago, migrated out of their ancestral home to the east, formed a sturdy wedge between Orient and Occident all the way from the Baltic to the Balkans, and century after century met Turk and Teuton in bloody onslaught. The Czechs, Slovaks, Moravians and Ruthenes pushed westward to the upper basin of the Elbe, where high mountain ramparts shut them off from their neighbors to the westward. Neumark Pass (Neugedein), leading from Germany through the Böhmerwald (Bohemian Forest), has been the scene of many a gory battle. Midway of the mountain backbone of

Europe, the northward sloping plains of Bohemia lie walled about by the mountain ranges where one may see pine and oak forested slopes and crystal torrents as lovely as anything in Tyrol.

© A. W. Cutler

RIBBON HEADDRESS OF A BRIDE

A bride in Slovakia does not wear pure white but crowds as many colors as she can on to her wedding-dress. Her headdress is composed of several layers of ribbons.

Within these mountain walls dwell the Czechs who form, roughly, two-thirds of the population of Czechoslovakia. The Carpathians to the north, rising in the Tatras to romantic peaks of eight thousand feet, shut Poland off from Slovakia and Ruthenia. To the south, rivers form the natural boundary for part of the way.

Fully a third of the land shows the deep green of conifers and other forest growth; the ax rings in the winter woods and aromatic rafts of pine logs—guided by tug boats—feed the paper mills. The woods which climb, sometimes to the very crests of the ranges, are haunted by the fleet shapes of deer and the whirring flight of pheasants.

SHEEPSKIN JACKETS, worn woolly side in and with the outside gaily ornamented, are the outdoor wear of both men and women among the Carpathians. This Ruthenian peasant, with his leather satchel and ribboned hat, is ready to go to market. Shoes are a luxury, but the trails are stony, and he has bound his feet, layer upon layer, with cloth.

FLORENCE FARMBOROUGH

WOMEN OF RUTHENIA put on their best sheepskin coats and tie their gayest handkerchiefs around their heads when they carry their home-grown goods to market. Market day is always a good gossip day, and many such groups of peasants may then be seen chatting by the roadside, with their wares, chiefly onions, on the ground before them.

CZECHOSLOVAKIA'S PARTS LEAD TO DIFFICULTIES IN GOVERNMENT

Over the springy turf, sharp-nosed foxes trail leaping hares and coveys of fat quail. Sheltered by the Ore and Giant mountains, the climate is less severe than in the countries to the north. The wooded uplands slope to wide valleys green with meadows and perfumed with orchards. Fields and roads are bordered by rank on rank of cherry trees. In the green pastures, which lie close to the pine forests, are scattered the farms of the Czechs. Many of the river beds are marshy and are used as grazing grounds for flocks of gabbling geese, which are tended by barefoot children.

Hidden away in the forests are lonely settlements where the people are almost completely cut off from the world. They have resisted the attractions of Pilsen and Prague, the capital city, which have taken so many people from the land to work in the factories.

Bohemia was once a powerful nation with a high culture, but unfortunately became one of the chief battlegrounds of Europe. The Bohemian crown passed from one family to another, and bitter religious wars divided the population. Finally the House of Hapsburg gained the crown permanently, and the Thirty Years' War deprived the Czechs and Moravians of political independence, though they stubbornly resisted Germanization. The Slovaks succumbed to the Magyars of Hungary.

In 1918 the Czechoslovak state was born. Under the great statesman Thomas G. Masaryk, the governments of the Czechs and the Slovaks united and Czechoslovakia began a period of prosperity. The products from her many rich farms—wheat, hops, and grains—the forests, and manufactured goods—woolens, glassware and steel—from busy mills found markets throughout the world.

Trouble for the new state began in the 1930's when Germans in Sudetenland, border province of the north, looked to the new Hitler regime for inclusion in Germany. German demands for the Czech territory as well as Polish and Hungarian demands for other parts of the nation were granted in 1938 at the Munich conference. Hitler soon annexed all of Czechoslovakia; the government under Masaryk's successor, Eduard Benes, fled to various Allied capitals.

After Hitler's defeat, Benes set up a new government. But Communists, who had the largest number of seats in Parliament, kept Benes and other non-Communists from taking up Czechoslovakia's former friendship with Britain and America. The Communists gained complete control in 1948, abolished all parties that opposed them, and rewrote the constitution of Masaryk. Since that time Czechoslovakia has been a satellite of Russia; its whole life—its trade, politics, even its religion—must fall into line with the plans of the U.S.S.R.

Bohemian glass has been famous for

Florence Farmborough

A LITTLE SHRINE UNDER THE BIRCH TREES OF A COUNTRY ROAD

Though the reformed clergy withdrew from the jurisdiction of the Pope in 1920, they founded a Czechoslovak Church and the country is still largely Catholic. One sees numbers of wayside shrines past which men walk with bared heads. Oxen yoked together with wooden yokes across their necks are commonly used instead of horses to draw the farm wagons.

many centuries. The glass was made first of all in the sandy districts on the northwestern border, but the first factories were built in the forests, as wood was wanted for fuel to heat the ovens. Later factories were moved to where coal could be obtained. It is well worth going into one of the factories in the Jablonec district, where we can see the great skill of the glassblowers and watch the care with which the glass is colored green, blue and purple. Bohemian glass is prized the world over. Goblets and flagons, imitation gems and buttons, colored beads and spangles now represent an industry

begun in the thirteenth century. In some of the factories the secrets of the trade have been handed down from father to son. Czechoslovakia has over two thousand glassworks.

Moravia is the central portion of Czechoslovakia and, although a quarter of it is covered with forests of oak and pine, it is one of the busiest manufacturing districts in the country. It has famous iron and engineering works. Factories for the production of cotton and woolen goods, glass, paper and chemicals are numerous. In Bohemia the villages are more like those of Switzerland, but

HOLIDAY CLOTHES are brightly colored and embroidered in the land of the Czechs. The skirts are short to show the high leather boots worn by mother and daughter alike. The child's flowered muslin looks very simple beside her mother's finery, but perhaps she has not put on her best frock. Yellow ears of drying corn are seen hanging from the eaves.

PAINTED BANNERS are borne high in the air by these six Slovak men who head the procession which, to celebrate the name-day of its patron saint, winds through the streets of a village in the present Slovakia. The men wear their gala clothes—sleeveless jackets with many buttons, full-sleeved white shirts and white embroidered trousers.

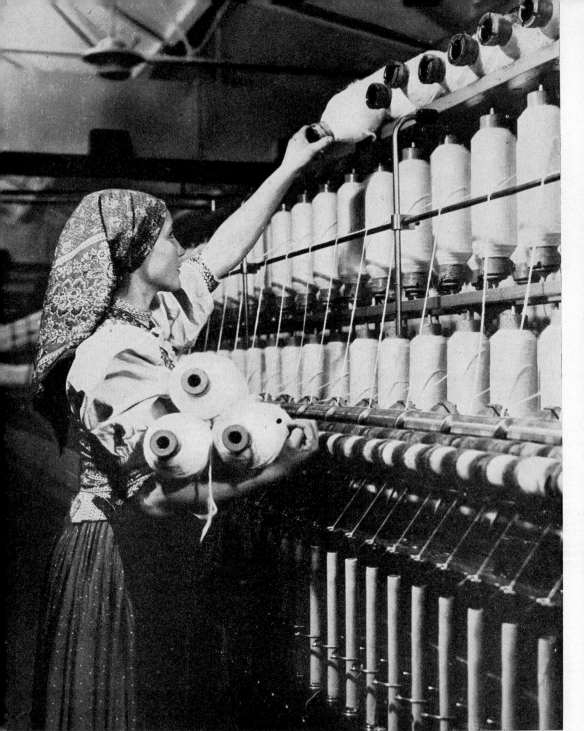

KOSTICH

A FAR CRY FROM GRANDMOTHER'S SPINNING WHEEL

A Czechoslovakian girl, in colorful native costume, prepares a modern loom in a textile mill. The textile industry is part of a state trust organization, as is almost all Czech industry. Under the communist form of economy, which is in force in this land behind the iron curtain, the state controls all the major industrial plants, as it does in Soviet Russia.

MAKING A NEW DRESS MEANS HARD WORK IN CZECHOSLOVAKIA

The hemp fibre that is used to make the peasant homespun is found in the stalks of the plant. These are gathered when ripe and soaked in water to destroy the cohesion of the woody fibres by rotting. This is called retting. When the rind comes loose the stalks are dried in the sun and are then beaten and broken with rough wooden implements.

PREPARING THE FIBRE OF THE HEMP FOR THE SPINNING-WHEEL

The next process is one in which the fibres are scutched—that is to say, they are separated from the wood in such a primitive way that it takes a long time to scutch an entire field. The short and tangled fibres which separate out in this process are called tow. The long ones are ready for spinning, after which process comes the weaving.

GOLD, RED AND BLUE are colors always found in the holiday attire of a Czech peasant girl, and part of her dress is likely to be spotlessly white. She does not usually wear silks and satins, but works on the commonest of materials with a needle and gold thread until she has a dress so rich that it enhances her peculiarly vivid beauty.

here they have the appearance of diminutive towns, with electric light in all the houses. The Morava River, which cuts the province in two, and its tributaries from the mountains on the borders provide water for the farms, on which wheat, flax, vegetables and fruit are grown. Brno, the capital of Moravia, is a busy town surrounded by hills and forests, and a population of whom about a third are German.

Slovakia occupies the eastern portion of the republic, which is formed by the mountains and valleys of the Carpathians. The province is wilder than Bohemia and Moravia, and includes the region known as the High Tatra, where there are mountains over eight thousand feet high. Their lower slopes, covered with pine forests and indigo lakes, lie hidden in mysterious valleys. In Slovakia the people devote themselves to cultivating their small farms or breeding sheep and cattle on the plain of the Danube here called the Little Alfold.

There are salt mines near Presov, and large estates on which sugar-beets are cultivated by the owners of the sugar refineries. Though Slovakia and Bohemia produce all the iron of the country, Slovakia has not been spoiled as yet by smoking factories. It has just one cotton mill that employs eight thousand people.

Where Savage Beasts Prowl

Ruthenia was the easternmost province of Czechoslovakia, separated from Poland on the north and east by the Carpathian Mountains. As in Slovakia, the summers are hot and the winters severe. The extensive forests of oak and beech are the haunts of bears, wolves, wild boars, and huge stags. Vines cover many of the hillsides, and when the grapes are ripe they are protected by armed watchmen and savage dogs.

Ruthenia was the most backward part of the republic, chiefly because so much of the land was owned by a few Magyar nobles before World War I, and the peasantry had no incentive to work hard. One of the most productive salt mines is at Slatina, and the government attempted to develop the oil fields as they also did in Moravia and Slovakia. Uzhorod is the capital of Ruthenia, and under the republic was changed from a dirty village to a town with asphalt streets. A corner of Silesia was attached to Czechoslovakia.

Railways that Ran the Wrong Way

For many years Czechoslovakia was handicapped by the fact that, when a part of the Austrian Empire, the railways had been built to connect with Vienna and Budapest, rather than with Prague or Brno. To correct this some new lines with double tracks were built.

Two streams find their way to the wharves of Hamburg and Stettin. The Danube leads to the Black Sea and the Vltava (Moldau)—branching into the Elbe—to the North Sea. The government has been promoting the building of a great ship canal which will connect these two rivers by a series of locks, crossing the divide between the two seas at an altitude of a thousand feet along the western frontier. The chief port is Bratislava on the Danube, an ancient capital of Hungary.

The Czechs form the greater part of the population of Bohemia, but where they came from is not clearly known. They conquered Bohemia in the fifth century, and are believed to be the descendants of Slav tribes which pushed westward from Russia. Much of the early story of the Czechs is a mixture of romantic legend and history. The first prince, according to a popular story, was Krokus, or Krok. He had three daughters, and at his death the youngest, Libusa, was chosen by the people to be their ruler. She is said to have foretold the future greatness of the city of Prague.

The Prophecy of Libusa

It came about in this way. One day she was called upon to settle a dispute between two nobles, and the one against whom she rendered her decision insulted her. She thereupon called together the representatives of the people and asked

BRATISLAVA, A CENTER OF DANUBE RIVER TRAFFIC

The kings of Hungary were once crowned in Bratislava, or Pressburg, but today it is one of the busiest transportation centers in Czechoslovakia. In addition to the river, it has good railroad connections; and these advantages make it a key point for trade with southeastern Europe. The low, flat cargo boats are loaded from piers that swing out from the bank of the river.

Both photos, Monkmeyer

A FARMING VILLAGE IN THE LEE OF A HILL

Farmhouses do not stand alone in Czechoslovakia, but cluster together in little hamlets. The houses are simple but comfortable, built with steep roofs so that the heavy snows of winter will slide off. Both men and women work in the surrounding fields or else take their cows and sheep to pasture on the neighboring hill. On holidays a village like this rings with merriment.

AN OPEN-AIR CONCERT ON A COBBLED TOWN SQUARE

The musicians stand in a circle, with the conductor in the center. Any true Czech would linger, as the people love music. Perhaps the band is playing some of their haunting folk tunes. These airs have been used by famous Czech composers such as Anton Dvorak and Bedrich Smetana. Smetana's lilting opera, "The Bartered Bride," shows how enchanting this music can be.

THE CZECHOSLOVAK GIRL LOVES EMBROIDERIES, AND CAN DO MARVELS WITH A NEEDLE AND THREAD

As this picture shows, the national dress of Czechoslovakia can be varied in many ways without losing any of its delightful individuality. In these seven dresses the only points that are alike in all are the natural waist-line, the full skirt and the loose elbow sleeve ending in a frill. Of all other details—trimming, shape of bodice, collar, material and even cap—there are as many different kinds as there are dresses shown. The colors vary as much as the styles, though all are bright, and are made still brighter by the wonderful embroidery.

EVEN THE RIBBONS OF HER CAP ARE RICHLY EMBROIDERED

When one sees such dresses as this it is easy to understand why the women of Czechoslovakia love their national finery. The sleeves are white and usually the neckerchief and cap as well, but the dress itself is brilliantly colored, chiefly in red or a bright, deep blue. The embroidery, too, is in every color; plenty of gold thread is sure to be used.

A MORAVIAN VILLAGE IN THE HEART OF CZECHOSLOVAKIA

Steeped in Slavic tradition since the seventh century, the province of Moravia in the central part of Czechoslovakia is a land of ancient custom and old architecture. It lies in a large, fertile basin surrounded by mountains and hills, and has a mild, genial climate. The Morava River, from the Sudeten Mountains, flows south through Moravia to the Danube.

them to choose a man to rule over them. Instead, they insisted that she select a husband, whom they would recognize as their king.

Libusa agreed. Pointing to the distant hills, she picked out a forested promontory on the river bank, and as in a trance prophesied:

"In that forest you will find a man fashioning a doorway. There will you build a city; and it shall be called Praha." (The word is said to have been taken from

the Slavonic *práh* meaning a doorway.)

"Behind those hills is a river called the Bellina, and on its banks, a town called Stadu. Near by is a farm, and in one of the fields of that farm is your future ruler plowing with a yoke of spotted oxen. His name is Premysl. Follow him!"

Her people accordingly followed her horse to the field where there was a peasant plowing with two oxen marked with spots, and this man said his name was Premysl.

They led him to Libusa, and eventually they married and lived happily ever after. Thus was founded a long line of Bohemian kings and princes.

Today the Castle of Prague, the Hradcany, combines a cluster of ancient buildings with the very modern and unromantic seat of government where the Hapsburgs had their vast palace. Here, too, rise the pure Gothic spires of the Cathedral of St. Vitus, where Bohemia's kings were crowned.

Prague consists of an Old and a New Town, and the tourist finds it strangely incongruous to ride on electric street cars through the Old World alleys of Old Town. There is a quaint theater called the Mozarteum where once Mozart waved his baton. One can also hear grand opera at either the Czech or the German opera house. The homeland of Dvorák and Smetana is a land of music lovers.

There are islands in the River Vltava where music and refreshments may be enjoyed together under the circling stars of summer nights. Or evening strollers may pause on one of the nine bridges that span the river to count the stars or lights reflected in the water.

Ancient Prague is a picturesque city that the Czechs have loved since the sixth century, when it was a center for their tribes. Today its modern districts and suburbs spread far beyond the old medieval portion.

Pleasure steamers in the red and white of the national colors used to ply upon the river, past old palaces with red tiled roofs set amid historic gardens or farmlands with barns of stone or brick cov-

PHILIP GENDREAU

EVERYTHING THAT GROWS HAS VALUE TO THOSE WHO TILL THE SOIL

This resourceful Moravian woman is gathering grasses and herbs left growing along the edge of a cultivated field. Moravia is a province in the central part of Czechoslovakia, where most of the people are of Slavic descent. With the Sudeten Mountains on the north and the Carpathians on the east, the Moravian countryside is really a large, fertile valley.

USTI, ON BOTH BANKS OF THE ELBE

Much of Europe, especially in the central parts, is crisscrossed by a network of rivers, canalized rivers and canals. These are busy highways, used both for passenger traffic and for carrying heavy freight, such as coal, in barges. Above is Usti, built along both banks of the Elbe, which is narrow at this point. The Elbe is navigable for about 470 miles.

ered with cement and tiled with red. One may also travel by air from Prague to Bratislava and elsewhere.

The wide streets of Prague are for the most part paved with wooden blocks, but there is a business section the broad sidewalks of which are set with black and white mosaics in inch squares arranged in patterns; and in places there are arcades lined with shops.

Prague has several choice legends. One relates that when Sophia, the pious daughter of one of the early Bohemian kings, was about to be forced into a marriage of state with a pagan king of Bavaria, she prayed to the Virgin to destroy her beauty, that her fate might be averted. The next morning people beheld her cross-eyed and possessed of whiskers falling well below her shoulders. A painting in one of the chapels of the Cathedral of St. Vitus, which stands within the maze of connected Castle buildings, shows her thus. It is not surprising that her lover withdrew his suit posthaste.

It is told of St. Vitus for whom the Cathedral was named that when he had performed many miracles of healing, the Emperor Diocletian called upon him to cast out a devil with which one of the princes was afflicted. St. Vitus cured the youth physically and mentally. At this, the Emperor urged the saint to abandon Christianty; but when he refused to do so, had him cast into prison. There St. Vitus was seen, the legend relates, night after night dancing with the angels. He thus became patron saint of dancers.

The Czechs have the reputation of being the most industrious of the Slav races. They are intensely patriotic, and, in the past, kept alight a burning desire for independence under generations of foreign rule. Before the iron curtain descended, visitors to Czechoslovakia were charmed by the national dress worn on holidays. Red was a favorite color, and skirts billowed over many petticoats. In southern Bohemia the men wore fur-edged jackets and the women had a special headdress, which is a close-fitting white cap with huge lace bows at the side. The people are good farmers and cultivate every available bit of land.

In the urban north the peasants work in their homes at jewel-cutting and bead-polishing. The roads through these hillside villages sparkle in the sunlight with many colors, because the bits of broken beads are thrown out of the windows. The frame cottages are built with wide overhanging eaves like those of Switzerland and often have only two rooms. But even the cooking utensils shine from frequent polishing. The Czechs realize the importance of education and when the children have left school they generally

go to an industrial training centre where they are taught some local industry.

Most of the young Czech men and women belong to gymnastic societies called Sokols, and the Czech rulers encouraged the Sokols not only to keep the young people physically fit, but also as a means of increasing their patriotism.

Horaks and Hanaks are other interesting Slav peoples who are found living in Moravia. They are expert dairy farmers, and ply such home industries as weaving and making wooden articles. They are not so progressive as the people of Bohemia, perhaps because when the Austrian nobles had vast estates here (to which they used to come to hunt wild

Florence Farmborough

THE HOUSE THAT BOASTS A STORK'S NEST IS LUCKY INDEED

On the cottage roof, where bundles of flax have been spread to dry in the sun, a pair of storks have made their nest and reared two long-legged youngsters; and though the great birds are extremely destructive to crops, they are welcomed by the Ruthenian peasantry as birds of good omen. Notice the high door-sill, designed to keep out cold draughts.

A STRANGE FASHION IN MEN'S ATTIRE: SKIRT-LIKE TROUSERS OF THE SLOVAKS

In parts of Slovakia, the peasants, men and boys, used to wear trousers exactly as extraordinary as those shown above, but the custom has largely died out. The garments are so wide that they look far more like skirts, and they are so full that it would seem as if any of these little girls could make a frock for herself from one of her father's trouser legs. The cloth of which they are composed is spun at home by the women of the household, and the mother of a large family of boys is obliged to work diligently at her spinning-wheel to keep them clothed.

THE SUNDAY BEST OF THE SLOVAK PEASANT WOMEN IS GAY INDEED

These sturdy women, who live near the little town of Pöstyén, in Slovakia, wear their bright beribboned costumes and embroidered aprons only on Sundays, or on high days and holidays. Their tall, shiny boots they likewise don only upon occasion, for unless they are rich enough to have two pairs, they go barefooted about their work.

Rudo Bruner-Dvořák

OPEN-AIR DANCE TO CELEBRATE A HOLIDAY IN PRAGUE

Even the busy city of Prague sometimes sees the national dress of Bohemia on a fête day, when the peasants go through their traditional dances with much stamping of boots.

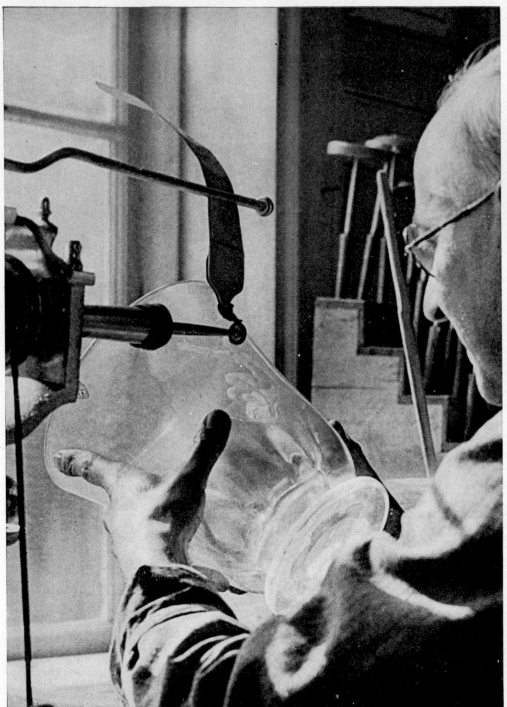

Kostich Photos

DELICATE BEAUTY FROM THE WHEEL OF THE GLASS-ENGRAVER

Bohemian glass has a long tradition, sprinkled with the names of gifted artists. In an earlier period it was often enameled or decorated with gold leaf, and the designs were elaborate. The modern glass, usually cut and engraved, has a simpler loveliness. Delicate as it looks, this glass is hard and can stand quite abrupt changes in temperature without breaking.

212

SOKOLS MARCH TO THE STADIUM THROUGH THE CITY OF PRAGUE

Every few years, notably in 1912 and in 1920, tens of thousands of Sokols gather together to hold a great display in Prague. Here a company of the men is marching through the city, bearing banners each topped by a falcon with open wings. The men wear red shirts with fawn-colored jackets, and in their round caps are two falcon's feathers.

WOMEN AS WELL AS MEN TAKE PART IN THE GREAT SOKOL DISPLAY

All Sokols, men and women, learn to fence, wrestle and keep themselves physically fit by drilling and athletics. They strive to be as active and as fearless as the falcon.

WHERE BOHEMIAN STEEL IS MADE: THE HEAVY FORGING DEPARTMENT OF THE GREAT SKODA WORKS

Pilsen, in Bohemia, is one of the chief manufacturing towns of Czechoslovakia, famous all the world over for two things—its great brewery and its huge engineering plant, the Skoda works. In 1859 it was a small factory, but by 1913 the concern, at that time in Austrian territory, had an area of 360 acres, besides coal mines and a proving-range for guns. It was the largest steel works in Central Europe and one of the largest arsenals in the world. During the two world wars it was busy turning out guns and other arms of many kinds

214

KOSTICH

WALKING ACROSS THE FAMOUS CHARLES BRIDGE IN PRAGUE

The ancient and picturesque city of Prague is built on both sides of the Vltava River, and each of the nine bridges that spans the winding stream has a history all its own. With its Gothic style, statues and guardian towers, the Charles Bridge is probably the one best loved by Czechs. It is the oldest, having been built in the fourteenth century.

boars), the trade of the province was in the hands of the Jews and Germans who had settled in the towns. The national costumes are most often seen in Moravia.

The Slovak language is nearest the Old Slavonic. The Slovaks are more superstitious than the Czechs of Bohemia and Moravia and speak a different language. Contented and industrious, they are mostly small farmers, using old-fashioned implements rarely seen elsewhere. Many of the men come down from the mountains at harvest time and work on the plains or in Germany and Denmark. Others wander about Austria, Hungary and southern Russia as traveling tinkers, mending pots and kettles by the wayside. Slovak girls used often to go as nursemaids to Vienna and other cities, where their national costume attracted much attention.

Slovakia is the most rugged part of the whole country. In the High Tatras, the chief mountain group of the central Carpathians, the peaks rise to more than 8,000 feet above sea level. Highest of all is Gerlsdorfer Spitze, 8,737 feet. Sprinkled among the mountains are a number of lovely little lakes. In more carefree days, city people flocked to the charming lakeside inns for summer holidays.

Winter is a bitterly cold season in the High Tatras. Then only the sound of a solitary woodsman or shepherd crunching through the snow breaks the hushed silence. There are no towns of any size and few villages. The chief highway in these mountains goes to Sanok, in the southeastern part of Poland, through the Lupkow Pass.

CZECHOSLOVAKIA: FACTS AND FIGURES

THE COUNTRY

The Republic of Czechoslovakia was created from parts of the old Austro-Hungarian Empire in 1918. Bohemia, Moravia and Silesia, and Slovakia banded together, drew up a constitution and declared themselves a republic. Ruthenia, formerly a part of Hungary, joined them to be governed as a trust. The republic was broken up and divided between Germany, Poland and Hungary as a result of the Munich Conference of 1938. All of the states, except Ruthenia, reunited under a new constitution after World War II. Ruthenia was ceded to Soviet Russia. Area and population (1948) of the present republic are 49,355 square miles and 12,409,000.

GOVERNMENT

With the adoption of a new constitution in 1948, Czechoslovakia became a so-called people's democratic republic. The two principal political parties—Communist and Social Democratic—merged and became the National Front party, dominated by the Communists. The country is governed by an elected National Assembly of 300 members, a president and a prime minister.

COMMERCE AND INDUSTRIES

All industries employing 50 or more people were nationalized in 1948, and a five-year Economic Plan of Development was begun to increase industry, agriculture and trade. Agriculture is well developed. Principal crops are potatoes, sugar-beets, oats, wheat, rye, barley, corn, hops, fruit (apples, pears, stone fruit). Livestock-raising is important. Forests, covering 33% of the whole area, are a source of wealth, and the minerals, of which there are rich deposits, include soft and hard coal, iron, graphites, garnets, gold, silver, copper and lead. Industrial products are refined sugar, beer, spirit, malt and foodstuffs, textiles (cotton, linen and woolen), glass, imitation stones, paper, furniture, machinery, metal goods and chemicals.

The main exports are sugar, cotton and woolen goods, flax and jute products, timber, coal, glass, iron goods, fruit and vegetables, leather and leather goods, porcelain and pottery. The imports are cotton and cotton goods, wool and woolen goods, cereals, live cattle, fats and tobacco.

COMMUNICATIONS

There are now about 8,157 miles of railway operating in the four states. The river Elbe and its navigable tributary, the Vltava, connect Prague with Hamburg. Bratislava, on the Danube, was formerly the headquarters of the International Danubian Commission. In 1937 there were 90,195 miles of telegraph wire and 683,882 miles of telephone wire. Prague was connected with the rest of Europe by fifteen different air routes, and motor transportation was being established in the mountain districts.

RELIGION AND EDUCATION

The majority of the population is Catholic. Education is obligatory between the ages of 6 and 14. There are 15,924 elementary, higher grade, secondary and vocational schools. There are ten universities and technical universities at Prague, Bratislava, Brno, Olomouc, Plzen, Hradec and Ceske Kralove.

CHIEF TOWNS

Prague (Praha), capital, in 1947, 922,284; Brno, 273,127; Ostrava, 180,960; Bratislava, 172,664; Plzen (Pilsen), 117,814; Olomouc, 58,617.

AUSTRIA: GATEWAY TO THE EAST

Album of Alpine Austria

Austria, once the domain of the Hapsburg rulers and the leading nation of central Europe, is today a weak state split by the iron curtain. In the days of greatness before World War I, Austria's Emperor Francis Joseph ruled over 51,000,000 subjects in a land of more than 250,000 square miles. Austria's population is now but 7,000,000 and her area 32,000 square miles. Made up of eight provinces and the city of Vienna, she hugs the southern border of Germany and stretches from Switzerland in the west to Hungary and Czechoslovakia in the east. A multitude of problems that beset the republic after World War I made the way easy for the march of Hitler, who annexed Austria in 1938. After 1945, French, British, Soviet and United States occupation forces controlled Austria. She gained considerable freedom in the sectors under the Western powers, and through hard work and outside aid she is struggling to rebuild her trade and industry.

AUSTRIA has been a republic with a president and parliament only since 1918 when the last Hapsburg emperor was forced from the land, which his family had ruled since 1282. The German name for Austria, Oesterreich, means eastern realm and was first used to mark off the eastern frontier of Charlemagne's vast Frankish empire. Far from being a frontier, however, Austria has usually been in the center of the stage. Barbarian tribes, first the Huns, then the Avars, the Goths and the Slavs, pressed in from the north and east while German princes tried to drive them off from the west. Later, due to the power and influence of the Hapsburgs, Austria was the ruling state of the Holy Roman Empire.

The Napoleonic Wars brought an end to the Holy Roman Empire, in 1806. The Hapsburg Francis II took the title of Emperor of Austria. In 1867 the emperor became by treaty also the king of Hungary, and the realm was known as the Austro-Hungarian Empire. The first World War swept that empire away.

The reigning Hapsburgs were exiled, much territory was taken away from Austria, and the state was left only a faint shadow of its former self.

The country was reduced to less than the population of New York or London, shorn of markets, and shut off by customs barriers from the markets upon which her factories depended. Hungary and the north no longer sent their leather,

iron, coal, and piano wood. There was unemployment and starvation. In 1923 the League of Nations secured an international loan for the little state; this, with some financial reforms, helped for a short time, but restlessness grew as poverty once more stared the little republic in the face. In 1934 there was a crisis, and blood was shed. In 1938 Adolf Hitler, with a show of force, in a single day "captured" Austria and made it a province of the German Reich. (As a matter of fact, many Austrians had wished to unite with the German Republic after World War I, but the Allied Powers had refused their consent.)

After Germany's defeat in 1945, Austria was forced to accept military occupation by Allied forces that were not always in agreement among themselves.

Much of the Austrian territory is mountain land. First come the Alps, which stretch from Switzerland into Tyrol and far to the east of Austria. Then there are the Dolomites, than which nothing could be more picturesque.

Close to Vienna we shall find beautiful mountain resorts. In the old days these places were isolated and difficult to reach for months of the year. But now electric railways whisk the tourist thence. Thousands of visitors come each year from all over Europe to enjoy the winter sports. Long, steep tracks for toboggans have been made down the hillsides, as in Switzerland, and are kept so smooth

HOCH-OSTERWITZ CASTLE near the village of Launsdorf, in the province of Carinthia, stands on the summit of a rock five hundred feet above the level of the surrounding country. Rebuilt in sixteen hundred, it is even to-day a magnificent example of the strongholds occupied by the Carinthian nobles. It is reached by a path that winds across three drawbridges, and through fourteen turreted gateways. The girl in the foreground is wearing the short, sleeveless jacket over a white blouse— part of the traditional costume of Carinthian women.

© E. N. A.

AUSTRIA HAS A GENEROUS SHARE of the glories of the Alps. Above the Seebach Valley towers the Ankogel, 10,705 feet in height, one of the most notable peaks along the central Alpine ranges that extend into western Austria. Ankogel is not far from the resort town of Badgastein in the massive granite range, Hohe Tauern, which forms an almost impassable frontier between the provinces of Salzburg and Carinthia. The Seebach Valley is typical of many in the Hohe Tauern. Watered by a rushing stream, it affords excellent pasture for the grazing of cows and sheep.

219

GASTEINER VALLEY FOLK IN THEIR TRADITIONAL COSTUME

These hearty, Alpine peasants linger to drink from a highly polished steer's horn, as they enjoy a holiday from work. Gasteiner Valley, high in the Austrian Alps, is famous all over the world for its health-giving mineral springs, its lakes and magnificent scenery. It is less than fifty miles from Salzburg, birthplace of Austria's great composer Mozart.

that the tobogganist could outrace the swiftest express train.

One of the chief amusements of the Tyrolese is their peasant plays, and the villagers toil for months, sometimes for years, to prepare a spectacle which tells something of their own life or history. The favorite play is one dealing with the life of Andreas Hofer, the national hero of the Tyrol.

Andreas Hofer was an innkeeper living near the town of Meran. When, in 1797, Napoleon Bonaparte sent a big army into the Tyrol to conquer it, the peasants came together and chose Hofer as their leader. Under him they defeated the French and drove them out of the country. Napoleon, however, made a treaty dividing the country between Bavaria and France. The French had their police spies all over the land, and anyone who whispered a word against them might find himself arrested, put in prison and shot.

But Andreas Hofer could not be subdued so easily. He worked secretly among the peasants, found arms, and told them to make ready to try again to win their freedom. Many of these peasants had no weapons except scythes, pitchforks and sledge-hammers. One day Andreas

Hofer sent a messenger to all his neighbors: "The time has come." That night he and his friends lit a big bonfire on the Alps above Meran, to show that they were going to attack their enemies.

Several thousand men gathered around Hofer: he led them over the Alps to Innsbruck, where, after hard fighting, they defeated the powerful Bavarian army. Napoleon, who had conquered nearly all Europe, did not like being defeated by these peasants. He therefore assembled an army of fifty thousand men under Marshal Lefebvre and sent it to Innsbruck. Andreas Hofer fought this great French army and defeated it also. The Tyrolese then elected him governor of their country.

He ruled the country wisely. But Napoleon made another great effort against him, and this time defeated him. Hofer, nearly all his friends having forsaken him, had to flee and hide himself in a mountain hut. There he was betrayed and made prisoner. The French took him to Mantua and there shot him. He would not allow the soldiers to bind his eyes and he would not kneel, but stood up and cried: "Long live Kaiser Franz! Aim straight!" While it has been many years since Hofer, the patriot, was shot, he is by

THE REPUBLIC OF AUSTRIA AS RE-ESTABLISHED AFTER WORLD WAR II

AUSTRIAN LEGATION

BESIDE THE TRAUNSEE, a lovely seven-mile lake in Upper Austria, lies the village of Traunkirchen. Rising precipitously from the opposite shore is the snow-flecked Traunstein, the summit of which is more than four thousand feet above sea level. The lake is, indeed, encircled by magnificent mountains, and mirrors their inverted cones.

IN TYROL one may sometimes see strong girls hauling branches for firewood down the hillsides to the farmhouses of the Alpine valleys. All the lower slopes of Tyrol are covered with tall forests of pine, fir and birch, and these forests are protected both because of the value of the timber and because they diminish erosion by the spring floods.

223

A LOW BUILDING THAT IS A SKYSCRAPER

Perched nearly ten thousand feet high in the Austrian Tyrol is the Ramolhaus. It commands a superb view of the Seelenkögl Peak that tops it by another fifteen hundred feet. This peak is in the Ötztaler Alps, a mountain range that extends through Austria and Italy and has numerous glaciers. The name is derived from the Ötztal Valley of the Inn River in the Tyrol.

RELIGIOUS PLAY PERFORMED BY TYROLESE PEASANTS

The mountaineers living in villages around Innsbruck, like the people of the Bavarian village of Oberammergau, used to compose and perform religious plays. In this photograph we see a man intended to represent Adam wearily plodding through life, while Death, inscrutable of face and armed with a wooden sword, dogs his footsteps.

BY TRAIN THROUGH AUSTRIA'S ALPINE SCENERY

The Semmering railway runs from Gloggnitz in Lower Austria to Mürzzuschlag in Styria, and between these two towns, a distance of thirty-three miles, it traverses fifteen tunnels and sixteen viaducts. It is the oldest of the great Continental mountain railways and the culminating point of the line is approximately three thousand feet above sea level.

OLD SALZBURG boasts this interesting gateway into a Franciscan monastery, with a sacred painting above the arch. There is also a Capuchin monastery. Salzburg was once the most powerful ecclesiastical principality in south Germany.

IN THE OLD QUARTER of Innsbruck one may see many an ancient building. This famous house facing Herzog-Friedrichstrasse, with its roof of gilded copper, dates from the early sixteenth century. Behind rise great snow-capped mountains.

MOZART'S GEBURTSHAUS.

© E. N. A.

HOUSE WHERE MOZART WAS BORN

Mozart, the world-famed musician, was born at No. 9, Getreidegasse, Salzburg, in 1756. The house now contains the Mozart Museum. His home in the Makart-platz has also been preserved.

to the days of long ago, with their rich copper decorations, quaint towers and cellar cafés. Innsbruck is also a modern city with a fine university. Salzburg, on the River Salzach, has an old castle on a high wooded hill. Two of the most delightful of the smaller towns are no longer Austrian, for Botzen and Meran, in southern Tyrol, were in the territory assigned to Italy. Even their names are changed, for now they are called Bolzano and Merano. But the Tyrolese people still hope that some day these towns will be returned to them.

A delightful trip can be taken down the River Danube on one of the river steamers, in which one can have one's own cabin and live in as great comfort as on an ocean liner. The chief difference is that the river steamers never have to face really rough water. One embarks at Passau and travels through quaint cities such as Linz, Melk and Krems, to Vienna. In summer, every hour of this journey is a delight. One passes hillsides covered with trees and picturesque old castles, each with its own story. Caum Castle, for instance, had once an owner who was so cruel and who so oppressed the people around him, that his name is hated to this day.

Linz is a city of flowers and sunshine. The Streuden (Rapids) here was once considered dangerous for people trying to navigate the river, but it does not trouble a modern steamer. The city is faced on one side by the Island of Mirth —about which many legends are told—and on the other by an ancient castle. Next we come to Melk, made famous by Wagner.

Vienna was the home of many famous composers—Gluck, Mozart, Beethoven, Schubert, Brahms, Johann and Richard Strauss—and was the inspiration for many fine compositions. The city that gave birth to Franz Schubert, was once noted for its unusually fine shops and gay life of fashion. It still has the famous

no means forgotten by the people of the Tyrol.

Everyone who travels through the mountain villages of the Tyrol is delighted with the simplicity and kindness of the inhabitants. In this region we may see ruins of the castles of the barons and of the great houses of bygone days. Big crosses have been erected at many points on the mountain roads, especially at any spots where someone has been accidentally killed. Many of the old churches are beautiful, but the finest buildings in Tyrol are seen in Innsbruck, which stands at the foot of the Alps at the beginning of the Brenner Pass.

Innsbruck is a charming city placed with the heights of the Alps looking directly down upon it. Many of the buildings in the main streets seem to belong

WOMAN TOY-SELLER AWAITING CUSTOM BENEATH HER UMBRELLA

During the long, snow-bound winter the peasants living in the Alpine villages of Austria spend most of their time indoors and busy themselves in making simple, wooden toys, like those this woman is selling in a street of Vienna. Sturdy Bohemian women may often be seen in the streets of the city selling apples or presiding over stalls at the open-air markets. The chief grain and cattle markets of Austria are held in Vienna, which is also the great manufacturing centre of the Austrian republic.

BESIDE THE DANUBE at Melk is this vast Benedictine abbey, situated two hundred feet above the river. The abbey was founded in 1089, but it was re-erected early in the eighteenth century. The domed church is lavishly decorated with gilding and red marble. Just below Melk the Danube enters a gorge which is famous for the wild beauty of its scenery.

THE HOHEN-SALZBURG, a fortress-palace overlooking the surrounding country at Salzburg (Zälts börg), was once the residence of the archbishops of Salzburg, but was later used as barracks. The fortress was founded as far back as the ninth century, but rebuilt in the sixteenth. Its chapel presents the twelve apostles amazingly sculptured in red marble.

SALZBURG, CITY OF RARE BEAUTY

The new garden restaurant in the foreground overlooks Salzburg. The white building toward the left is the cathedral, a replica of St. Peter's at Rome. The citadel of Hohen-Salzburg stands high above the old quarter of the city. Monchsberg in the background rises so steeply that some houses in its vicinity have rooms that are hewn out of the solid mountainside.

ORNATE TRINITY COLUMN RISING IN THE GRABEN, VIENNA

In more prosperous days, some of the best shops in Vienna were found in the Graben, which dates from the thirteenth century. The Trinity Column, sixty-nine feet high, was erected to commemorate the end of the great plague of 1679. After World War II, Vienna became the seat of the Allied Council, and the city was divided into four zones.

233

McLeish

KÄRTNERSTRASSE, VIENNA'S CHIEF BUSINESS THOROUGHFARE

Vienna was originally a Celtic settlement on an arm of the Danube. It consists of an inner
city, Altstadt, and a number of municipal districts. St. Stephen's Church, the spire and tiled
roof of which are shown, is a rare example of Gothic architecture. The tourist should also
see the university, the medical faculty of which has made it famous; and the museums.

park known as the Ring that circles the inner city. Vienna seems to be first of all a city of palaces, for the Hapsburg monarchs dwelt for more than six centuries in the buildings of the Hofburg.

The palace of the old Emperor Francis Joseph, to-day a National Museum, is rather a gloomy place. Visitors are taken through endless rooms, splendid with rich decorations, where the Court ceremonies were held. They see also the surprisingly simple rooms where the old emperor himself lived.

The Viennese relish good cookery. People like to meet in cafés, where they will sit for hours over a cup of coffee and a few pastries. The Viennese coffee, with its rich layer of whipped cream on top, is unexcelled. The Viennese shops are full of luxurious leather and metal work and embroideries, and the Viennese are famous dressmakers and designers of artistic furnishings. For centuries the sparkling climate has attracted people of wealth from other countries. These have supported the gay cafés and the luxurious shops of the Graben and the Kärntnerstrasse. Vienna has ever been a city of music and dancing. The city celebrated the two thousandth anniversary of its founding on August 26, 1929, with patriotic demonstrations and special programs of its numerous singing societies.

Vienna, the music-loving capital, shared the musical spotlight with Salzburg. The Viennese have been ready patrons not to music alone but to all the arts.

Austria has been the patchwork union of a dozen nationalities. Position and location have brought many wars and occasional wealth and power to this mountain-core-country of Europe. Austria has known little but war's desolation for a number of years.

AUSTRIA: FACTS AND FIGURES

THE COUNTRY

Austria is bounded by Germany and Czechoslovakia on the north and northwest, Hungary on the east, Yugoslavia and Italy on the south and Switzerland on the west. The Treaty of St. Germain, signed in September, 1919, gave to the Federal Republic of Austria the following territories (or "Lands") of the old Austro-Hungarian Empire: Upper Austria provinces, Lower Austria and the City of Vienna, Salzburg, Tyrol, Styria, Carinthia, Vorarlberg and Burgenland. Census of 1948 showed a population of 6,952,744 and an area of 32,375 square miles.

GOVERNMENT

Following Austria's liberation by allied forces, the country was divided into four occupation zones controlled by the United States, France, Great Britain and Russia. Elections by the people in November, 1945, returned 165 deputies to the National Assembly, of whom eighty-five were members of the Austrian People's Party. Next in strength was the Socialist Party with seventy-six members. As a result, the People's Party formed a government which was recognized by the four powers. 1949 elections retained the party in power.

COMMERCE AND INDUSTRIES

Agriculture is the principal occupation of the people, and the chief products are potatoes, turnips, rye, oats, wheat and barley. The foodstuffs produced are not sufficient for the population. Cattle-raising and sheep-raising are carried on. Minerals, including lignite, iron, copper, zinc, lead and salt, are important, and the forest wealth is notable. Other industries are manufacture of pianos, motor cars, furniture and textiles, especially knit goods (sport knitted goods and hosiery). The chief exports are timber, ores, fruit, sugar-beet, furniture and chemicals, and the imports include wines, fuel. grain, flour and rice, building materials and cotton. Many industries have been nationalized.

COMMUNICATIONS

There are about 3,700 miles of railways, mostly state-operated, in Austria. It is intended to electrify the entire system, which is expected to take about 12 years.

RELIGION AND EDUCATION

About 90 per cent of the people are Roman Catholics. In 1948-49 there were 4,956 elementary and private schools; ten commercial schools; three state-controlled universities, at Vienna, Graz and Innsbruck; a Roman Catholic theology school at Salzburg and a number of agricultural and technical schools.

CHIEF TOWNS

Population (1948): Vienna, 1,731,557; Graz, 219,974; Linz, 181,532; Salzburg, 105,407; Innsbruck, 97,221; Klagenfurt, 65,799; St. Polten, 40,711; Steyr, 38,041; Wels, 36,528; Leoben, 35,785; Wiener Neustadt, 31,894.

HERDSMEN BEFORE THEIR SHELTER ON THE HORTOBÁGY PLAIN

In eastern Hungary lies the Alföld, or great plain, of which the Hortobágy Plain forms a part. Herds of cattle and horses and flocks of sheep graze over its rich pastures, attended by herdsmen such as those above. The man on the right is wearing an embroidered sheep-skin cloak, with the fleece inside, a custom reminiscent of Tibet.

A Link Between East and West

The Magyars and Gipsies of Hungary

Hungary has led a long and varied existence of alternate freedom and oppression. Hungarians, who call themselves Magyars, are descendants of Finno-Ugrian tribes that came in the ninth century and for centuries held the plains against the Turks—not always successfully. For less than fifty years, Hungary was a part of the Austro-Hungarian Empire; between the two world wars she was a kingdom without a king. After the war a republican form of government was adopted, and Hungary came within the Russian sphere of influence. The gipsies who are dealt with in a feature article, have long roved the plains. Hungary has been termed the gateway of the East, and the people still retain many Eastern characteristics. Indeed, the influence of the East is everywhere manifest.

THE Hungarian plains and sun-baked steppes are sheltered on the northeast and southeast by the Carpathians, and on the west and southwest by a long arm of the Alps, known as the Bakony Wald. This mountain encircled basin contains an area of wide treeless steppes where graze vast herds of horses, cattle, buffaloes, sheep and swine. Rich fields of wheat flourish on cultivated land, and the hill slopes are fragrant with wine grapes. The mountain slopes of the Bakony Wald are heavily forested. The Danube and the Theiss (Tisza) afford water transportation. The Danube is navigable in its entire course through Hungary.

The division of land for the past thousand years—two-thirds of it into large estates—had preserved feudalism; and until Hungary procured independence from Austrian oppression there was little incentive to manufacturing. For over a thousand years this fertile land has been occupied by an Asiatic people somewhat related to the Finns. According to legend, hordes of nomads came in 895 or 896, led by Khan Arpád, and drove out the Slavs; and these Magyars are still the dominant race, though varied peoples long menaced national stability. Hungary's charter of liberties, the Golden Bull, is older than Magna Carta and she celebrated her thousandth anniversary in 1896. Early in the eleventh century King Stephen knitted the tribes into an organized state and established Christianity. Hungary then became a bulwark against the Asiatic invasion of Europe: for in 1353 the Ottoman Turks crossed the Hellespont and for three centuries terrorized all of Europe. In 1443 John Hunyadi became a national hero when he defeated the Sultan before Sofia. In 1526, however, the Turks made murderous onslaught at Mohács, securing central Hungary; and soon after, the Hapsburgs secured the throne, with supremacy in western Hungary. The Turks were finally driven out in 1683 by the kings of Austria and Poland.

Though the Magyars strove desperately in 1711 to regain their freedom, thirty years later they made a gallant sacrifice for the young queen, archduchess Maria Theresa of Austria, when she asked aid in repelling the invasion of Austria by the French. Wearing the iron crown of St. Stephen, she addressed the Hungarian Diet at Pressburg (Bratislava). In reply, the hall re-echoed to the sound of sabres half drawn, then thrust back into scabbards, and with one voice they cried: "We consecrate our life and blood to your most sacred majesty!"

During Maria Theresa's reign a pontoon bridge was built across the Danube to connect Buda and Pest. The two ancient cities had long been rivals. But not until 1873, under the Dual Monarchy, that the law was passed decreeing that they should henceforth be one. Some twenty-one years later Budapest became a royal city, equal in rank to Vienna. It is a city of fine churches, wide streets and handsome bridges. The Opera and National Theatre belong to the state and Shakespeare is frequently played. There are numerous moving picture houses,

MAP OF THE GREAT PLAINS OF HUNGARY

good cafés, and the library of the National Museum is one of the most valuable in Europe.

The Dual Monarchy was established in 1867 when the Austrian emperor Francis Joseph became the king of Hungary. This benevolent monarch endeared himself to the Hungarian people; and though the national spirit had never been quenched, it lay quiescent until his death in 1916. Then the embers of discontent burst into flame and on November 16, 1918, independence was declared and the Hungarian People's Republic came into existence.

Two years later, the old monarchical constitution was restored and the country became, in effect, a kingdom without a king, governed by a regent.

Hungary sided with Germany during World War II. Upon Germany's defeat, Russia occupied Hungary and exacted large reparations from the already impoverished nation. Hungary fell victim to inflation. In 1947, America offered to stabilize the tottering finances with a loan, but withdrew the offer when the Red army of occupation helped the communist minority in Hungary's Parliament stage a coup d'etat. Since that time Hungary has been a Russian satellite.

The Hungarian, tall, high cheek-boned and slightly oblique of eye, loves dueling, horse-racing and games of chance, and can dance for hours, fairly intoxicated by the gipsy music of the country. The Czárdás alternate from rhythms of wild exuberance to those of drooping sadness. The shepherds play a flute, the *tilinko,* and the villagers, the ancient lute. The tziganes—gipsies—believed to have originated long ago in India, have for hundreds of years roved the lowlands of Hungary, though the government has tried to make them settle down. Many of them are horse traders and some are thieves, but nearly all are musicians. The wild rhythms of Franz Liszt's Hungarian Rhapsodies have preserved elements of gipsy music; while the German composer, Johannes Brahms, based his Hungarian songs on their haunting melodies.

The peasant women of Hungary are nothing if not picturesque, with their red stockings, full petticoats—of which they sometimes wear ten or a dozen—their gay aprons and beribboned hair. They never miss an occasion for donning this finery. Easter, Christmas and New Year's Eve are the great events. At Easter, the first young girl to be met must be sprinkled,

FISHERMAN INSPECTING HIS NETS ON THE BANKS OF THE RIVER HORTOBÁGY

When the fisherman takes up his nets he spreads them over wooden frames to dry and mend. Hungary has important fishery preserves in the Danube and the Theiss and on Lake Balaton, a body of water fifty miles in length. Perch, carp and pike are taken, also shad and sheatfish —a sort of catfish. Hungary is well fed, what with her fish and her sheep, hogs and cattle, her vast fields of wheat and maize and the vines from which her "Tokaj" wine is made. The chief commercial need of her people is to secure the means for buying manufactured goods.

239

DANCING THE HUNGARIAN NATIONAL DANCE BEFORE A VERY CRITICAL AUDIENCE

© E. N. A.

The Csárdás, as the Hungarian national dance is called, has two movements—one slow and stately, the other gay and whirling. These Magyar peasants are passionately fond of dancing, and they seem to become fairly intoxicated by the emotional music. While the ancient lute is still played for village dances, and the flute is carried by every shepherd of the plains, it is the violin, with its wild gipsy dance rhythms, which characterizes Hungarian music. Only strings could express the sharp alternations of the Csárdás, melancholy cadences and frenzied delight.

HUNGARIAN CHILDREN IN HOLIDAY FINERY

This serious little boy and his sisters are dressed in elaborately embroidered clothes, copies in miniature of the festival garments their parents wear. The blouses, vests, skirts, aprons—even the tablecloth—are stiff with the famous Hungarian needlework, done in the most vivid colors possible. Hand-made fringe finishes off the edges of the tablecloth and the girls' aprons. All of these pieces represent months of work by the children's mother.

whether she likes it or not, with scent-water, or if she is daring enough to venture out of doors she will promptly be seized and taken to the nearest well, and she will be lucky if she escapes with having only one bucketful of water emptied over her. The men dress as gaily as the women. They wear small, round hats ornamented with feathers and flowers, black sleeveless jackets over loose white undershirts (often with embroidered sleeves) and white trousers that look like petticoats. They also wear bright aprons. The women wear the sleeveless bodice and white blouse and a full, embroidered skirt, with often a handsome shawl, a

kerchief for the head, but usually with bare feet. The *suba* and the *szur* are two garments especially beloved by the shepherds and peasant workers. They are the garments in which they live and sleep. The *suba* is a long cloak of sheepskin with the wool worn inside, and the leather elaborately embroidered. The *szur* is also an ornate long cloak, but is made of a felt-like material.

In former years great contrasts of wealth and poverty existed. Most Hungarians are poor today, however, partly as the result of defeat in World War II and partly due to the great political changes that have taken place. Hungary

© Cutler

HUNGARIAN WOMEN CARRYING THEIR GEESE TO MARKET

It is as customary in Hungary to raise a few geese as for Western farmers to raise chickens for a side line. Sometimes goose girls drive their flocks to town; but a single bird is harder to manage as it never wishes to leave its fellows. The character of the roads makes it necessary for peasant women to wear high boots like the men's.

FAMILY MAKING JELLY IN THE VILLAGE OF CZINKOTA

In the autumn, when the plums have been gathered, everyone seems to be busy at the same task—jelly-making. The whole family has to help, because the stirring must go on throughout twenty-four hours without a stop. Appearances to the contrary, the man is not wearing a petticoat, but trousers cut wide and loose.

is behind the iron curtain today. It is very difficult to know for certain how the people live. We do know that the army has been built up to frightening proportions. We also know that the present communist Government stresses the need for building heavy industries.

There are too many people living in the farm regions. Though the Great and Little Alföld are among the most fertile plains of Europe, there is not enough land to go around. There is not enough food harvested to satisfy the hunger of the people. And because Moscow gives the orders, what food there is, is not always eaten in Hungary.

243

Kankovszky

EVERY YEAR IS LEAP YEAR IN THE BAJA DISTRICT OF HUNGARY

According to a peasant custom of South Hungary, while the men are harvesting, the unmarried young women go into the fields to cook for them, taking bouquets of flowers to bestow on the objects of their esteem. If a man likes the girl whose offering he receives, he gives her a piece of crystallized sugar as a sign of their betrothal.

TIME TO PLANT POTATOES

Once this field was part of a large manor. After the war the big Hungarian estates were taken away from their owners and parcelled out in small lots. In 1950 the Government instituted a Five Year Plan, with agricultural quotas for peasants. Potatoes are a mainstay in the diet, especially in rural areas, and the Hungarian wife knows many ways of cooking them.

AUTUMN—AND THE CORN IS RIPE

A short length of stalk is left on the ear when corn is gathered in Hungary. The stalks are then braided and the golden garland is hung from the rafters, up under the thatch, to dry. Corn is good family food and excellent feed for livestock as well, during the winter. Most farming in Hungary is now done on the collective pattern. The country is becoming increasingly industrialized.

245

© Cutler

REED HOUSE OF A FISHERMAN ON THE BANK OF THE HORTOBÁGY RIVER

With mild winters and food in abundance, life is comparatively simple in Hungary. Those who cannot obtain timber from the forested areas for building purposes make adequate shelters from the reeds that grow tall and thick along the banks of the rivers, tying them together in bundles and plastering them with mud. Thick mats of reeds thatch the roof, a chimney for the fireplace is made of plastered stones and only the door is of plank. There are no windows, but the inmates spend most of their waking hours in the open air.

FINE CHINA FIGURINES READY FOR A BATH

When the delicate, ornamental figure is first produced it has a porous, dull surface. Then it is dipped into a vat of liquid glaze, a substance similar to glass, that penetrates the figure and clings to the surface. After that the statuette is baked in an oven at extremely high temperatures and emerges at last with a glossy and durable surface.

AN OLD MASTER AT PAINTING PLATES TEACHES APPRENTICES

This experienced artist is one reason why Hungarian porcelain is so well known for its fineness and variety of design. In spite of his years, his hand is steady and sure, his motif original, and his colors delicate. His trainees will learn a deep pride of craftsmanship as well as a fine art from him, and some day they may be skilled masters teaching others.

SUSPENSION BRIDGE OVER THE DANUBE JOINING THE TOWNS OF BUDA AND PEST

The city of Budapest was formed in 1873 by the union of Buda and Pest. The older town, Buda, climbs a hill on the top of which stand the ruins of a citadel where once the flag of the Crescent waved. Pest, the more important part of the city, spreads over the plain on the far bank of the Danube. The dome is that of St. Stephen, named for the first Christian king of Hungary. Along the river bank is a promenade, the Corso. Budapest has a large trade, especially in grain, wool and hides, though all the products of Hungary go forth on her busy waterway.

UPON CASTLE HILL IN BUDAPEST RISE THE WALLS AND TOWERS OF THE FISHERMEN'S BASTION © E. N. A.

Overlooking the Danube, on a bluff in Buda, is the handsome Fishermen's Bastion and behind it the impressive, historic St. Matthias, or Coronation, Church. Begun in the thirteenth century by King Bela IV and once used as a stable by invading Turks, St. Matthias has long been an important national shrine. The Bastion is a rebuilt section of the old city wall of Buda. Though house-to-house fighting and heavy artillery and aerial bombardment at the close of World War II destroyed much of Budapest, these structures escaped without suffering serious damage.

KANKOVSZKY

ALONG THE DANUBE, where even in the driest summer the wells fed by the river cannot fail, the well-wheel is a favorite meeting place for lovers; and a girl who has an affianced sweetheart places two huge pieces of sugarloaf in her window. The costume shown above is that of the countryside near Kalocsa. Hungarian women all do elaborate embroidery.

WEDDING GARMENTS are worn by the Hungarian peasantry in exact imitation of those of mediaeval times. The bride's flowery head-dress, her embroidered panels and handkerchief the size of a dinner napkin may have taken years to make. The bridegroom's surplice-like robe is heavy with handwork and the flowers in his hat are to be regarded with entire seriousness.

© Cutler

PEASANT LADS PROUDLY WEARING THEIR SUNDAY CLOTHES

The wide sleeves and rich embroideries of the Sunday attire of these Mezökövesd men are reminiscent of both the vestments of the Catholic Church and court costumes of the East.

HUNGARY: FACTS AND FIGURES

THE COUNTRY

European state bounded by Austria on the west, Poland and Czechoslovakia on the north, Rumania on the east and Yugoslavia on the south. The present territory, as settled by the armistice of 1945, covers 35,902 sq. miles; population (est. 1948), 9,201,158.

GOVERNMENT

Hungary entered World War II as an ally of nazi Germany and finally was occupied by German troops. In 1944, Russian troops entered Hungary and succeeded in driving out the Nazis. A provisional government was set up, which was ratified by the National Assembly, and Hungary declared war on Germany in 1945, after signing an armistice with the Allies. Free national elections were held in 1945 and the anti-Communist Small Landholders Party was victorious. However, in 1947, pro-Communists gained control of the country.

COMMERCE AND INDUSTRIES

Agriculture is the chief industry and it occupies about 56% of the people. Wheat, corn, rye, barley, oats, potatoes, sugar-beets and grapes are the principal crops. Livestock raising is important and also fishing. The chief mineral products are coal and lignite, and the bauxite mines are among the largest in the world. Other industries are lumbering, milling, distilling and the manufacture of sugar, hemp, flax and textiles. There are also iron and steel works. The chief exports are wheat, livestock, flour, rye, poultry, eggs, sugar and corn, and the imports include cotton and woolen fabrics, machinery, paper, metals and mineral oil. Since 1946, many industries have been nationalized.

COMMUNICATIONS

Railway, 5,416 miles, of which 4,409 are state owned; telegraphs, 4,570 miles; telephones, 13,289 miles.

RELIGION AND EDUCATION

Most of the Magyars are Roman Catholic. Elementary education compulsory between ages of 6 to 12 years. In addition to extended facilities for secondary education, there are special schools and six state-maintained universities.

CHIEF TOWNS

Budapest, capital (estimate 1948), 1,058,288; Szeged, 136,752; Debreczen, 125,933; Miskolc, 109,433 (1941); Cluj, 100,272; Kecsketemet, 83,732; Oradea, 80,872 (1939).

SWITZERLAND AND THE SWISS

Beautiful Countryside of the Alpine Republic

Switzerland, birthplace of the Red Cross, is the Mecca of the mountaineer and the paradise of the winter sportsman, and the Swiss have made it their chief industry to care for tourists. They are also famed for their watch-making, wood-carving, lace-making and embroidery and for their fine cheeses. The people show varying proportions of German, French and Italian descent, and the newspapers and government reports are printed in four languages.

SWITZERLAND is a tiny country composed of two great mountain ranges with a narrow tableland between. Fir-clad slopes hem in lush valley pastures and blue mirrors of Alpine lakes between glittering snow peaks that reach skyward for two miles and more. This lovely land, with but four million people save as it attracts visitors from America and Europe, becomes one gigantic white setting for the winter sports. The lakes become natural ice-rinks; the meadows, the best of "bob runs," and the steep slopes, the ideal courses for the ski-jumper. It is the Alps that make Switzerland unique.

On the south lies the Swiss portion of the higher Alps, walling off France and Italy from Lake Geneva to Lake Constance; and on the north, the Jura Mountains, united with the main range of the Alps in the west. Between these two high ranges flow two mighty rivers, the Rhone, flowing westward, on the side nearest France, and the Rhine, flowing eastward, toward the Austrian boundary, with the River Aar and that tributary of the Rhine, the Thur, in undulating valleys that dent the plateau between. The rivers are mountain torrents that have to be embanked as a measure of flood prevention; the Rhone has falls of considerable height, and the Rhine, shorter falls of greater volume. In marked contrast to their sonorous turbulence, more than a thousand glaciers creep imperceptibly down the grooves of the ranges, feeding three large lakes and innumerable Alpine tarns. Of these glaciers, there are three in the north which are over ten miles in length—the Great Aletsch, a thousand feet deep, the Fiescher and the Unteraar. Lake Geneva in the

southwest is cut by the borderline between Switzerland and France, and Lake Constance, in the extreme northeast is only in part Swiss, but Lake Neuchatel lies wholly within the little mountain republic. Of the snow caps which rise violet-shadowed above all, Mt. Blanc is 15,781 feet high; the Matterhorn, 14,703; and the Aletschhorn, 13,713; while hundreds of less famous peaks are really high mountains. The Alps reach their greatest altitude on the Bernese Oberland. The Great St. Bernard Pass—over which both the armies of Caesar and those of Napoleon passed—is 8,111 feet in altitude and covers a distance of 53 miles.

The mountaineer passes through many climates, beginning with that favorable to vineyards and olive groves; and as he reaches higher slopes or those more exposed to winter storms, through oak and beech woods, pines and firs and the zone of dwarfed Alpine plants, and on—above the clouds to the eternal snows.

An hour before sunrise the challenge of the guide's horn echoes from peak to peak. As one climbs, pale clouds go smoking up the canyons, and the towns beneath become more and more toy-like. At last one looks out over a sea of peaks capped, billow upon billow, with dazzling ice. One of the most memorable sights in all the Alps is the Jungfrau, rising white and solitary, encircled with clouds.

The tableland between the ranges, deep with the silt of centuries, is incredibly rich soil that can be cultivated intensively. Fully half of Switzerland is under grass, however; for every opening in the forest is cleared of stones and made into pastureland. Half of the area is either forested or too rocky to yield anything but scenery.

253

MC LEISH

A WORLD OF SNOW lies above the green valleys and pine woods of Switzerland, a world where everything that the eye can see is dazzling white. Four adventurous amateur climbers, led and followed by trained guides, are approaching the summit of the Allalinhorn, 13,000 feet above the sea, across a treacherous snow-covered glacier, where a slip would be fatal.

MC LEISH

THE MATTERHORN, rising solitary and majestic 14,703 feet above the sea, bears on its sheer slopes the blossoms of the edelweiss and the alpenrose, while the meadows at its feet are starred with buttercups. Those who climb must carry pack-baskets or pack-harnesses, that their arms may be free, and a load of more than twenty pounds soon becomes irksome.

SKIERS RACING OVER WAVES OF SNOW IN THE BERNESE OBERLAND, AT MURREN, SWITZERLAND

With lungs tingling to the crystal air, eyes narrowed to the white glare and the knowledge that a fall in the soft snow will not hurt, though one moves with speed, one climbs with the clouds left far behind and the ice-clad peaks rising on every side like the rim of a frosted bowl. Every year the winter sports attract so many tourists to the mountain republic that the hotel and guide business amounts to one of Switzerland's leading industries. The Bernese Oberland (above) is the climax of a range to the north of the main chain of the Alps.

256

TERRACE ON TERRACE OF THRIVING VINEYARDS

As one sails on Lake Geneva, the vineyards that climb the steep hillsides of the Lavaux region are an impressive sight. This district is on the northern shore, in the Vaud canton, and produces fine white wine. Lake Geneva is formed by a natural damming of the Rhone River; and the lake's clear, blue waters mirror a mountain region of surpassing beauty.

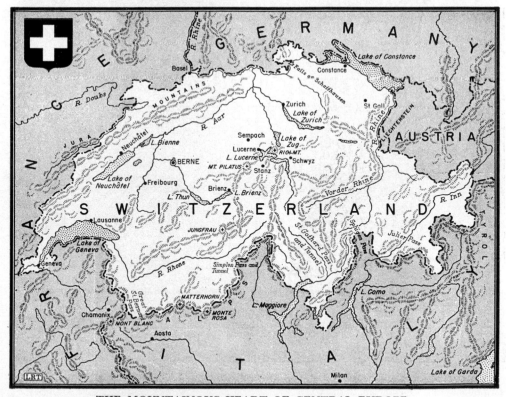

THE MOUNTAINOUS HEART OF CENTRAL EUROPE

THESE SWISS GIRLS are wearing the costume typical of Hallau, a diminutive village in Schaffhausen. This small canton, lying a little to the west of Lake Constance, is the most northerly of the Swiss cantons. Indeed, it seems to dip into Baden, Germany. It also possesses the distinction of being the only canton entirely north of the Rhine River.

THESE LITTLE PEOPLE dwell at Unterschächen in Uri, William Tell's native canton, nearly a tenth of which is covered with glaciers. It is autumn and the boys apparently have to wear hoods to keep their close-clipped polls warm, though the girl is barefoot. The wooden carrier on the back of the older boy is a Swiss back-pack, or pack-basket.

A STUDY IN BRIEFING

A monk at the Great St. Bernard Hospice receives rapt attention from one of his "pupils." Here, atop a mountain pass in Switzerland 8,111 feet high, the monks train their famous dogs to rescue travelers who lose their way in the snow. In recent years, however, modern methods of transportation have left few opportunities for these animals to practice their skill.

TROUSERED WOMEN OF CHAMPÉRY, NEAR THE FRENCH FRONTIER

Swiss peasant women are rarely idle, for they do most of the work involved in cultivating
the steep little fields that dot the lower mountain slopes. Those of the Val d'Illiez, at the
head of which is the little town of Champéry, have a sensible workaday costume that includes
trousers of local cloth and, almost invariably, a scarlet headkerchief.

BY A TINY CHALET which is the stable of their long-horned goats, a peasant of the Bernese Oberland and his wife gaze intently, perhaps at a chamois, the wild antelope of the Alps, leaping from rock to rock on the height above them. The hunter who kills a chamois has a dangerous time tracking his prey among the crags, and a laborious one bringing it back.

THE MOUNTAIN PASTURES are usually communally owned. At twilight the chorus of cow-bells sounds a musical tink-a-tonk that is heard in the villages far below. The cattle are driven higher as the summer comes on, while their owners manure the cropped meadows and grass patches ready for another season. Every farm makes many cheeses for export.

263

Allied for Mutual Defense

What effect have these mountains had upon the history of the Swiss and how do people wrest a living from this Alpine land? The history of Switzerland is, in effect, that of the drawing together of groups from Germany, Italy and Burgundy for mutual defense against the Hapsburgs. In 1291 three little German forest districts formed a league for self-defense. The league thus formed, in which at first the Teutonic interest was strongest, gradually won its independence during the one hundred and fifty years preceding 1648. Though the French Revolution had its influence on the Swiss mind, it was not until 1803 that the French-speaking subjects were accorded political equality—nor were Italian-speaking people till 1815. In that year the perpetual neutrality of Switzerland was guaranteed by Austria, Great Britain, Russia and other countries.

Originally only an alliance of several small states, gradually the idea of Swiss nationality grew, and in 1848 a proper federal state was formed. The Swiss were ever an independent people, and to-day few are more democratic. Thrifty, inclined to be blond and stocky (with the exception of those nearest Italy, who show evidences of the southern blend), they are finely educated and make the most of their limited resources.

Typical Swiss Châlet

The peasant as a rule has a rough but comfortable châlet built of pine which weathers to a rich light brown. When it is in an exposed position, heavy stones are placed on the roof to prevent its being torn off by the fierce winter gales or by the melting snows of spring. A gallery runs around the house. This is sheltered by the broad eaves, which jut out sometimes ten feet beyond the walls. The stone basement is utilized as a storeroom for the produce of vineyard or dairy. The eaves and galleries are often elaborately decorated with carvings. The living-rooms are large and airy. The furniture is homemade. Large benches and dressers of walnut made by the owner or by the local carpenter are the chief pieces. The dressers are sometimes decorated with painted plates. The house is warmed by a large green tiled stove which stands in a corner of the living-room and is kept burning throughout the winter.

In districts where sheep are reared, the housewife, with the help of her daughters, weaves the wool into cloth; in some places the women make beautiful lace. In winter the menfolk occupy themselves with wood-carving, at which they are most skillful, making anything from furniture down to miniature châlets. These things, like the lace, are sold to tourists.

In addition to the hotel-keepers who offer tourist accommodations of the finest, a large number of the Swiss add to their incomes by acting as guides. Nor can these Swiss guides be excelled the world over; for every school child learns to climb the peaks. Groups go with their teachers for days at a time armed with ice axes, ropes and rucksacks, and in many places the military authorities lend them blankets.

Swiss Alpine Club Huts

The Swiss Alpine Club has erected stone huts where climbers may take refuge when violent thunderstorms and sudden blizzards overtake them among the peaks. It is significant that these huts contain not alone fuel, but first-aid equipment and clogs for the foot-sore.

Those who take their vacations less strenuously may, however, reach high altitudes on the trains, which often tunnel through rock and under glaciers, stopping at intervals to allow passengers to walk to some point from which they may enjoy the view. In Switzerland everything possible is done for the accommodation and pleasure of the visitor, and thousands from every part of the world come every year.

The presence of the mountains has a vast influence on the lives of those who live among them. In winter the postman goes his rounds on a toboggan and the housewife goes to the store with one, dragging it back loaded with her supplies. Farmers wait for the snow that they may transport their firewood by guiding it over

©E.N.A.

CROSS-BOW REDUCED IN SPREAD AND ATTACHED TO MUSKET STOCK

As legend has it, in a ballad written before 1474, William Tell was "the first Confederate," and his feat of shooting the apple which the tyrannical Austrian bailiff had ordered placed on the head of his little son is treated as the reason why the tyrants were driven out of the land, wherefore the archer became to many the most famous Switzer.

THE PORT OF BRUNNEN ON LAKE LUCERNE, SWITZERLAND

Summer tourists frequent this place, on Lake Lucerne, in the canton of Schwyz. Lake Lucerne, in the heart of the Alps, is believed by many to be the most magnificent of all the Swiss lakes. It stretches for nearly twenty-four miles through breath-taking mountain scenery. In spite of its high altitude the lake never freezes over in winter.

A CORDIAL GUIDE FOR THE MOUNTAIN HIKER IN SWITZERLAND

Artistic road signs such as this one are made in the city of Brienz, the famous wood-carving capital of the Bernese Oberland. Wood carving is one of the many handicrafts for which Switzerland has long been noted. The city is on the northeast shore of the Lake of Brienz, at the foot of the Bernese Alps, and the spot is very popular with tourists.

TOYS THAT WILL GLADDEN THE HEARTS OF CHILDREN

This young employee in a Swiss toy factory looks, at this smiling moment, hardly more than a child, as she adds final hand touches to a tray of toy donkeys. Toys come in all sizes and shapes; they imitate all sorts of things; but animals seem to be popular with children everywhere. The toy industry in southern Germany and Switzerland has long been important.

the slippery white crust, and in places they lower it on wires stretched from the high cliffs to the valleys below and operated by windlasses. Everyone skates, but the first skis were brought from Norway in 1883 by the monks for use in life-saving work.

The government has not only subsidized the farmer but aided him by such agricultural engineering works as cableways for the transportation of milk from inaccessible mountainsides.

Danger of Sudden Avalanches

The one ever present danger of the mountains is that of the avalanches, huge masses of snow and bowlders that come sliding down upon the valleys, sometimes crushing entire villages. A rockfall crushed the village of Elm in 1881. That was due to quarrying for slate on Mt. Tschingelberg. Mt. Arbino has been left unstable by the retreat of glaciers and for forty years has been slowly collapsing. Since the days of Æsop's Fables the idea has prevailed that mountains do not move, yet the Swiss topographical authorities had discovered by annual surveys both the speed and the direction of the movement of Arbino, and so were able to give warning in 1928 to the village of Arbedo and the Ticino Valley through which runs the important St. Gotthard railroad to Italy. Of course the movement has been too slow to be observed by the layman save for the almost constant sound like rolling thunder and the haze of dust over the mountain from the falling of stones and bowlders.

Conservation of Forests

The forests are well policed in accordance with a conservation policy which aims at a perpetual timber supply. At the same time, the commune permits everyone a sufficient quantity of wood ripe for cutting to be used in building and for winter fuel. Incidentally, if there were no other reason for preserving the forests, it would be necessary as a means of holding the soil of the mountainsides and so preventing landslides and destructive floods. The government also controls the waters, with their potential electric power

—so important in the case of the federally owned railways, which are almost entirely electrified. For irrigation, miniature aqueducts carry glacial waters along the precipices to the vineyards below.

Switzerland employs the initiative and referendum, enforces insurance against illness and old age, as well as industrial, accident and military insurance, and provides work for the unemployed.

Switzerland's Army

Switzerland depends for her defense upon a national militia. Service in this force is compulsory. Only the physically disabled and a few people belonging to special classes of the population are exempted; those who are exempted pay special taxes. The training period for recruits does not extend throughout the year; it ranges from 88 to 102 days, depending upon the branch of the service.

Switzerland's army is small but very efficient. She has a wonderful mountain brigade of infantry and engineers trained to ski over the deep snows, and she maintains an aviation service which is organized in ten squadrons with over two-hundred airplanes. Incidentally, the state aerial service has been gradually developed as it is a favorite mode of travel with many of the tourists.

As Switzerland is almost the least self-sustaining nation of Europe, her people make the most of their skill in manufacturing. In the canton of Appenzell people have been making lace for centuries. On Lake Brienz is a village of wood-carvers and toy-makers; in Zurich, a community specializing in the weaving of silk textiles. The metal workers in the world-famous watch factories can make timepieces the size of a dime, with 170 parts to each one. Where four hundred years ago Swiss watches were made in the homes of the workers, one part by each family, now factory methods are employed. Heimberg manufactures majolica ware and Valais has aluminum works.

Berne, the capital city, named for the bears that are the town emblem, lies in central Switzerland in a crook of the River Aar, where it faces half a dozen peaks

YOUNG GOATHERD GIVING A TIT-BIT TO HIS FAVORITE CHARGE

Switzerland has well over three hundred thousand goats, which thrive on the scant forage of the clearings where the grasslands meet the pine trees and on slopes too steep for cattle. The tinkle of their bells sounds from the mountainsides with musical good cheer and every now and again the tourist comes upon a little herd of agile creatures.

NATIVES OF OLD ZERMATT ARE ACCUSTOMED TO HILLS

Zermatt, in south Switzerland, is a popular holiday resort and a favorite starting-point for mountaineers. This sturdy lad, who is giving his sisters a ride, is as likely as not to follow the perilous profession of mountain climbing when he grows up, for several of his fellow villagers have been among the most famous of Alpine guides.

MAKING THE MOUNTAINS RING WITH THE ECHO OF HIS NOTES

The wooden alpenhorn, by means of which the Swiss peasants were wont to communicate with each other from a distance or call in the cattle at sunset, is now rarely used except when a tourist is willing to pay a few centimes to hear its mellow notes. The herdsman lives here in the mountains all summer, his roof anchored from the wind with stones.

over ten thousand feet in height. In the medieval part of town the narrow streets are overhung by tiled roofs, arcaded stores and cross tunnels; while the sight of draft dogs pulling the milk carts, men in aprons and school children in black over-dresses adds to the quaintness. *"Leb' Wohl"* (good health to you) is the greeting heard on every side.

The name Lucerne means lantern. There was a great lantern in the watchtower of its old fourteenth-century bridge. The high walls and nine watch-towers catch the eye as one comes in by steamer across the lake. The Lion of Lucerne is a splendid piece of sculpture. Cut in the solid rock in 1821, it is dedicated to the memory of the Swiss guards who died defending the Tuileries in Paris at the commencement of the French Revolution. The cathedral is noted for its wonderful organ.

One of the best centres for seeing the beauties of Switzerland is Interlaken, at the head of the valley of Grindelwald overlooked by the Jungfrau. The road near Interlaken is one of the most picturesque in Europe. In some places one drives along the edge of a rushing mountain torrent, in others through pine forests;

and sometimes the road winds along with a solid wall of rock on one side and a precipice on the other.

When Mark Twain visited Interlaken more than a generation ago he predicted that the day would come when every mountain in Switzerland would have a railway up its back like a pair of suspenders. That prophecy is fast coming to pass. Moreover, these and the major portion of all the Swiss railways have been electrified from power provided by the mountain waterfalls. That makes it possible for a tourist to climb mountains by rail. The greater part of the Jungfrau railway tunnels through the rock directly beneath the glaciers, as it worms its way upward through the very substance of the great peak and its neighbor the Mönch.

Grindelwald, a village at the foot of the Wetterhorn is a centre for skiing. Lausanne has a special school for training chefs and hotel-keepers. Zermatt is famous for its guides. From this town the Matterhorn can be seen, its peak outlined against the vivid sky in solitary grandeur. Many lives have been lost on this mountain, but every year fresh enthusiasts set out to conquer its precipitous sides.

MEN OF A DELIGHTFUL PASTORAL DISTRICT THAT IS QUITE UNKNOWN TO THE AVERAGE TOURIST

These men from Appenzell are cowherds and dairy farmers who keep large herds of milch cows, most of which resemble Jerseys. Those at the left are carrying the enormous cow-bells suspended from broad buckled collars. The women of this district are noted for their fine embroidery. Old customs are still observed and the distinctive old-time costumes still worn in this canton of northeast Switzerland, which is only ninety-three square miles in area. The men wear waistcoats bright with numerous buttons and have braces joined across chest and back.

ZURICH CLIMBS THE HILL ABOVE THE LAKE

Zurich, Switzerland's largest city, is pleasantly situated at the northeastern end of Lake Zurich. It was a town in ancient Roman times, and there are buildings still standing that go back hundreds of years. Yet the main part of Zurich is modern and progressive. There is a university, several colleges and numerous schools for special instruction.

PHOTOS, SWISS NATIONAL TOURIST OFFICE

GALA PARADE AT ZURICH'S SPRING FESTIVAL

Beduin horsemen on handsome mounts lead the grand parade of the Sechselauten festival in Zurich. This traditional spring fete has come down from feudal times. It celebrated the pealing of bells at six o'clock in the evening (Sechselauten means six o'clock bells). The bells were silent in the dark winter evenings, so the first ringing in spring was a joyous occasion.

CASTLE OF CHILLON AT MONTREUX ON LAKE GENEVA, SWITZERLAND

The castle, built on a rock close to shore, is the one about which Lord Byron wrote in his *Prisoner of Chillon*. It is near the east end of Lake Geneva where the Swiss Alps rise in sheer beauty all around, and where the mild, pleasant climate and clear air attract travelers and vacationers from far and wide to the hotels of Montreux.

Geneva, famous city where the International Red Cross Society was founded, is located on Lake Geneva where the Rhone River flows from its blue waters. Though the lake is but ten miles at its widest, and forty-five miles long, it lies quite 1,230 feet above the sea. Its assemblage of craft, lateen sails of red or white floating across its surface, appear at a distance like so many gigantic butterflies.

In the old part of Geneva, where close-packed medieval buildings once stood within walled fortifications, stands the tenth-century Protestant Cathedral of St. Peter, and near it, the Arsenal, which contains an historical museum. On two islands may be seen the statue of Rousseau and the Castle of Chillon (where Bonnivard was held prisoner by the Duke of Savoy).

Some idea of the theological controversies that once tore Geneva may be acquired from the fact that it has one monument to Calvin and one to Servetus. For the two men had a controversy in 1553 after which Servetus would have fled to Italy but that he was apprehended at Calvin's instance and burned at the stake for heresy. Calvin published his great work at Basel in 1536 and, banished from Paris, took refuge at Geneva. He founded the Academy of Geneva in 1559.

Geneva has at various times been the sanctuary for religious and political refugees (not all of them welcome), the gathering place of scholars and the focus of humanitarian movements. To this cosmopolitan city came John Knox, Dostoevski and Andrew Melville. The International Red Cross, initiated here after the horrors of the Battle of Solferino by Henry Dunant, appropriately chose for its flag that of Switzerland with the colors reversed. During World War I Switzerland might almost have been

IN THE HEART OF BERNE, SWITZERLAND'S SEAT OF GOVERNMENT

Berne (the name means bears) stands on a high bluff overlooking the Aar. Berne retains its medieval character, with its narrow streets flanked by arcades and its old buildings. The clock tower, once the west gate of the city, marks each hour with a procession of bears and the crowing of a cock. At the left of the picture is a famous old bear statue.

called one great internment camp. In addition, it acted as intermediary for the exchange of seriously wounded prisoners. The country steadfastly maintained its neutrality during World War II, and successfully escaped invasion of its boundaries.

The newcomer, having established himself at one of the excellent hotels that line the banks of Lake Geneva and the Rhone, will approach the Palais des Nations by the quay, a tree-lined promenade behind which the four-story building, designed along unpretentious classical lines, graces the lawns of a beautiful park. When the League disbanded in 1946, its assets were transferred to the United Nations. The Palais des Nations became the headquarters of the European Office of the UN. The International Labor Organization continued to hold meetings in the building. Since the war, Geneva has been the site of several momentous world-trade meetings that have advanced the cause of economic co-operation among many nations.

The tourist ought to see an Aelplifest some Sunday, in spring. This pageant, representative of the moving of the cattle to the Alpine pastures, is one in which people don their local folk costumes and march through the streets with their cattle, sheep and goats and carts laden with their shining copper cheese caldrons, while sometimes floats that look like châlets carry women engaged in cheese-making or men operating the winepress.

Every village has its choral society, and singing competitions are held at Lucerne and elsewhere to which singers come from all over Switzerland.

SWITZERLAND: FACTS AND FIGURES

THE COUNTRY

Land-locked state of Europe, bounded north and east by Germany, southwest and west by France, and on the southeast by Italy. To the south is the central section of the Pennine Alps, comprising some of the greatest heights in Europe. Principal rivers are the Aar, Rhone and Rhine. The lakes include those of Geneva, Constance and Maggiore (these three are not wholly Swiss), Neuchatel, Lucerne, Zurich, Lugano, Thun, Bienne, Zug, Brienz Morat, the Walensee and Sempach. Total area 15,944 square miles, with a population of 4,714,992 according to the census of December 1950.

GOVERNMENT

Legislative power is vested in a parliament, consisting of two chambers—a Council of State with 44 members (2 for each of the 22 cantons) and a National Council of 194 members elected by proportional representation (one deputy for every 22,000 inhabitants). Executive authority is exercised by a Federal Council consisting of 7 members, elected for 4 years by the Federal Assembly. A president and a vice-president, who are the chief magistrates of the Swiss Confederation, are elected by the Federal Assembly for a term of one year. For purposes of local government Switzerland is divided into cantons and demi-cantons.

COMMERCE AND INDUSTRIES

About 22.5% of the soil is unproductive, and of the production area 32% is forest. Arable land covers the greatest acreage, and dairying is the chief agricultural industry. Switzerland is noted for her cheese and chocolate. Wheat, potatoes, sugar-beets, vegetables and tobacco are grown. Apples, pears and grapes for wine are the principal fruits. There is salt-mining and a slight output of iron ore and manganese. Electric-power production is over 10 billion kilowatt-hours per year. Leading manufactures are processed foods, clocks and watches, machinery, metalware, chemicals and dyes, textiles, knitted goods and embroidery. The leading exports are machinery, clocks and watches, textiles and clothing, instruments and parts, dyes, drugs and chemicals. The leading imports are cereals and other foodstuffs, iron and iron manufactures, motor vehicles, machinery and chemicals. Tourist trade is important.

COMMUNICATIONS

Railways, 3,245 miles; of 1,844 miles of state railways, 1,708 miles are electric. Main auto roads, 10,200 miles. Merchant marine, based at Basel, has 16 vessels. Domestic and foreign air service. Telegraph wires, 2,025,929 miles; 845,471 telephones.

RELIGION AND EDUCATION

Protestants are in majority in 12 cantons and Catholics in 10. There is absolute freedom of worship. Elementary education is free and compulsory. There are 7 universities, at Basel, Zurich, Berne, Geneva, Lausanne, Fribourg and Neuchatel, a technological institute and a school of economics and public administration.

CHIEF CITIES

Population (1950 census): Berne (capital), 146,499; Zurich, 390,020; Basel, 183,543; Geneva, 145,473; Lausanne, 106,807; Winterthur, 66,925; Lucerne, 60,526; St. Gall, 60,011.

THE TOY STATES OF EUROPE

Tiny Countries and Their Self-reliant People

There are pin-points of color on the map of Europe. You have to look closely to see them. Though almost invisible, the tiny states these dots represent hold up their heads among the free nations of the world. Andorra balances between France and Spain in the Pyrenees. Vatican City, the home of the Pope, is a free state of one hundred acres within Rome. Monaco, a principality, is a famous pleasure resort on the lovely blue coast of the Mediterranean. Luxembourg, a grand duchy, is a busy little triangle enclosed by Belgium, France and Germany. Another principality, Liechtenstein, is in a mountain valley between Switzerland and Austria. And San Marino perches proudly in the Italian Apennines. These states may be Lilliputian in size, but they cherish their independence as much, if not more, than many larger ones.

IN thinking of Europe our thoughts naturally turn to the Great Powers, such as France, Germany and Russia, whose territories practically cover the continent. We forget that among these mighty nations there are the baby states of Europe still existing as semi-independent lands, with curious customs of their own, and in some of which the people live much as they did in medieval days.

Perhaps the most interesting of these is Monaco, which owing to its situation on the Mediterranean, has become the most popular pleasure resort on the French Riviera. Monte Carlo, although not the capital of this tiny state, is the town that attracts most attention, and it is certainly one of the most beautifully situated and fascinating places on the shores of the Mediterranean.

One element that makes Monte Carlo the paradise of the pleasure-seeker is the sunny climate of the Riviera and its location between a background of high Alps, rising in snow-white points above the purple mountain wall. The perfume of orange and lemon blossoms greets one in January, and the whitewashed villas that cling to the green velvet hillsides add rose-colored roofs to the picture. Man has also done his utmost to bait the gold of cosmopolitan tourists, as evidenced by the luxurious wines of the restaurants that line the boulevards, the gaiety of night clubs, theatres and concert halls, to say nothing of the lure of the famed Casino, established in 1863 by a notorious gambler.

Quaint superstitions actuate many of the gamblers, of which there are fully as many women as men. It is, for instance, thought to bring good luck if one stumbles while going upstairs, or if one meets a hunchback and can manage to lay a finger on his hump. Some gamblers also believe that an evil spirit may, when it so elects, preside over the roulette board and cause the ivory ball to behave in a manner contrary to the laws of chance.

Monaco has an area of just about eight square miles, and an average width of six hundred and fifty yards, so that we might in three strokes send a golf ball right across the state. Its population is approximately twenty-three thousand. Within its limits it manages to compress more excitement and tragedy than probably any other place in the world. The one great source of revenue is the Casino at Monte Carlo, where fortunes are lost and won.

Monaco has its own coinage and postage stamps, its inhabitants are practically free from every form of taxation, and the ruling prince and his council direct the fortunes of the state. It has had a constitution since 1911, and there is a semi-military police force. Monaco suffered during World War II because its prosperity depends on the pleasure-seeking crowds of peacetime.

The late Prince Albert of Monaco, who died in 1922, was not the kind of man we might expect to find as the ruler of such an extraordinary land. He was intensely interested in all that pertains to the sea and the fishes and vegetation in it, and in his yacht he frequently made expeditions in the interests of scientific research and

GRANDE CORNICHE DRIVE FROM NICE TO MENTON IN FRANCE

The motor highway along the French Riviera, part of which was built by Napoleon as a military course, passes through the tiny principality of Monaco. Above it rise the steep Maritime Alps. The Monacan farmers in the foreground are cultivating perfume flowers. In Monaco is the famous resort Monte Carlo, which people visit from all over the world.

oceanography. His museum is the finest of its kind in the world. La Condamine, one of Monaco's three towns, is a bathing resort, set in orange groves on the shore of the bay.

If we travel to Austria through Switzerland we come across another of the independent principalities of Europe—Liechtenstein—set in the midst of high peaks between the Austrian mountains of Vorarlberg and the Rhine. It is larger than Monaco, being about sixty-five square miles in area. It has one claim to distinction in that its inhabitants are exempt from military service, and free to pursue the pastoral life their forefathers led for centuries before them.

Once a Roman camp on the site of Triesen—before that town was wiped out by a landslide—Liechtenstein formed part of the great German Confederation of States; but in the Council of the Diet it maintained its practical independence by holding a separate vote; and when the Confederation was dissolved, Liechtenstein became independent (though economically allied to Switzerland).

In Prince Johann II, whose death in 1929 occurred soon after the fête in honor of his seventy years' reign, Liechtenstein had a benevolent monarch. He not only asked no taxes, but spent of his own fortune for improvements within the boundaries of his toy state, and even kept his palace and garden open to the public. Prince Johann had come of one of the most ancient families in Europe. He had a palace in Vienna with an unexcelled art collection and a telephone line to the capital of his little principality on the Rhine. He also paid out of his own pocket the major portion of the cost of the electric lighting of Vaduz and the hamlets, and the founding of electric sawmills, flax and cotton weaving industries. In 1921 Liechtenstein accepted of him a free constitution with a parliament of fifteen members. Swiss money is used, and the posts, telegraph and customs are managed by Switzerland.

LOOKING ACROSS THE YACHT BASIN AT MONTE CARLO

Monte Carlo is in the principality of Monaco on the southern coast of France, not far from the Italian border. The famous resort has luxurious hotels for wealthy visitors.

TRANS WORLD AIRLINES

CLERGY AND MILITIA UNITE TO HONOR SACRED RELICS

St. Dévote is the patron saint of Monaco. Her dead body, according to various legends, was washed ashore or brought there from Corsica. Annually, on January 27, her relics are carried in their casket, as seen above, from the fortalice to the vale of Gaumates, her original burial place behind Monte Carlo. On the way, the port receives a blessing from the sacred casket.

CLOSE-HAULED ON THE STARBOARD TACK AT MONTE CARLO REGATTA

With taut mainsail and bellying jib, the yacht leans to the push of the breeze. Monaco includes the regattas at Monte Carlo as not the least of its varied attractions. There is also an oceanographical museum on the headland of Monaco, a Romanesque-Byzantine cathedral and a modernized Renaissance palace, and at La Condamine, orange groves.

BEFORE THE HYDROPATHIC PORTION OF THE CASINO TERRACE

The Casino Terrace, with its hydropathic establishment, for which the space of several stories has been excavated in the rock beneath. Curiously enough, it is the company that calls itself the Sea-Bathing Society of Monaco which operates the roulette and other gambling at the Casino at Monte Carlo. Sometimes those who lose commit suicide.

VADUZ, CAPITAL OF THE TINY PRINCIPALITY OF LIECHTENSTEIN

Overlooking the city from the high promontory is the Castle Liechtenstein, with a back curtain of lofty Alps. Liechtenstein, one of Europe's smallest independent states, has only sixty-five square miles; it is flanked on the west and south by Switzerland and on the east by Austria. Its economy —trade, finance and so on—is closely related to that of Switzerland.

LUXEMBOURG, CAPITAL CITY OF THE GRAND DUCHY

A view of the old prison in the lower part of the city which borders on the Alsette River. The upper part of the city is built on a plateau and was once called the "northern Gibraltar," because it had such a strong military position. The newer parts of Luxembourg, with modern and costly buildings, are laid out along wide, attractive thoroughfares.

A VENDOR'S STAND AT THE NUT FESTIVAL, VIANDEN

The first Sunday in October is nut festival day in Vianden, a village in the Grand Duchy of Luxembourg, near the German border. Children have worked hard gathering the nuts from the hilly countryside; these are carefully washed and sold along with other traditional goodies at the roadside stands. Vianden is an ancient town, dating back to the fourteenth century.

MOUNTED SMUGGLER-FIGHTERS AT THE CUSTOM HOUSE END OF THE ANDORRAN VALLEY   Canon J. T. Parfit

The feudal republic of Andorra, the Hidden Valley, high in the fastnesses of the Pyrenees on the borderline between France and Spain, is a country in extent less than seventeen miles across by eighteen miles in length. For a thousand years it has been given over to agriculture and latterly, it is hinted, to the smuggling of tobacco, for which reason mounted guards patrol the frontier paths. A French syndicate has acquired the right to establish a gambling casino similar to that at Monte Carlo, together with a luxurious hotel, golf grounds, cabarets and so on.

284

McLeish

PORTA FRANCISCANA, THE MAIN GATE OF THE CITY OF SAN MARINO

San Marino, the capital of a state which finds itself a lone speck of independence in the midst of Italian territory, stands on the summit of Mount Titano, and the main gate is so narrow that it barely permits the passage of an ox-cart. The gates were purposely made thus in the olden days when the inhabitants were fearful of Austrian and other invasion,

Vaduz is an old-world village through which goose-girls drive their flocks. The castle, on a hilltop, has walls twenty feet thick and contains a splendid collection of armor. Though bicycles and even automobiles are seen in this mile-high country, oxen draw the carts and plows.

San Marino is reputed to be the oldest state in Europe. Located on spurs of the Apennines about twelve miles from the Adriatic, it lies between several Italian provinces. Its customs and constitution are survivals of the Middle Ages. The miniature country has had a part in many events of Italian history. It placed itself under the protection of the Italians in 1862.

Founded, according to tradition, in the third century by St. Martin, during the persecutions of Diocletian, the history of San Marino includes the founding of the monastery of St. Marino in 885. The independence of the diminutive republic was confirmed by the Pope in 1631, and it has been the only one of the Italian states to retain its independence. The town stands on Mt. Titano, a rock 2,437 feet high, each summit of which is fortified, and the fortifications of the state consist

Parfit

SMUGGLER OF ANDORRA, A REPUBLIC IN THE PYRENEES

Andorra, a valley of the high Pyrenees between France and Spain, has a good road from the Spanish frontier and makes smuggling its chief industry. Nearly every man has smuggled at some time. New hotels are projected to increase the tourist industry. The native shown above, nearing the custom house, became a traveler's porter.

LIBERTY PRESIDES OVER THE SQUARE IN SAN MARINO'S CAPITAL

The majestic statue is in front of the government buildings. San Marino City perches on the western slope of Mount Titano just below the summit, which has three peaks. Each of the peaks is crowned with towers, connected by ramparts, where long ago the San Marinos defended themselves in turn against Hungarians, Saracens and Normans.

of three peaks each crowned with a tower, at the base of which stands Borgo, where oxen are the chief means of transport. The government is democratic.

The Grand Council of sixty is elected by popular vote, and two Regents appointed from their number every six months act as executives.

On the first day of April in San Marino one must be up by sunrise, otherwise there is risk of being hauled out in one's nightdress, placed upon a mule and paraded through the streets to the music of bells and jangling instruments and the jeers of the crowd. San Marino issues its own postage stamps. Tobacco, by international agreement, is not allowed to be grown within the state, but every year a supply is received from Italy, which, in addition, gives a large quantity of white salt.

Jamieson

CAPTAINS REGENT OF SAN MARINO

Two Captains Regent, appointed twice a year from a Grand Council of sixty members, rule the independent republic of San Marino. The oldest state in Europe, it has a treaty of friendship with Italy.

The feudal state of Andorra, the Hidden Valley, lies high in the Pyrenees between the borders of France and Spain. Twelve hundred years ago, when the Moors swept down upon the Visigoths who had for three hundred years ruled Iberia (the present Spain), a group of Catalan peasants fled from the foothills of Urgel, up the Segre and Valira rivers into a remote valley of the mountains that guard the northern frontier of their mother country. There, silent amid the deep undertones of mountain torrents, the dark-eyed refugees took up their lives. There Charlemagne came upon them on his way southward to attack the Moslem hordes. Andorra still treasures a document signed by him enfranchising the state. The present capital was once the scene of a battle in which Charlemagne's son Louis achieved a hard-won victory over the swords of the Mohammedans.

Louis placed Andorra under the protection of the Spanish Bishops of Urgel. Three hundred years later neighboring French counts disputed it with the Spanish Bishop until 1282 when suzerainty was divided between them. Thus it happens that the tiny state finds itself under the joint authority of the French President and the Spanish Bishop of Urgel.

To-day Andorra has but five thousand people scattered among half a dozen villages. They speak Catalan, and few of them have ever crossed the rocky frontier. The self-governing state is neutral, although under the joint protection of France and the Spanish Bishop of Urgel. It is a primitive spot, its laws are unwritten and few of its inhabitants can read.

Government is by an executive known as the First Syndic, nominated, with a Second Syndic for deputy, by a council of twenty-four members who receive ten shilling per annum and meet in a council chamber resembling the loft of the barn in which they stable their mules while deliberating. No one can serve unless he is married. Taxation is light and, as the people are largely agriculturists, they pay a certain proportion of their profits to the landlord.

Andorra is astride the crest that separates the waters flowing toward the Atlantic in the west and the Mediterranean in the east. The passes leading to France are inaccessible for more than six months in the year, as they are then blocked by snow and all transport has to come from

THIS PEASANT GIRL of Vaduz (Vallis Dulcis, Sweet Valley), in Liechtenstein, lives among pastures musical with the bells of cattle on the pine clad slopes of Vorarlberg.

POLICE HEADQUARTERS IN ANDORRA LA VELLA

The little village of Andorra la Vella is the capital of Andorra, the isolated and romantic little state that perches high in the Pyrenees Mountains on the border between Spain and France. Today a good road crosses Andorra, connecting the Spanish and French frontiers. Andorrans speak Catalan Spanish, and use both Spanish and French currency.

the Spanish side from which there is a good road. Vividly colored shrines carved of native stone are found everywhere.

Until recently the cultivation of tobacco was the leading industry. The plantations in the valleys are watered by a primitive system of irrigation consisting of tiny canals hollowed out of tree trunks. The tobacco grown is smuggled across the frontier. Indeed, smuggling is regarded in Andorra as an honorable profession. The smuggler must have not only the acuteness to avoid the officers of the law, but the physical fitness to carry loads up the mountainside. The natives are pastoral. They drink the acid and slightly sour wine of the country from leathern bottles similar to those their nomadic forbears used centuries ago. There is, however, this difference, that where the latter drank in the ordinary way, the Andorran holds the bottle a few inches from his mouth and lets the liquid pour into it.

The Andorrans have many quaint beliefs. Their fields must each have a sprig of cypress placed in the ground at one side and be blessed by the priest, that evil spirits may be warded off. If an Andorran sets out on a journey and he sees a white cat, he will turn back.

Sheep- and cattle-breeding are important occupations of the Andorrans. The women spin and weave the clothing worn by both sexes, and the home industries include boot-making, pottery and other crafts to supply the simple wants of the community. Andorra's isolation is coming to an end, however.

The Duchy of Luxembourg

The Duchy of Luxembourg is on the heavily wooded Ardennes plateau—a rising shelf of land a few hundred miles back from Europe's northwestern coast. Luxembourg is a land of gently rolling pastures marked here and there with castle-topped hills or steep river valleys. The streams of the north wind through slight highlands and rush into the Sauer, which also wends its way eastward to the Moselle, the river of the Luxembourg-German border. The principal river of the south is the Alzette. It flows northeastward

across the southern plains, watering the small farms and providing transportation to the mines and mills of industrial towns.

The minette iron ore of this region is Luxembourg's richest resource. Most of the people of the Duchy work in the iron and steel industry.

Only one man in five now lives off the land. The farmers grow oats, wheat and potatoes and also raise horses, cattle, sheep and hogs. Those along the banks of the Sauer and Moselle tend lovely orchards and vineyards.

The story of Luxembourg begins in the eleventh century when it became a principality in the Holy Roman Empire. Several noblemen of Luxembourg were elected emperor; the son of one of these emperors was the adventurous King John of Bohemia. Made a duchy in 1354, Luxembourg came under the sovereignty of the house of Burgundy in the fifteenth century and later became a possession of the powerful house of Hapsburg.

Freedom Is Won, Bit by Bit

After the French Revolution, Luxembourg was a part of France. In 1815, after Napoleon's defeat, the Duchy passed on to the Netherlands. When Belgium broke with the Dutch King in 1830, she annexed a large part of Luxembourg. The remaining part—what we know today as Luxembourg—became virtually free, though the crown still remained with the royal family of Holland. Upon the death of William III, king of the Netherlands, in 1890, the house of Nassau inherited the Grand Duchy and made a complete break with Holland.

In 1867 the great powers of Europe declared Luxembourg neutral. The following year the people of the Duchy drafted a constitution and wrote this principle of neutrality into the document. Germany defied the declaration in both world wars. Her troops swept through the Alzette and Sauer valleys on their way into France. In World War II, Luxembourg suffered particularly heavy damage.

Luxembourgers themselves abandoned neutrality in 1948 when they amended their constitution and joined the Western

LA ROCCA, the citadel of San Marino, founded in the third century, stands on one of the three peaks of Mt. Titano in the Apennines. Of all the Italian states, San Marino alone has retained its independence. The stronghold is now used as a prison. Like other buildings of the republic, it is made of stone quarried out of the slopes of the mountain.

PARFIT

SAN JULIAN, an important town in Andorra, though it is really but a village, manufactures large quantities of tobacco. It is also the headquarters of a band of smugglers who take the tobacco into Spain. Roman Catholic Andorra was one of a chain of miniature states established by Charlemagne along the Pyrenees, and it still prizes a document with his signature upon it. Its parliament house is a barn-like building, its laws are unwritten, and until recently it had no school system. Its transportation is by mule-back and woman is man's hard-working chattel.

European Union and the North Atlantic Pact. By these acts of co-operation they stood firmly with their neighbors, contributing troops and products of iron and steel.

Vatican City

In the city of Rome, there is an area that contains less than 110 acres and yet forms an independent and a very important state: the Vatican City. It has its own government, its flag—yellow and white— its diplomatic service and all the requisites of a sovereign country. To 400,000,-000 Roman Catholics of the world, it is the residence of their spiritual leader, the pope. To tourists, the Vatican is a treasure house of the arts. The Palace of the Vatican and the Basilica of Saint Peter date from the Italian Renaissance and they are splendid examples of the architecture of that period. They contain paintings, frescoes and sculpture by the most gifted artists of the time: Michaelangelo, Raphael, Titian, Botticelli. There are also magnificent collections of Greek and Roman statuary and Egyptian antiquities. The Vatican has an astronomical observatory; and its library, particularly rich in manuscripts, is one of the most important in the world.

TOY STATES: FACTS AND FIGURES

ANDORRA

Occupies a valley in the Pyrenees between France and Spain and is under the joint suzerainty of the head of the French state and the Spanish Bishop of Urgel. It is 17 miles in length and 18 miles in width; total area is 191 square miles with a population of 5,231 scattered in 6 villages. The government is in the hands of a council of 24 members elected for 4 years by the male citizens. Tobacco-growing and sheep-raising are the most important occupations. A department under a permanent French delegate controls services established by France, as education, post, telegraph, etc.

LIECHTENSTEIN

A principality on the east bank of the Rhine between Switzerland and Austria. Area, 62 square miles; population, 13,000. The crown passes by inheritance through male line of the house of Liechtenstein. A democratic constitution of 1921 establishes the right of all citizens to elect Diet of 15 members. Capital and largest town, Vaduz (population, 2,020). Roman Catholicism, predominant religion; 14 elementary and 3 advanced schools. Main products are agricultural—corn, wine, fruit and wood. Livestock numbers more than 10,000 head. Small industries produce cotton, pottery and leather goods. Good roads connect the villages. Member of Swiss customs union, uses Swiss currency and telegraphic and postal services; but issues own postage stamps.

LUXEMBOURG

A Grand Duchy ruled by heirs of the house of Nassau, is bounded by Belgium on the north and west, by France on the south, by Germany on the east. The twice revised constitution of 1868 sets up parliamentary government, recognizing social, political and economic rights of the citizens. Principal legislative house, Chamber of Deputies, has 51 members elected by electoral delegates. The sovereign also appoints 15 members to an upper house, the Council of State. Area, 999 square miles; population, 290,992. Primary education compulsory. Farming by about 25% of the people; principal crops: potatoes and grain. Livestock, over 200,000 head. Iron ore, pig iron and steel are the principal products of the very important metals and mining industry. Road mileage, 2,673; 340 miles of railway. Chief towns: Luxembourg (capital), 62,000; Esch-Alzette, 26,851.

MONACO

A principality on the Mediterranean near the Italian border, surrounded by the French Department of Alpes Maritimes. Constitution of 1911 provides for National Council of 10 members elected for 4-year terms by universal suffrage. Council assists prince in legislation. Prince and State Ministry have executive control. Area, 370 acres; population, 19,242. Excellent small harbor. Independent postage system; in French customs union.

SAN MARINO

Is within the area of Italy on the Emilia-Marches border near the Adriatic. The area is 38 square miles and the population, 12,100. The republic is governed by the Grand Council of 60 members elected by popular vote. Two of the members are appointed to serve as Regents for a term of 6 months. The chief exports are wine, cattle and building stone. There are several elementary schools and one high school.

VATICAN CITY

Independent papal state on the right bank of the River Tiber within the city of Rome, the capital of Italy. Executive, legislative and judicial authority rests with pope, the spiritual head of the Roman Catholic Church. Temporal powers are delegated by the pope to church dignitaries and to the College of Cardinals, which acts as a senate and meets at the death of a pope to elect his successor. The Vatican maintains a railroad station, postal and monetary systems, radio station and official papal journals. Area, 108.7 acres; population, 940.

PEOPLE OF SUNNY ITALY

Folk Whose Forebears Were Makers of History

When the Romans were at the height of their power Italy was the head and heart of Europe, and during the golden period of the Italian Renaissance, which began in the fifteenth century, it was the centre of the world's new culture. As Italy was so long divided, much of its history is that of the independent states, such as Genoa, Florence and Venice. Many relics of the country's former greatness still remain. Italy is about twice as large as the New England states and contains five times as many people. The peasants of this romantic land are gay and devout, and find Nature kindly in the matter of yielding them a living, whether on the plain of Lombardy or in the south.
Stories of Rome, Venice and Sicily appear elsewhere in this volume.

THE map of Italy *(Regno d'Italia)* is shaped like a high-heeled boot with piratical wide top. Sicily is a triangular stone that the boot is about to kick. Naples lies in front of the ankle; Rome, halfway to the knee; Florence, high on the calf; Genoa on, and Venice underneath, the knee. The River Po embroiders the top. Save for the extensive river plain, Italy lies along a mountain background which is a spur of the Apennines thrust into the Mediterranean between the Adriatic and the Tyrrhenian seas, with the Gulf of Taranto under the instep and the Strait of Messina barely separating Sicily from the mainland. Volcanic Mount Etna rises from the east coast of the island; Mount Vesuvius behind the Bay of Naples. To the north, the high Alps wall Italy off from Austria, Switzerland and France.

Italian territory has been acquired little by little, Turin as far back as the eleventh century, the province of Rome in 1870, and portions of Austria since World War I. In 1935 Ethiopia was taken by conquest, but early in World War II Italy was forced to withdraw from this territory.

When Greece was the leading power of the world, the southern half of the Italian peninsula contained many Greek colonies. Meanwhile, farther north, a certain Latin tribe was sending out young colonists who settled on one of the hills overlooking the River Tiber. This settlement became Rome. The tiny country was ruled first by kings, we are told, then became a republic, and finally an empire. Its power steadily increased, more and more territory was brought under control, until

finally imperial Rome sat in majesty upon her seven hills and ruled the known world. In the fourth century the Roman Empire was divided into the Eastern and the Western Empires. The Eastern Empire, with its capital at Constantinople, was to last for more than a thousand years. The Western Empire broke up under the assaults of barbarians from the north— Goths, Vandals, Huns and Lombards— who, at one time or another, poured through the passes of the mountain barrier to take and hold the city of Rome and to seize the riches of this favored land.

Though Rome was sacked again and again, her vitality was indestructible: the city of the Cæsars became the centre of a rapidly spreading new religion—Christianity—and the Bishop of Rome, as Pope, became the spiritual ruler of all Christians in the West. As the Church grew wealthy it fostered learning and the arts, and when Constantinople fell in 1453 and its scholars fled from the Turks, it was Italy that welcomed them and that stood foremost in that revival of learning known as the Renaissance.

After the Western Empire began to fall apart, the history of Italy is confused for nearly fifteen hundred years. It was sometimes the playground of barbarian tribes, sometimes under the Eastern Empire (though the Pope ruled in Rome from an early date). Through the favor of Pepin, the father of Charlemagne, his territories were much extended and finally they formed a broad band across Italy. Though Charlemagne and his successors claimed to rule Italy, their power was generally

LAKE COMO, famous for its loveliness, is over thirteen hundred feet deep. Between its blue waters and the forest-clad mountains that rise steeply from its shores lies many a village amid its vineyards and flower gardens; and also many a stately palace, with its flight of steps to the water. A bit of the Villa Balbianello is shown above.

MC LEISH

ACROSS LAKE MAGGIORE, from the woods above Arona, in the province of Novara, we see one of the Borromean Islands, with a castle dating from before 1440. Its grounds were converted into pleasure gardens in the seventeenth century. On the west side of the lake is a bronze and copper statue of St. Carlo Borromeo, Cardinal-Archbishop of Milan, 1538-84.

THE LONG PENINSULA OF ITALY AND ITS ISLANDS

Extending into the Mediterranean Sea in the shape of an enormous boot, the mainland of Italy seems about to kick Sicily. Italy is a natural unit, with the sea on three sides and the Alps looming to the north, forming a zigzag border. The Po, which flows all the way across the Lombardy plain, below the Alps, is the most important river.

298

small and dozens of almost independent states arose.

Many of the cities ruled themselves and the country around them. Some of these city-states lived under dictators, some were rather democratic, but more were ruled by a few aristocratic families. Some of these, as in Venice and Genoa, were rich merchants. These city-states were in frequent wars with their neighbors, but as the people were too busy to fight they often hired soldiers to do their fighting for them. The Othello of Shakespeare was this type of soldier.

The Saracens overran southern Italy and also Sicily. Later the Normans united southern Italy and Sicily. Then Naples, southern Italy and Sicily became the kingdom of Naples, or of the Two Sicilies, as it was often called. As the other nations of Europe grew strong, many of them, such as France, Spain and Austria, conquered and ruled parts of Italy, and many battles were fought on Italian soil.

Considering the almost constant fighting it is a wonder that medieval Italy found time for anything else. Yet the fact remains that her architects have given us some of the finest cathedrals and palaces in the world, her poets rank among the "immortals," and her artists have left a wealth of pictures and statuary.

In the nineteenth century the movement for the unification of Italy under the king of Sardinia began and gathered strength. There was considerable fighting, but one by one the states were annexed and in 1861 Victor Emmanuel was proclaimed king of Italy. Only Venetia and the Papal States remained outside. The former was annexed in 1866, the Papal States in 1870 and the modern Italy was born.

When we take account of the many different peoples who have lived upon the soil of Italy it is easy to believe that the blood of all Europe runs in Italian veins, and it is not surprising that there are many physical types among the Italian people. Olive skin, dark hair and eyes are found in the south, red-gold or auburn hair in Tuscany and Venice, and north of the Apennines it is easy to see that the people have in their veins some northern blood.

The larger part of northern Italy is an alluvial lowland that was once a gulf of the Adriatic. It consists chiefly of the great valley of the eastward-flowing Po, the tributaries of which race precipitously down out of the forested Alps to the north or more leisurely out of the barren Apennines to the south. The broad plain is sheltered by the curving wall of the Alps, the southern slopes of which are almost perpendicular walls richly forested in their lower reaches but rising to a sea of jagged peaks and pinnacles patched with glaciers and pierced by narrow canyons down which foaming rivers tumble. These swift streams provide water and electric power, the mountain pastures are unexcelled for milch cattle, and the making of cheeses—especially Parmesan and Gorgonzola—is an important industry of the region. Sheep forage exists in the hills, and on the lower slopes one finds chestnuts —a favorite food of Italians—wine grapes, mulberries for the silkworms that supply

Kodak Snapshot

A LITTLE DAUGHTER OF ITALY

This child of Naples, beautiful both in feature and expression, is a fitting representative of lovely Italy. Italian women have long been renowned for their beauty.

MC LEISH

THE ISOLA SAN GIULIO lies like the enchanted island in the turquoise waters of Lake Orta or Lago Cusio, a little west of Lago Maggiore in northern Italy. The church we see is said to have been founded in the fourth century by St. Julius, who came to convert the residents of the town of Orta, the roofs of which we overlook.

MC LEISH

WASHERWOMEN OF OMEGNA, a small town at the northern end of Lake Orta, kneel
upon their back doorsteps and wash their clothes in the Nigulia. The waterway, after
draining the lake, joins the River Strona, which flows into Lake Maggiore, on which Locarno
is located. Thus water from the small lake is always being poured into the large one.

IN THE VIA SAN GIUSEPPE, A THOROUGHFARE OF OLD SAN REMO

San Remo, northeast of Nice, is a health resort on the coast of the Riviera. This street in the old quarter of the town is so narrow and the crumbling houses are so tall that little light can enter through the windows, and the rooms are dark and ill-ventilated. Much of the life of the people is lived in the open.

the silk-mills, olives and tangerines. The Lombardy Plain, favorable to the vine and mulberry, is also patched with fields of the wheat of which the native macaroni and the round crusty loaves of Italian bread are made. Here one sees the blue flower of the flax for the linen industry, and in the wet lands corn may be garnered in time for a crop of hemp for ship cordage. Around Pavia and Mantua it is even warm enough for rice. The one thing most feared by plains farmers is the too frequent hailstorms that sweep down out of the Alps at the time of harvest.

After United Italy was born, Italians looked with longing eyes toward Italia

302

FISHERMEN'S QUARTER AT SORRENTO AND A FEW FISHERFOLK

The fishermen of Sorrento, on the Bay of Naples, bring their laden boats to the west end of the town, to the Marina Grande, or large harbor. Most of Sorrento, as we see on another page, is built on the cliff tops high above the sea; but here room has been found for a few humble houses at the harbor's edge.

© E. N. A.

THIS OLD FISHERMAN, in green woolen stocking-cap, dwells in Salerno, when he is not sailing in search of sardines, anchovies or tuna-fish. Salerno is in south Italy on a beautiful gulf to which it has given its name. The port city is not far from Naples and Mount Vesuvius. It is a delightful old town, lying beneath a hill crowned by the ruins of a castle.

Irredenta—"unredeemed Italy." This was the term applied to sections in the north, and also on the east coast of the Adriatic where people Italian in blood, and for the most part in language, lived under Austrian rule. The promise of being able to unite these Italians to the Motherland was the chief reason why Italy entered the first World War on the side of the Allies.

Italia Irredenta

In spite of all the objections of some of the other powers this dream was in large measure accomplished. The northern boundary was pushed up to the Brenner Pass, taking over a large part of Tyrol. The final boundary gave to Italy a total gain of 8,900 square miles (nearly 6,000 of which were in Trentino), with not only all the Italians in the region but about 230,000 German-speaking people. The Italian government first set out to Italianize these people. It forbade them to speak their native tongue in public and it required them to Italianize their place names, changing the term South Tyrol to Trentino. It even ordered the inscriptions on German and Austrian tombstones to be changed to Italian. Finally, Mussolini and Hitler agreed to allow the German-speaking people in Trentino to migrate to Germany; almost 200,000 did so in the next few years.

For the first time in modern history Italy had a political frontier which followed the high Alps from end to end of her northern boundary, with the two passes of the Great and Little St. Bernard and Brenner Pass as the chief means of approach by land.

The Triangle of Trentino

Trentino, a triangular territory which reaches, roughly, from Lake Garda to Brenner Pass, is an Alpine district traversed by the upper valley of the Adige and reaching to the Inn. Its Dolomite Alps (named for the French geologist Dolomieu), with their limestone pinnacles, their dry summers and cool nights, are world-famous with tourists. There are forests of fir, pine and larch in which the chamois and the red deer still are hunted. There are tiny farms on the valley floors on which the hardy, independent people like to raise their own living, from the oil that dresses their salad to the wool and flax with which to weave their clothing. The lower slopes are utilized for vineyards and the mountain pastures, which belong to the communes, afford summer feed for numbers of cows and goats. Butter- and cheese-making is a leading industry. Three quarters of the people live in the cities and towns that dot the river valleys, where there are textile and other manufacturing plants.

Distances of Time

Italy has been the home of republics and empires, kingdoms and cities, for so long and has had so high a civilization that it is strewn with ruins and ancient buildings. Castles once held by feudal lords, princes, and even kings still adorn hundreds of hills and crags. Monasteries on hills or in protected places on valley walls bear witness to the long religious history of the land. Roman roads, many of them over two thousand years old, can be traced far and near over the country. Roads bound people together as nothing else can. Conjure up the commerce on these roads but picture perhaps pleasure-seekers too. Among them is the elderly Roman, clad in toga and sandals, shambling with mincing steps on the approach which reaches to the hot springs and baths where he pursues, not pleasure, but relief from rheumatism.

The Istrian Peninsula, across the northern arm of the Adriatic from Venice, was ceded by Austria to Italy after World War I. After the second World War, the peninsula, with the exception of Trieste—now a free territory under United Nations supervision—was granted by treaty in 1947 to Yugoslavia. Under the terms of the same treaty, Yugoslavia also took control of Fiume (Rieka) to the east of the Istrian Peninsula, and of Zara, now known as Zarad, on the Dalmatian coast.

Before World War II, Italy extended her rule to Albania, east of Italy across the Adriatic, and south of Yugoslavia. Italian interests had huge concessions in

MC LEISH

THE TRADITIONAL COSTUMES of the boys of the Roman Campagna, the wide plain surrounding Rome, reflect the colorfulness of Italian art, landscape and temperament. Local feeling is everywhere strong and the traditions of the days of the city states have been preserved. The malaria that is the scourge of the district in summer sends people up to the mountains in May.

A DAUGHTER OF ABRUZZI, this laughter-loving girl comes from Ciociaria, a land of forest and pasture, mountains and fertile valleys. Originally named for the peasant custom of wearing sandals, in the old days of warfare between city states, the inaccessibility of the district made it important as the natural protector of Naples on the north.

A GODSPEED FOR THE FISHERMEN

In beautiful Portofino, a small town on the Italian Riviera, a blessing is invoked on the fishing fleet. In a solemn procession that extends around the bend of the water front, the priest under the canopy in the foreground carries the monstrance. With it he will bless the fishermen and their boats before they set sail, and he will offer prayers for their success and safety.

FESTIVITY, MEDIEVAL STYLE, IN FRONT OF THE CATHEDRAL IN SIENA

The thirteenth-century Italian Gothic cathedral is outstanding among Siena's works of art. Color-fully garbed members of the Giraffe Club are waving their banners in anticipation of the annual Palio horse race dating from the seventeenth century and dedicated to the Virgin Mary. Ten of Siena's districts, chosen by lot, send one horse each to compete for the prize banner.

RIVA (REIF), IN TYROL, is a drowsy tourist town sheltered by the steep mountains surrounding it, not alone from cold winds, but also from the hot afternoon sun. It stands at the northwesternmost point of narrow Lake Garda, the largest lake of northern Italy, which lies before it enclosed by precipitous walls, like a Norwegian fjord. In the south, Lake Garda widens and its banks are low, but the azure waters are rarely as still as those of the other Italian lakes; and when a sudden squall races down from the north, it becomes almost as rough as an angry sea.

© E. N. A.

WHITE WALLS OF SORRENTO rise, from amid orange and lemon groves, on precipitous cliffs above the Bay of Naples. As the city lies exposed to sea breezes, summer heat is tempered, and it is therefore a popular resort the year around. An old town—the Surrentum of the Romans—it was an important trading centre in the Middle Ages, though it has not many relics of those bygone days. Torquato Tasso, the poet, was born here in 1544, but his house has been swallowed up by the sea. Here we see the town from the Capo di Monti.

© E. N. A.

THE GREAT PORT OF TRIESTE AT THE HEAD OF THE ADRIATIC SEA

The old town is built on the slope of a steep hill and is crowned by a castle. The new town occupies the plain that fronts the sea. Between these two divisions runs the Corso, the chief thoroughfare. Trieste was made a free port in 1719 by Charles VI which date marks the beginning of its importance. It finally became the commercial rival of Venice.

OLD, WALLED TIVOLI ABOVE ITS THUNDERING CASCADES

Tivoli has been famous for its beauty since the building of the Temple of Vesta. It was a summer resort of the Romans, who built villas and temples here. Even the Emperors Hadrian and Augustus had palaces near by. Below Tivoli the River Teverone, issuing from a ravine, divides into a number of enchanting waterfalls.

© E. N. A.

NAPLES, THE "SIREN CITY," on the map, at the instep of the boot, lies upon the shore of a lovely bay, north of Mount Vesuvius' smoking cone. It is a beautiful city in a beautiful position, but it is noisy and, in many parts, squalid. In the great harbor lie all kinds of vessels— warships, liners, cargo steamers, pleasure and fishing boats. It is the last that we see here, graceful craft with huge lateen sails that overtop the buildings, craft manned by sailors whose fishing ground is the blue Mediterranean. Notice the colors shown both in the boats and in the sails.

THE CASTLE OF ARCO, from its lofty crag 930 feet above the River Sarca, once protected from all enemies the town that lies in a half moon at its base. Destroyed by the French in 1703 during the War of the Spanish Succession, its ruins remain to crown the jutting peak. The town of Arco, there among the olive groves, has prospered well enough without its protection, however, and is now, owing to its sheltered position, a thriving winter resort. Were it not for Mount Brione in the distance we should see the lovely Lake Garda.

THIS STREET OF BORDIGHERA WAS NOT DESIGNED FOR VEHICLES

In olden days, towns were built, for safety's sake, in the most inaccessible places. That is why the ancient quarter of a town so often scrambles up a hillside, and the new part spreads over level ground at its foot. That is true of Bordighera, on the Riviera coast, near Monaco. Needless to say, this narrow, arched street is in the old quarter.

Albania's timber and mineral regions and in 1939 the stronger nation moved troops into Albania, declared the King deposed, and took over the country. During the war Italy managed to get control also of the Yugoslav coastline, and thus she was mistress of the Adriatic Sea. However, she had to loose her hold on Albania and also on Yugoslavia, when the Axis failed to win the war.

The River Arno flows through Tuscany, and on its banks, a few miles from the sea, lies Pisa, once a great maritime republic, and important for having fostered early sculpture and architecture. A leading Ghibelline city, it lay midway between two

SHOES THAT ARE WORKS OF ART

This painstaking worker in a shoe factory in Florence reminds us that industry and art have always been closely allied in this city. Its hand-made shoes are world-famous. Although Florence was organized commercially into seven guilds as early as the thirteenth century, its products, even in the modern machine age, bear the unmistakable stamp of the true artist.

IN OLD SAN REMO, on the Riviera, made fashionable by the Crown Prince, Frederick III, the narrow houses crowd together along steep lanes and even flights of steps. The arches that span the thoroughfares are designed for support in case of earthquakes. Modern San Remo is a seaport and health resort that basks between the hills and the Ligurian Sea.

THE SLENDER TOWER of the Palazzo Vecchio, the battlemented town hall of Florence, begun in 1298, is seen here from the banks of the River Arno. On either side of the quiet street that leads to it are the arcaded buildings that compose the Palazzo degli Uffizi, which now houses a famous picture gallery, a library, the post office and the Archives of Tuscany.

powerful enemies, Genoa and Florence. The odds were overwhelming. The Pisans were defeated by the Genoese in a naval battle in 1284, and in 1509 the possession of the city passed to Florence. The magnificent cathedral of black and white marble was built to commemorate a naval victory. Though it was begun in 1067, it was not completed and consecrated until 1118. Near by is the cemetery known as the Campo Santo, a beautiful cloister surrounding a greensward.

About fifty miles up the Arno lies Florence—the city of flowers—the intellectual and artistic centre of Italy for more than two centuries. In its narrow streets, where the palaces of the nobles stand like fortresses, papal Guelph and imperial Ghibelline (the popular and the aristocratic factions) fought out their differences in the thirteenth century. Dante, "the first Italian" in having tried to recon-cile the two, was banished for a year in 1302. Greatest of Italian poets, his love of Beatrice has been immortalized in the Vita Nuova and the Divina Commedia.

The cathedral is a stately building of marble. Beside it rises perhaps the most beautiful campanile in Italy, a thing of delicate tracery called The Shepherd's Tower, because its architect, Giotto, was a ten-year-old shepherd lad minding his flocks when the artist, Cimabue, found him drawing a picture of a lamb on a flat stone. Cimabue took the boy to Florence and had him taught art.

Many Italian cathedrals have beside them a building called the baptistery. This was needed during the centuries when everybody in the diocese was baptized by the bishop. The baptistery at Florence is famous on account of two of its bronze doors that Michelangelo said were "fit for the gates of Paradise." The

© E. N. A.

WHERE OIL AND WINE WERE BOUGHT AND SOLD IN OLD POMPEII

From Pompeii, now being cleared of the volcanic ash from Vesuvius, beneath which it has lain buried for eighteen centuries and more, we gain an idea of the lives that people led in 79 A.D. We see the narrow, paved streets, the shops and taverns, dwelling-houses, theatres and temples, and even the posters in red letters on the walls.

EASY-CHAIR FISHING IN THE TIBER

The machine age inspires fishermen at the mouth of the Tiber to construct hammock nets on pulleys that can be raised and lowered from the edge of a mole. In ancient times the Tiber emptied into the Tyrrhenian Sea at Ostia, but that port has filled in with sediment brought down by the stream. The opening (in two branches) is now a little to the west.

making of these doors occupied a celebrated goldsmith for fifty years.

In the older streets may be seen little shrines, each containing a sacred picture in a frame with a lamp always burning before it, reminders of the ancient practice of praying at the street corners. Here, too, we may see the sick carried to hospital on a litter borne by men who wear black robes and curious pointed hoods which conceal their faces. These men are the Brothers of Mercy. The members are drawn from all classes, and a certain number are always on duty that they may be ready to help the sick and injured or to carry the dead to burial.

The carnival in Florence lasts from Christmas to Lent and is a time of merrymaking. Florentine children do not hang up their stockings on Christmas Eve, but at the Epiphany, or Twefth Day, which is the children's festival, they put their shoes out overnight, hoping that La Befana, an old woman who in the Italian nursery takes the place of Santa Claus, will fill them with presents.

On Easter Eve there comes the Feast of the Dove, which has been celebrated in Florence for eight centuries. From early morning the peasants flock in from the country and join the crowd of townspeople in front of the cathedral. Then appears a huge wooden car festooned with fireworks and drawn by four milk-white oxen whose horns are tipped with gold. It halts in front of the cathedral, within which Mass is being celebrated.

When the Archbishop comes to the words, "Glory to God in the Highest," he releases a little, white, artificial dove which, carrying a light in its mouth, slides along a wire from the High Altar through the open door to the car. The dove is greeted with tremendous shouts of welcome, and

ON THE BANKS OF THE RIVER RECINA WHERE, AT FIUME, IT FLOWS BENEATH MONTE CALVARIO

© E.N.A.

The great port of Fiume, which lies on the Adriatic Sea east of the Istrian peninsula, used to be in Austria-Hungary. After World War I Italy and Yugoslavia both laid claim to it, and the soldier-poet, Gabriele d'Annunzio, seized it for Italy and ruled it for over a year, without the authority of his government. At last, in 1920, it was made an independent state. It did not remain so long, however, for Italy took it again in 1924, leaving Yugoslavia the tiny port of Susak. Fiume changed hands once more after World War II, and returned to Yugoslavia.

STRAW-PLAITER OF FIESOLE WORKING AT HER WOODEN LOOM

This woman is making lace out of straw. Fiesole, four miles from Florence, has many straw-plaiting industries. An old Etruscan city, it was the headquarters of Cataline in 62 B.C. La Badia is its Renaissance monastery, and a villa near by was once the favorite residence of Lorenzo the Magnificent, ruler of Florence.

the people watch to see whether it will set alight the fireworks.

The Benedictine monastery on Monte Cassino, above Cassino, celebrated its fourteen hundredth anniversary in 1929. Through its centuries of existence, this historic shrine has suffered much. The barbarians who poured over Italy in the sixth century, later the Lombards, and then the Saracens sacked the place, and in other wars it suffered damage. But always the monks rebuilt it. In 1944, however, Monte Cassino was a war target, and when the bombing and shelling were over, the monastery was left a heap of rubble. A new monastery is being erected on the site, but the treasures of the old building—works of art, ancient manuscripts and rare medieval volumes of untold value—can never be restored.

In Umbria is Assisi where St. Francis gathered together a little band of men vowed to poverty, and sent them out as preaching friars to work among the poor and wretched. Thus the Franciscans, or Greyfriars, were founded, 1210-23.

Over the Apennines to the east lie the Marches, the granary of ancient Rome. It is still mainly an agricultural district. North of these is the toy republic of San Marino, about which we read elsewhere.

In the Apennines themselves, especially in the upland valleys of Abruzzi, the winters are extremely cold. Sometimes in winter the villages are cut off from each other for months by deep snow. Naturally, the hill folk differ from the people of the sunny plains. Too isolated for a free exchange of new ideas, they cling to the old ways and, where the ground is level enough for plowing, use the same form of plow as did their Roman ancestors. The hillsides are clothed with Spanish chestnut trees, which are an important

RAW MATERIAL FOR A WORK OF ART

The marble quarries of Italy, especially those of Carrara, have been famous for more than two thousand years. They still yield the precious material for sculptures and monumental buildings. Mechanical methods of quarrying have been introduced to some extent, but the stone is easily broken and blasting must be done with the greatest care, if at all.

BLACK STAR

MILAN'S CATHEDRAL WITH ITS FOREST OF MARBLE PINNACLES

The cathedral of Milan, capital of Lombardy, is one of the wonders of the world, with its white marble traceries, its delicate pinnacles and its flying buttresses and thousands of statues.

food to the people, for in these districts chestnuts, dried, ground and made into flat cakes, largely take the place of bread. An earthquake in the Abruzzi in January 1915, cost thirty thousand lives.

In one town of the Roman Campagna, Marino, there is a fountain which flows with free wine for one hour each year. At the height of the vintage season a gigantic grape basket owned by the town is set up in the market place and filled with the fruit to be made into wine for the next year's celebration.

On the coast, about halfway between Rome and Naples, lies Terracina. Here southern Italy may be said to begin. Thence around the coast to the Adriatic runs a series of bays where blue sky, bluer sea and golden sunshine are well-nigh everlasting. But groves of fruit trees alternate with vast stretches of land which have been abandoned.

Along here, before Rome had risen to power, a series of prosperous Greek city-states sprang up amid cultivated fields and orchards. When the Carthaginians fought the Romans for the mastery of the world, most of these cities, especially those in the far south, sided with the Carthaginians, and were destroyed by the victorious Romans. Then the land went uncultivated, the rivers silted up and overflowed, and malaria completed the ruin. Paestum (originally Posidonia), once a city famous for its temples and for its roses, brought under Roman rule in 273 B.C., dwindled until in the ninth century it was utterly destroyed by the Saracens. It is today but a mighty ruin in a wilderness. But neither Lombardy nor Tuscany can vie with the coloring and climate of Naples and the surrounding country.

Milan, the most important city of the plain, is a thriving commercial center. Its cathedral, adorned with turrets and pinnacles and some 4,000 statues, is like a carven mountain of marble. Indeed, the design for it is supposed to have been suggested by the appearance of Monte Rosa away to the north.

Leonardo da Vinci's Masterpiece

In a former monastery, adjoining another church in Milan, is what was once one of the great art treasures of the world —The Last Supper, by Leonardo da Vinci. The masterpiece is faded and peeling now, a pathetic ghost of its former greatness. Milan is the city in which Mozart's first opera was produced.

Milan streets radiate like the spokes of a wheel, with concentric boulevards outside its ancient moat. At its heart its most important arcade, Victor Emmanuel Arcade, rises to about a hundred feet. Lined with shop windows, it affords a favorite promenade and at night its glass ceiling is brilliantly lighted.

Monza, a few miles from Milan, is connected with the history of Theodolinda, a Bavarian princess who, in the sixth century, became the wife of a Lombard king, and the mediator between the Lombards and the Catholic Church. For her missionary zeal Pope Gregory the Great sent her a most precious relic—a thin circlet of iron, made, so it was claimed, from one of the nails used at the Crucifixion. This iron band, set in a circle of gold and jewels, is the famous Iron Crown of Lombardy. Charlemagne, Frederick Barbarossa, Charles V and Napoleon I have all worn it. It is kept at Monza, in the cathedral where Theodolinda is buried.

Where Virgil Was Born

The Lombardy Plain is rich in interesting cities. Mantua, near which the poet Virgil was born, appears to rise from a lake, because the River Mincio completely encircles it. Piacenza, Cremona, Bologna, Modena and other Lombard cities were Roman colonies planted here, in the generation preceding 220 B.C. when the people of the plain were Gauls.

From Roman times the Via Emilia has been an important highway. To-day it provides a motor road from Rimini (near which Cæsar crossed the Rubicon), via Bologna, to Milan. Bologna controls the major passage of the Apennines from the plain to the peninsula. The town, seat of an ancient university, has two grotesque leaning towers which date from the thirteenth century. Other stations on the old Via Emilia were Piacenza, Parma, Reggio and Modena. The tourist will find it worth while to visit Padua if only to see the frescoes by Giotto and the tomb of St. Anthony; and Verona because it was the home of Romeo and Juliet. It has one of the most impressive amphitheatres in all Italy.

Northern Italy is well supplied with railways. From Milan two lines run into Switzerland, one through the Simplon Tunnel and one through St. Gotthard Tunnel; while from Verona—the fortress that holds Brenner Pass—a third line runs to Austria.

Home of Stradivari

Cremona was the home of three generations of the Amati family and of their pupil Antonio Stradivari, who, about two centuries and a half ago, made violins that have never been equaled. To-day the quiet Lombardy town, with its thirteenth-century bell tower, is a centre for silk manufacture.

As the plain rises toward the snow-clad Alps of the north and west, one finds long lakes formed by the widening of the tributaries of the Po as they rush down from the snows. The Lombard Lakes (Como, Garda, Lugano, Maggiore and others famous among tourists) are romantically beautiful and on their shores, as in ancient Roman times, people of means have built their villas and terraces. The town of Como, with its marble cathedral, lies in an amphitheatre of mountains.

In the upland villages the peasant tends his vines and makes wood into charcoal. Like his brother of the plain, he lives mainly on *polenta*, which is cornmeal cooked and cut into slabs to be eaten as bread or crumbled into soup. This *polenta* and a soup, flavored with a variety of vegetables and meat, forms the staple food

FLAG-WAVING DAY IN SIENA

Boys in Renaissance costume take part in an old-time festival at Siena. The city, built on three hills, is one of the most venerable in Italy, for it was founded by the Etruscans, who built a wall around it pierced by nine gates. Siena had her greatest glory in the thirteenth and fourteenth centuries, when she was the center of early Renaissance art.

of the working classes of the north. It is varied occasionally with eggs and cheese and on fast days with fish.

In every cottage an attic is reserved for the rearing of silkworms. Here, with a fire always going to keep the air at the right temperature, caterpillars (silkworms) are spread out on frames covered with mulberry leaves. As their size and appetite increase, the mother, father and all the children are kept busy supplying them with fresh leaves. The yellow cocoons produced are sold to keep busy the silk looms of the manufacturing cities. Italy is one of the greatest silk-producing countries of the world.

The Wine Industry

Another big source of income is the wine industry. The vine-growing peasants have to combat hailstorms which, coming with startling suddenness, may strip the grapes from the vines and destroy the year's harvest in half an hour. Lately the practice has been adopted of firing cannon at the dark clouds that precede a hailstorm, with the hope of making them precipitate snow and sleet instead of hail.

In winter, bitter winds sweep down from the Alps, and the Apennines keep the warm air of the Mediterranean from the northern plain. Along the coast from east of Mentone to Spezia is the contrasting mildness of the Italian Riviera, with its pleasure resorts of San Remo and Bordighera.

So fertile is the soil that oranges, lemons, olives and other fruits thrive, and the mountain sides are cultivated in terraces. Genoa has a long history as a seaport. Christopher Columbus was a Genoese mariner.

West of the Apennines in the northern half of the peninsula lie two fascinating provinces, Tuscany and Umbria, to which artists flock, for here the land is a picture of loveliness.

Farming is profitable and over half the population of the country is directly engaged in agriculture, and another quarter in the industries directly dependent upon the products of the soil. In spite of this Italy must import grain and cotton. She also imports fish and timber, and the iron and coal needed for her industry and fuel. This need of imports has led to the development of her Merchant Marine. The land is two-thirds mountainous or so hilly that roads are continually washed away by spring freshets.

A Traveling Agricultural College

The five hundred thousand small farms occupy but one-seventh of the agricultural lands. These incredibly small holdings everywhere adjoin the large estates of the hill slopes, on which skilled methods, pedigreed animals and selected seeds, together with more fertilizers, are coming to be employed. In places the soil is impoverished by three thousand years of cultivation, but Italy is, on the whole, extraordinarily fertile. This is especially true of parts of the Campania and Sicily and the plains of Lombardy and Venetia. Even sun-scorched or marshy areas can often be made to yield olives, oranges, lemons and tangerines. To encourage a movement of more city dwellers back to the land, agricultural experts have been formed into a traveling college, and in addition, large projects are afoot for reclaiming waste lands, especially swamps in need of drainage, for generations abandoned because of malarial mosquitoes, and arid lands in need of irrigation. By a recent survey Italy had between four and five million acres which might be so reclaimed, and state aid is to be tendered individuals who sho.. initiative in the matter. Italy also has many co-operative credit associations.

Electricity for Many Purposes

The swift mountain streams of the Alps will permit the development of electric power on a large scale. Part of this power is to be used for the drainage of water from bogged areas, and part used for industries and transport.

Despite her farming and industrial possibilities, Italy's wealth per capita is low. For years before World War II she had a surplus of workers, and there was considerable emigration to other countries. For a long time Italy's extensive possessions in northern and eastern Africa were not much of an outlet for her surplus population, since a comparatively small number of Italians migrated there. The Fascist regime, headed by Benito Mussolini, made extensive plans for the development and colonization of Italy's African territory, particularly after the annexation, in 1936, of Ethiopia. These projects had to be abandoned in the course of World War II, since North Africa became one of the fighting areas of the war.

On the island of Capri, near the southern extremity of the Bay of Naples, everyone goes to visit the Blue Grotto and to see the effect of yellow sunlight filtering through azure water. Here the Emperor

THE AMPHITHEATRE at Pola, a port of Istria, is a relic of the ancient Romans, and could seat 25,000 people. The Venetians, who took the town in 1148, used its stone seats as building material. Taken by Austria in 1850, Pola became, thanks to its fine harbor, an important naval station, as in Roman times. Its foreign population is largely Slav.

Tiberius spent the last half of his life in riotous living. Baja, the ancient Baiae, nestling in the northern corner of the bay, was a fashionable bathing resort of Roman society in the time of Nero, and the coast is rich in remains of ancient villas. Pompeii, buried twenty feet deep beneath the ashes of Vesuvius, was one of these pleasure resorts, and from its ruins we can reconstruct much of the early Roman life.

Naples, with its pink or blue or violet stucco houses climbing the hills behind the Bay, is crowded, noisy and most particularly smelly. Despite its artistic treasures, people are for the most part unpleasantly crowded together. Even in the new buildings that the city is providing for the working classes, a family may live in a couple of rooms, and frequently hens or turkeys share the apartment. To the poor Neapolitan the house is merely a place in which to sleep; his real life is lived in the sunny streets. There children play amid panniered donkeys and men take their siestas on the sidewalks.

Life in the Streets of Naples

Early in the morning the milkman comes along and drives his goats up four or five flights of steps, and there and then milks them into the jugs. Cows are milked in the street, the customers from the upper floors letting down the necessary receptacle in a basket. Stalls heaped with flowers vie with fruits and vegetables, and food of all sorts is cooked and eaten, hot from the pot, in the streets. Macaroni takes the place of the *polenta* of the north, and such queer dishes as snail soup, roast chestnuts, starfish, sea-urchins, and octopus tentacles appear on the menu, while the air is richly scented with the all-pervading odor of unrefined oil and garlic.

The southern Italians, with their mixed heritage, are a handsome, vivacious people, happy, musical, fond of color, easily moved to anger, and addicted to games of chance. Many Italians are good horsemen. They have lately adopted football. Italy is the native home of the Punch and Judy show. Indeed, her people delight in every form of drama from marionettes to tragedy.

Mussolini and Fascism

A vast working-class movement began in 1901, which at the end of the World War became a general strike of revolutionary character. In this crisis Benito Mussolini came forward as dictator. He founded the first black-shirted Fascio at Milan, and these defeated the Reds, later receiving reinforcements from the poet and airman, D'Annunzio. By the end of 1921 Fascism had become a political party, and a year later the King invited Mussolini at Rome to form a Fascist government.

For over twenty years Fascists were in control, but for a time, old forms of government were observed. Benito Mussolini was made prime minister with all power, though decrees were issued in the name of the King. The government was entirely centralized. All mayors of towns, heads of provinces and of smaller divisions were appointed by decree. Only the Fascist party was allowed to exist. Parliament had been succeeded by the Grand Council of Corporations. Industry and all other elements of national life were organized into twenty-two corporations, with Mussolini at the head of each and of the Grand Council as well. No student in a higher school could be promoted or graduated unless he had completed the military courses.

A King of the House of Savoy

Italy had, in King Vittorio Emanuele III, a representative of the ancient house of Savoy. The ancestors of the reigning house, probably Germans, acquired territory in Italy, and at one time were lords of Sicily, but exchanged the island in 1720 for Sardinia, gained the Genoese territory in 1815, and in 1851 most of Lombardy, then in 1860 Parma, Modena, Romagna and Tuscany, Sicily and Naples (including part of the Papal States), the Marches and Umbria. In 1861 the first Italian Parliament declared King Victor Emmanuel of Sardinia King of Italy. In 1866 the rest of Mantua and Venetia, and in 1870 the rest of the Papal States (Rome) were annexed. After the first World War, parts of Austria were added.

VIEW FROM TSCHAMIN VALLEY LOOKING TOWARD THE ROSENGARTENSPITZE

Worn and broken into sharpened peaks that notch the skyline the Dolomites, sometimes called the Limestone Alps, are a prime favorite with tourists and mountain climbers. Here well marked trails and shelter huts established by the Swiss Alpine Club and other mountaineering organizations enable one to reach heights from which one sees a panorama of jagged peaks and forested slopes, interspersed with green valleys in which white dots of hamlets punctuated by church spires lend life to the scene. The sharp summits daily gather streamers of white mist.

331

MC LEISH

THE LEANING TOWER of Pisa, the cathedral's bell-tower, is famous, not for its beauty nor yet for the tone of its seven bells, but because it is 16½ feet out of perpendicular.

MANSELL

THE DUOMO, the handsome cathedral of St. Maria del Fiore in Florence, is the fourth largest church in Europe. The square campanile is considered to be the finest of its kind.

The Italian population has increased very rapidly over the last hundred years. The people have had a hard lot on the overcrowded peninsula. Many have lifted themselves from poverty by breaking all ties in the homeland and migrating to all parts of the world, principally to the United States and Latin America. Others left their families at home and came to America by cheap passage rates under contract with a padrone, or employment agent, to work for a season and return. Even those who did set up new homes continued to nurse fond dreams of some-day journeying back to Italy. In all, some 4,700,000 Italians emigrated to North America in the period from 1851 to 1940. In the year 1940 nearly 1,800,000 people of Italian birth were living in the United States. This figure, of course, does not include American-born persons of Italian descent; they add several millions more.

Between Rome and New York there is a distance of 4,172 miles. In time there is a difference of five hours forty-five minutes, so that when it is midnight in New York it is 5:45 a.m. in Rome, and the sun is already above the horizon.

ITALY: FACTS AND FIGURES

THE COUNTRY

Central peninsula of Southern Europe. On the east is the Adriatic Sea; on the south, the Ionian Sea; on the west, the Tyrrhenian and Ligurian Seas; on the north, forming a natural boundary, the Alps. Area, 119,800 sq. miles; pop. (est. 1949), 45,871,000. Because of World War II, she lost 4 border districts to France; Zara, Pelagosa and most of Venezia Giulia to Yugoslavia; Dodecanese Islands to Greece; Saseno to Albania; Trieste became a free territory. Eritrea unites with Ethiopia in 1952; Italian Somaliland under Italian trusteeship is to become completely independent by about 1960; and Libya, including Cyrenaica, Tripolitania and Fezzan, has become a sovereign state ruled by a king and national assembly.

GOVERNMENT

Italy became a republic by a vote of the people in 1946. At the same time, a general election was held to form a constituent assembly of 556 members for the purpose of drawing up a constitution. Local elections were held and the pre-Fascist type of communal government was restored. The new constitution was approved by the assembly in 1947, and took effect January 1, 1948. It provides for a strong central government, a Parliament of two houses, a president to hold office for 7 years and equal voting rights for all over 21. The Vatican City of 109 acres became an independent state in 1929.

COMMERCE AND INDUSTRIES

Agriculture occupies more people than any other industry. About 41.4% of the total area is under crops, 21.9% under meadows and pastures, 4.8% devoted to horticulture, 18% to forest, 4% is not cultivated, but is productive, and 8.1% is unproductive land. Fruit, wheat, corn, potatoes, olives and sugar beets are grown.

The textile industry (silk, rayon, wool and cotton) is the largest and most important. Dairy-farming and cheese are also important industries. Manufactures include lace, machinery, food-stuffs, lumber and woodwork, art goods, wine and automobiles. Minerals found are sulphur, building and decorative stone (granite and marble), zinc, iron, mercury and lead.

The chief exports are vegetables and fruits, rayon, cheese, felt hats, rice, olive oil, gloves, marble and alabaster. Imports are meat, wheat, coffee, fish, wool, raw cotton, coal and coke, machinery, mineral oils and crude rubber.

COMMUNICATIONS

Railway lines, 13,371 miles, of which 10,127 are state owned. Telegraph lines, 37,254 miles. There are 10,150 telegraph offices. Total length of national highways, 105,938 miles. In 1948, 7 airlines were in operation with regular flights to Tunis, Tripoli, Athens, Cairo and Istanbul.

RELIGION AND EDUCATION

Roman Catholic is the established religion, but freedom of worship is allowed. Education is regulated by the state, which maintains public schools of every grade, but only the lower grade instruction is compulsory. In 1931 21% of the population was illiterate. There are 27 state and free universities, technical schools, higher institutes, and a national institute for the instruction of illiterate adults.

CHIEF TOWNS

Populations (1949): Rome, capital, 1,638,226; Milan, 1,284,564; Naples, 1,013,710; Turin, 722,592; Genoa, 670,460; Palermo, 485,429; Florence, 380,221; Bologna, 336,700; Venice, 316,253; Catania, 289,549; Bari, 265,988; Messina, 224,914; Verona, 196,510; Taranto, 189,976; Padua, 167,591; Brescia, 149,958; Livorno (Leghorn), 144,729; Reggio di Calabria, 141,308; Ferrara, 137,069.

THE CITY THAT RULED THE WORLD

Rome and the Ruins of Its Ancient Splendor

Rome, the capital of a united Italy, is even more interesting as the former centre of the Roman Empire and headquarters of the Christian Church. The antiquarian finds ancient palaces and temples, forums and circuses, arenas and triumphal arches, baths and aqueducts in all the beauty of colored marble and architecture reminiscent of Etruscan, Greek and Roman days and the romantic splendor of the greatest empire of antiquity. Now one may visit a Cathedral of St. Peter's which was built on the site of an older structure; one will find the Forum Romanum a pillared ruin and the Campagna, once the haunt of brigands, become an artists' mecca. The heart of present-day Rome is the Piazza Venezia, which leads to the most important street, the Via Nazionale, an imposing street opened in modern times.

A S we approach Rome we enter what is known as the Roman Campagna, a sparsely peopled plain which extends like a sea to the walls of Rome. Bare acres stretch endlessly, mile upon mile of rustling grass and reed, with here and there a group of umbrella pines, and lines of willows hanging low upon the banks of the Tiber.

Paved roads, which have borne the wear and tear of twenty centuries, cross the plain. Here is a ruined tower—remnant of family feuds in medieval time; yonder are the gaunt remains of an old Roman aqueduct, or the conical huts of shepherds, and lines of weather-worn tombs.

Legendary stories tell how Romulus founded a city on the Palatine Hill, and how early Rome was governed by kings who fortified the city with a wall and trained the hard-working farmers of the country around to be well-disciplined, invincible soldiers. Later the Romans drove out their king and established a republic which endured for five hundred years. This small city-state gradually overpowered the neighboring tribes one after another until it ruled the whole Italian peninsula. As Rome grew in strength, she came in contact with the powerful empire of Carthage, a Phœnician city on the north coast of Africa. For over a century the two cities struggled against each other; in the end Carthage was destroyed and Rome became the strongest nation on the Mediterranean. Her great generals extended her territory from Asia Minor to Spain and from Britain to Egypt.

But with world power came wealth and luxury; Romans no longer worked their own farms and fought their own battles, because slaves were plentiful. The people failed to govern themselves well, and so one remarkable man, Julius Cæsar, was enabled to seize power in his own hands. He was assassinated, but his nephew Augustus became the first Emperor of Rome. Augustus Cæsar lived just at the beginning of the Christian era. In his day were built many of the temples and monuments which now stand in ruins, and under him Roman literature reached a height which it never equaled afterward. He organized and governed the vast Empire so well that his subjects were proud to become Roman citizens.

Many great rulers followed Augustus, but the empire grew so large that it was unwieldy. Even the military genius of the Romans could not protect it against the attacks of barbarians from the north and east. The Goths even captured Rome itself, the city which all the world had long considered impregnable. And the growing force of Christianity steadily undermined the old religion, until in the fourth century the Emperor Constantine became a Christian. From that time on the empire changed more and more rapidly. Finally it broke apart, but its prestige and some of its power were handed down to the Bishop of Rome, who as Pope came to be the head of the Christian Church.

If the day of our arrival at Rome is clear, presently the eye is caught by what looks

MC LEISH

THE ETERNAL CITY shows clean, red roofs after a shower. We can stand on this terrace of the enormous monument to King Victor Emmanuel II, and look across Rome toward the domes of St. Andrea della Valla and St. Peter's. It is interesting to compare the new buildings of the city as it stands today with the many wonders that it displayed in olden times.

IN THE COLOSSEUM men fought animals before audiences of forty thousand. The tiers of seats were reached through corridors lighted by the arched openings shown above. The Romans enjoyed many spectacular performances, since the more cunning Emperors found they could buy the good will of their subjects with free circuses, as well as gifts.

IN THE DAYS WHEN FASCISM WAS RAMPANT IN ITALY

These young Black Shirts, as the Fascisti were called, annually filed past the Porta del Popolo on their way to be reviewed by Mussolini and to celebrate the anniversary of the foundation of Fascism. This political philosophy at one time was identified with Mussolini's regime in Italy although it later spread with aggressive militarism into other totalitarian states, notably Germany and Japan. Fascisti marched where Caesars tramped and conquered princes walked in chains, and chariots rolled and helmeted legions clanked.

LOOKING OVER ROME FROM THE GREAT DOME OF ST. PETER'S

From the dome of St. Peter's we see beside the Tiber the rounded Castle of Sant' Angelo, the remodeled mausoleum of Emperor Hadrian. It was rebuilt as a fortress by Pope Boniface IX; and when their safety was threatened by the turbulent factions of the city, the Popes fled from the Vatican by a covered passage to the massive stronghold.

THE NOBLE WAY TO THE MOTHER CHURCH OF CHRISTENDOM

The great domed Cathedral of St. Peter's was built on the site of a yet older church that had been erected to mark the burial place of the Apostle Peter. The present building slowly took its vast and unsymmetrical shape during a period of 120 years, under the care of some of the greatest Italian artists, such as Bramante, Raphael and Michelangelo.

FROM THE PINCIO GARDENS we look across a modern quarter of Rome to the glittering white mass of St. Peter's on the farther bank of the Tiber, and, to the left of this church, to the Palazzo di Giustizia. The Pincio, which is a favorite resort of the Romans in the cool eve- ning, was turned from a vineyard to pleasure-grounds at the beginning of the nineteenth century; but it was not the first time that it had been laid out in such a fashion, since Lucullus, a Roman soldier and epicure who died in 57 B.C., had a garden here.

© EWING GALLOWAY

THE TEMPLE OF SATURN, now reduced to eight meaningless pillars, looms above the triumphal arch of the Emperor Severus on the Capitoline Hill. In early times the public treasure was stored in the Temple of Saturn, which, from the remains still existing, must have been a magnificent building. It was approached by a lofty flight of steps. The splendid church of Santa Martina e Luca, which was first built in the seventh century on the ruins of the hall in which the Senate of ancient Rome held its secret meetings, faces the temple.

DOME OF ST. PETER'S GLEAMING BEYOND THE SUN-DRENCHED GARDENS OF THE VATICAN PALACE

The palace of the Popes, built at the same time as St. Peter's, is said to have eleven hundred rooms. Many of them are adorned by frescoes by Michelangelo and other great Italian artists. They are open to the public. The tourist will be enchanted with the museums and libraries, the Sistine Chapel containing paintings by Raphael and the galleries enriched by his masterpieces. The extensive gardens are laid out in the Italian style on the hillsides; statuary and shrines adorn walks and groves; and everything is arranged to produce stately harmony.

like a cloud on the horizon. This is our first glimpse of Rome. It is the dome of St. Peter's, and in those marks against the sky, like pencil scribblings on a slate, is the eternal city of the empire of the Caesars, of the dominion of the Popes and now of the Republic of Italy.

The city by the Tiber is a strange admixture of old and new. The drive from the station reveals a street which might well be found in any modern city. Street cars rumble, newsboys shout—and there are more newspapers than can be counted in New York City. Sturdily built flower girls give color to the scene. Gowned priests push through bustling crowds— for all Rome hurries in these busy days, and tourists with red guide-books add to the bustle.

Every now and then we come upon a piazza or public square, with obelisks, columns, fountains and perhaps a few trees. We are impressed by the many squares, the balconies of the palaces, and the colonnades, the fine churches, the obelisks, the ruins, no less than by the colorful gardens, the cafés, the bookstores and the smart shops. Above all looms St. Peter's gigantic dome, while the columns of the Caesars brood over all.

MAGNIFICENT GARDEN OF THE HISTORIC PALAZZO COLONNA

The Palazzo Colonna, an impressive reminder of the greatness of the Colonna family, stands on the broad Corso Umberto, near the center of Rome. The construction of the Palazzo was begun in the 15th century by Pope Martin V, one of the Colonna. The Palazzo has a fine gallery. It also boasts of beautiful gardens, of which the above photograph gives us some idea.

MC LEISH

SWISS PONTIFICAL GUARDS are always on duty at the Vatican, and form part of the Pope's train in processions. Their uniform had altered considerably through the centuries, and had become really ugly. In 1914-15, the above distinguished garb was provided for them. It is an exact reproduction of the uniform worn more than three hundred years ago.

STONE RELIEF RECENTLY FOUND AMONG THE RUINS OF THE TRAJAN FORUM

The vanished splendor of Imperial Rome appears again in the stone sculptured in high relief recently found among the ruins of the Trajan Forum. Last and most magnificent of all the fora of ancient Rome, it was built early in the second century A.D. The griffin represented above was supposed to watch over hidden treasure. It was consecrated to the sun.

The Palatine Hill (Palatium) overhangs the Forum. This is the hill on which Romulus built the first Rome. To-day the place is a mass of débris, but we may trace the Servian Wall (which was probably built by Servius Tullius), as it has been disclosed by excavations reaching from the Tiber straight to the Capitoline Hill, thence to the Quirinal, and see how it was made of two-foot blocks of tufa quarried on the spot. We may even see the cave—known as the Lupercal—in which the twin founders of the city were supposedly suckled by the wolf.

The Forum Romanum, which begins in a hollow of the eastern slope of the Capitoline Hill, was the heart of ancient Rome and the meeting-place of the first citizens. It became in time the centre of the civic and political life of the city. On this spot were raised memorials to Roman heroes, temples to their gods and tribunals of justice.

Barbarian conquerors burned and pillaged it; the makers of Christian Rome took its stone to build their churches; ruin and neglect fell upon it, so that the greater part lay buried for centuries beneath forty feet of rubbish, and its surface was used as a cattle market and as a place for washer-women to hang out their clothes to dry.

Now, thanks to the excavators, a great deal of the ancient Forum has been revealed, and we shall stand before the relics of temples, prisons, tombs and basilicas. We shall see what remains of the Old Senate House, and the depression known as the Lake of Curtius. According to legend, in 362 B.C. a chasm had suddenly opened in the Forum and an oracle declared that it would close only if Rome's greatest possession were thrown into its depths. Marcus Curtius, believing that a good citizen was the city's greatest possession, mounted on his horse and in full armor leaped into the chasm, which instantly closed again.

The tourist season begins with Christmas. During the two weeks from Christ-

© Ewing Galloway

THE ROYAL PALAZZO DEL QUIRINAL SET ON THE HIGHEST OF THE SEVEN HILLS OF ROME

This palace, because of its airy and healthful situation on the Quirinal, was once a summer residence of the Popes. From 1870 to 1946 it was the home of Italy's royal family. In the square before the structure are two superb marble groups of horse tamers—fragments of the period of Rome's imperial greatness—over sixteen feet high. These sculptures, which are magnificent both because of their size and the energy that they express, have never been hidden from sight since they were originally set up in the Baths of Constantine.

SPLENDID RUINS OF THE FORUM ROMANUM, ONE OF THE FINEST RELICS OF ANCIENT ROME

Here ancient Roman orators like Cicero, or agitators like Catiline, harangued an eager crowd, composed of city merchants and worshipers coming from the many temples. On the left of the photograph is the line of pillars forming the portico of the temple built by the Emperor Antoninus in memory of Faustina. his wife. On the right, three columns remain of the great temple of Castor and Pollux, the warrior brothers of legend. In the background we see the Arch of Titus, built to commemorate the taking of Jerusalem.

347

THE COLOSSEUM, THE LARGER OF ROME'S TWO AMPHITHEATRES, ERECTED IN THE FIRST CENTURY A.D.

The Colosseum, built of large blocks of travertine, was said to be the scene of the massacres of early Christians. Certainly for four centuries it was the scene of gladiatorial combats and the fighting of wild beasts. A common sight was the match between a paid warrior called a Retiarius, armed with net and trident, and another equipped with the round shield and short sword of a Greek soldier. At other times lions, tigers, bears, giraffes and ostriches were killed. Even the emperor Commodus took part in these shows.

TRAJAN'S TRIUMPHAL COLUMN: NOW CROWNED BY ST. PETER

To commemorate his Dacian victories Trajan erected this marble monument, around which
runs a spiral band illustrating the emperor's campaigns, with over six hundred feet of the
figures of soldiers, animals and war-engines. Beyond is the church of Santissimo Nome di
Maria, a thank offering for Vienna's deliverance from the Turks in 1683.

mas to the Epiphany, the Romans give themselves over to feasting and merry-making. On New Year's Day everyone from the postman to the man who mends your typewriter must receive a gratuity, and in return, one receives gifts from the trades-people. The custom is traced to Janus, for whom the hill known as the Janiculum was named, and to whom after his death a temple was erected. The first month was also named in his honor. He it was who is supposed to have introduced the custom of giving gifts. In the old days bouquets, especially of verbena, were the usual gifts, but as Rome grew in splendor the practice of gift-giving grew to such proportions that in the time of

Augustus families were beggared by the necessity of distributing gifts beyond their means. To-day at both the Vatican and the Quirinal New Year's Day is spent in receiving calls of state.

The modern city promenades in the fashionable Corso. From the Piazza del Popolo one may retreat to the coolness of the Pincio Gardens, famous even in antiquity, on Monte Pincio. Around five o'clock the band plays and all Rome walks.

Along the Corso, one of Rome's principal streets, friend meets friend for a cup of coffee at a nearby restaurant, say, the Colonna or the Fagiano in the busy Piazza Colonna about halfway down the street.

Centuries now have passed since the

Chichester

LEARNED MEN WHO WRITE LETTERS FOR A FEW PENCE

In spite of their country's ancient culture and twenty-seven institutions of university rank, many Italians can neither read nor write. When they wish to send a letter they do as the woman in this photograph is doing, and dictate whatever they want to say to professional letter-writers, who set up their booths at the side of the street.

Forum swarmed with the busy life of ancient Rome and the Colosseum echoed to the cries of the gladiators and the roaring of hungry lions. Despite the ruin, they are still imposing and typify the city which once gave its laws as an example to every nation. The broken columns of the Forum and the ruined buildings are reminders of the days when ancient Rome was the mistress of a mighty empire and the center of civilization.

One thing we shall notice in our wanderings through Rome is the great number of churches, most of them handsome and impressive and many of them full of pictures and statuary. Rome is one great museum. One could spend years without exhausting its possibilities.

St. Peter's, with its great colonnaded piazza, its dazzling fountains and its yellowish-white stone glistening in the sunshine, is perhaps the most magnificent church in the world. The vast interior is a wilderness of gold and marble, presided over by colossal statues of the saints, past prelates of the church and great Christian kings. The dome, over 404 feet high, was built as a canopy above the tomb of St. Peter. The dome's four supporting piers are the work of Bernini who also designed the colonnade in the piazza, the pulpit and the baldachin, or marble canopy, over the papal altar.

The Vatican Palace

Near the Basilica is the Vatican Palace, which became the residence of the popes in 1377. Its galleries contain the largest collection in the world of Greco-Roman and Roman sculpture. The magnitude of the palace is staggering. There are twenty courts, two hundred staircases and more than one thousand rooms, including picture galleries, museums, chapels, libraries and the apartments of the pope.

Many of the world's great artists have assisted in decorating the Vatican. The Sistine Chapel with its ceiling and altar-wall frescoes by Michelangelo is a wonder of Renaissance beauty. Though Michelangelo dominates the chapel, there are also notable works by Botticelli, Domenico Ghirlandaio and other masters of a great age. The Loggia and Stanze are rich with tapestries and paintings designed or executed by Raphael; his Transfiguration is in the Pinacoteca, or Vatican Picture Gallery; and there are other paintings by him throughout the palace. Tapestries by Fra Angelico are in the Chapel of Nicholas V. In the Vatican Museum we find the original of the celebrated Laocoön group, supposed to have been sculptured in the first century B.C. There are also fine copies of other Greek statues, such as the Venus of Cnidus, the Apollo Belvedere and a Belvedere torso.

The Temporal Realm of the Pope

The Vatican, the Lateran Palace (the papal residence before 1377), other buildings in Rome, and the Castel Gandolpho, a summer palace ten miles from Rome have been outside the jurisdiction of the Italian Government since 1929, when the Pope gained temporal authority of the little state. More on Vatican City will be found on page 294 of this volume.

Across the Tiber from the Vatican toward the Colosseum are many famous monuments, churches and other buildings clustered about the Capitoline Mount, religious center of ancient Rome, and the Piazza Venezia, center of the modern city. Within the massive Palazzo Venezia is a museum containing works by Titian and Fra Filippo Lippi. Near by is a twentieth-century statue in memory of King Emmanuel II and the tomb of the Italian Unknown Soldier.

The Piazza del Campidoglio, in the vicinity of the Capitoline Mount, is largely the work of Michelangelo. In its center the equestrian statue of Marcus Aurelius, a fine example of second-century Roman sculpture, stands on a graceful base made from plans by Michelangelo. Michelangelo's artistry is further represented in the design of the near-by Senatorial Palace, modern Rome's city hall.

After just a short tour of the most famous parts of Rome we can easily see that it is, indeed, one great museum. Yet for all its antiquity and its superb treasure of art from the past, it is as alive today as it was two thousand years ago.

HOW A MAN IN AN AEROPLANE SEES THE TREMENDOUS CITY

In the centre we see the Capitoline Hill, on the northern slope of which the Italians have built their glittering white memorial to Victor Emmanuel II. On the right, in the immediate foreground, are two courtyards of the Palazzo Colonna. On the left of the Palazzo, and beyond the two smaller domes, we can see the lines of broken columns of Trajan's Forum.

WHERE ANCIENT HISTORY STILL LIVES IN MODERN STREETS

On the extreme left, in a line with the memorial, are the remains of the pillars of the Forum Romanum. Behind the memorial is the Palace of the Conservatori, with its open courtyard. The Corso stretches away from the memorial toward the right, and on the further side of this street we see the Palazzo Venezia, with its delightful tree-shaded garden and tower.

353

AS THE HOUR STRIKES ABOVE ST. MARK'S SQUARE

This is one of the two gigantic bronze figures of Moors that regularly sound the hours at the top of the Clock Tower. It is over an arch on the north side of the square. Below the Moors, in the façade of the tower, is a great gilt and enamel clock face. In the background, rising still higher, is the Campanile, bell tower of St. Mark's Cathedral.

BEAUTIFUL VENICE

Born of the Marriage of Land and Sea

Venice, Italy's chief port on the Adriatic, is a city lovelier than Turner's famous painting of the same name. It is therefore the more appropriate that she should have given the world such artists as Titian and Tintoretto. Her history is a brave one, as we shall see. Built on three large islands and the one hundred and fourteen small ones that lie in the Venetian Lagoon, the city proper is supplemented by a chain of sand dunes called the Lido which lie outside the Lagoon, on which are villas and a famous bathing beach, and by a new port on the mainland. The houses stand on piles driven into the mud and held in place with heavy blocks of stone, while the islands are separated by one hundred and fifty canals crossed by four hundred bridges.

VENICE (*Venezia*), "Bride of the Adriatic" and home city of Marco Polo, at first impresses the tourist with its silence. The only sounds are the lapping of the salt tides against the walls of the canals, the calls of the gondoliers and the chug of motor boats, or the slosh of the little steamers against the piles. It is a city of beauty and mystery, and its history has been a romantic one.

Located on three large and over a hundred small islands in the Lagoon between the Po and the Piave, its houses are built on poles secured by stones. The most charming villas will be found outside the city on the Lido, a chain of sand dunes reinforced by a thirty-foot wall with openings to admit the tides. Once a great sea power, Venice is to-day important for its shipping and ship-building and for its manufacture of jewelry and mirrors, mosaics, silks and laces, as well as for its exports of oil and wine.

The Veneti, perhaps Swiss lake-dwellers of the Stone Age who had pushed southward over the Alpine passes, were in the fifth century expelled from Padua, Altinum and Aquileia by the Lombards, the Goths and in particular, Attila the Hun. Led by a priest, directed, legend had it, by signs from heaven, the founders of Venice took refuge on the islands to the north of the far-spreading marsh at the mouth of the Po; and, for generations, each island retained its independence.

The assaults of Dalmatian pirates necessitated, at one time, the building of such strong castles as that of Petrarch, who has described it as having been flanked by two watch-towers, besides which the canals were guarded against enemy craft by chains stretched across their mouths. Indeed, the Torresella Canal was guarded by towers. The houses were built in groups around the churches, and these groups were not at first consolidated into one city (though in the seventh century twelve islands elected a common magistrate whom they called the Doge); and the canals between these village-like groups of dwellings were deepened. In places trees were even planted along the banks or land was reclaimed from the sea and vineyards and orchards set out. While most of the canals were crossed on wooden bridges the first bridge across the Grand Canal was carried on boats. The earliest of the stone bridges to be built was that of San Zaccaria, which is mentioned in a document dated 1170; whereas the original Rialto bridge, carried on pontoons, is recorded as having been designed in 1178. It was twice rebuilt in wood during the thirteenth century. The present Rialto bridge, designed by the same architect who built the Bridge of Sighs, was not completed till 1591. The early bridges had no steps but were for the most part inclined planes which could be crossed by the horses then in universal use. A law of 1392 ordered that all horses and mules carry bells as a warning to foot passengers and that no horses be ridden in the crowded Merceria. As early as the thirteenth century brick pavements began to be built and ferries run to the mainland at Fusina and Mestre and to some of the outlying islands like Murano and Chioggia. Gradually the city grew to be a power-

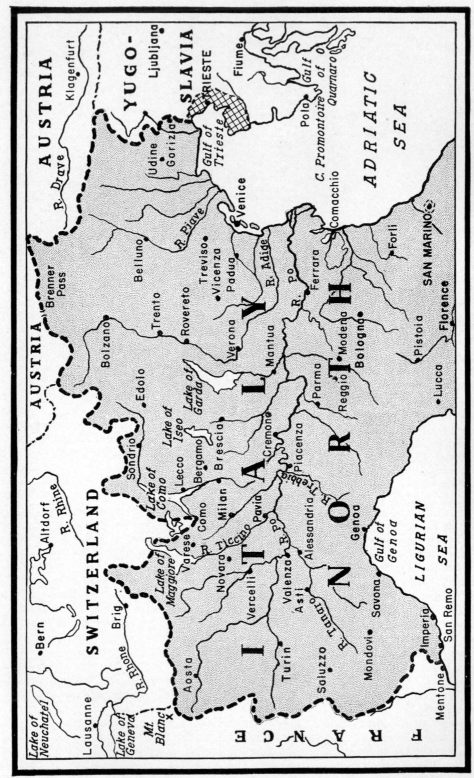

TWO SEAS AND THE LAKE-STUDDED ALPS GUARDING THE PLAIN OF NORTHERN ITALY

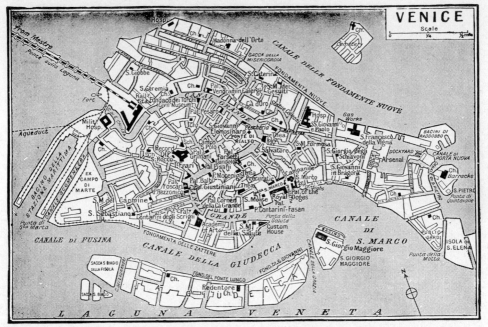

CANALS AND STREETS OF THE CITY BUILT IN THE SEA

ful republic, with a fleet that enriched itself on the commerce of the world. Great oaks were felled in the forests of the mainland for the building of ships. These vessels went to England for wool and to India and China for merchandise for Italy. They penetrated through the Black Sea for furs. By taking part in the Crusades, Venice even secured trading stations in the Holy Land.

As the Eastern Empire weakened, Venice obtained colonies in Cyprus, Crete and the Ægean Islands. When Genoa, aided by Greece, began disputing the trade routes, Venice established a Latin empire in Constantinople (1204-61). In 1379 the Genoese blockaded Venice: the island city in turn blockaded the Genoese fleet and compelled its surrender. The fall of Constantinople came in 1453, and thereafter Venice had to fight the Turks in defense of her eastern colonies. (This warfare did not, in fact, cease for over 250 years.) A body blow was struck at her commercial supremacy in 1486 by the discovery of a sea route to India.

Venice now acquired Padua, from which some of her people had fled so many centuries before, together with Cremona (home of the famous violins), Verona and certain other towns and provinces, and

ruled them wisely. Because of her growing power she was attacked by the League of Cambrai (aided by the rulers of France and Spain), and in 1508 lost most of her mainland territory. After about 1797 the government had become an oligarchy of wealthy families ruling through the Grand Council and the smaller Council of Ten. The latter body made the Doge a mere figurehead. Napoleon destroyed the republic in 1797, but by the Treaty of Campo Formio Venice fell to the lot of the Austrians. A revolt in 1848-49 freed her for a time, although, becoming weakened by the cholera brought about by poor sanitation, she again fell under Austrian domination, from which this time she struggled free in 1866. Her history from that date is united with that of the Italian people.

Picture the world in the days of the greatness of Venice. When Nicolo Polo and his brother Maffeo, jewelers, returned from their first wanderings in China, the empire of Kublai Khan reached from the Steppes of Siberia to the Punjab of India. Marco was but a stripling of seventeen at the time (1271) he elected to accompany his father and his uncle on their return journey. Little did he dream of the wonders he was to witness during the next twenty-three years. For not until he was

357

VENICE FROM THE STILL BLUE WATERS OF THE LAGOON

Venice, on her 120 islands, looks out upon a peaceful lagoon, or arm, of the blue, blue Adriatic. Most of the streets are canals and most of the buildings are erected on piles.

a bearded man of forty was he again to set eyes on the dome of St. Mark's, and not for several hundred years thereafter were the tales he told of the unknown lands of farthest Asia really credited.

Kublai Khan had requested oil from the lamp of the Holy Sepulchre at Jerusalem, and the trio made their way bearing a vessel of this oil through what is now eastern Turkey, Georgia and the Desert of Gobi. It is interesting today to reflect that they passed Mount Ararat but pronounced its ascent impracticable, that they noted in Georgia where petroleum has lately become important that "there is a fountain from which oil springs in great abundance," and that the oil was good to burn, though not to flavor a salad. They witnessed the recruiting methods of Moslem chieftains who administered hashish to their victims. Entering the region now known as Persia, they fingered the softness of the Kerman "shals" on which the shawls of Kashmir were later modeled. They were astounded by the fat-tailed Armenian sheep, the caudal appendages of which sometimes weighed thirty pounds. They plunged desperately into the unknown fastnesses of Badakhshan, where

salt was mined and rubies dug from the mountainsides. They crossed the Desert of Gobi, with its mirages of sight and sound and the peril of its sand-storms. The Great Sea of Sand, as the Chinese termed it, was vividly described by Marco Polo in a way that has been verified by subsequent explorers.

At Kanchow they found themselves in the homeland of the Mongol tribesmen who were riding into Russia, capturing Budapest, and even harrying the English. Not until four years of weary journeying did the travelers reach Chandu, the Xanadu of Coleridge's poem. The "stately pleasure dome" of the Khan's palace at Peking gleamed violet, green and vermilion above walls plated with gold and carved with the figures of dragons and Buddhas; and in the great hall the monarch of all Asia and Eastern Europe could entertain six thousand at dinner. It was said he had a million retainers. Within the walls of his summer residence he kept ten thousand milk-white horses. His New Year's parade included five thousand elephants, each of which carried two coffers of treasure.

Kublai Khan was pleased with Marco and the tales he could tell and made possible his further travels, and for seventeen years Marco roamed Cathay. In the end he returned with a small fleet, the seams of his garments filled with jewels of incredible value. Marco Millions was the nickname given him, and for years the Venetian carnivals contained the figure of a Munchausen who related tales on a par with Marco's. Since for the time the Mongols had beaten back the Moslems, it was possible for Venetian silk merchants to profit by the route Marco had blazed across Asia. The tale of his travels, which added greatly to Europe's knowledge of the strange lands he visited, came in this wise to be preserved. During a battle between Venice and her rival Genoa, in 1298, Marco was taken prisoner and passed the

MONKMEYER

PIGEONS THAT HAVE ACQUIRED WORLD FAME

From their roosting places among the pillars and arches of buildings that line St. Mark's Square, Venice, pigeons flutter down in their thousands to the piazza to be fed by tourists. Hawkers sell grain to those who wish to feed the birds, which fraternize fearlessly with visitors from all over the world. No traffic is permitted in the square.

time dictating his reminiscences to a fellow prisoner who was gifted with the pen. The story was translated into many languages, but not till 1447 could it be printed.

Gondolas Are Painted Black

To-day Venice is beloved of tourists. Leaving the mainland, the jog-trot Italian train seems to run straight into the sea. Presently we espy a vision of domes and towers rising sheer out of the water, with never a trace of land so far as eye can see. At the station there are no cabs, only black gondolas and motor boats. A law was passed in the fifteenth century requiring gondolas to be painted black. On a star-lit summer night the lights gleam across the waters and even a whisper carries.

One might spend a month in Venice and scarce set foot on land, for 150 canals lead to almost every doorway. But behind the waterways lies a maze of narrow streets and paved squares connected with one another by curved bridges like those of which Marco Polo told on his return from China. It is puzzling, though, to find one's way about afoot, when so many areaways come to a sudden end, perhaps against the blackened walls of some old palace with iron-barred windows. In few places would it be so easy to disappear without a trace. One's thoughts turn to abductions and assignations, secret societies, conspiracies and deeds of darkness.

Banishment for Outsize Bread

The old republic of the Doges was cruel in a way that would now be regarded as absurd. For instance, between St. Mark's, the great cathedral, and the Rialto bridge over the Grand Canal, is a sort of tombstone on which is an inscription that threatens everything from penal servitude and torture to banishment and fines of many ducats, for anyone who baked round loaves exceeding a certain weight and offered them for sale to the public in any square, street, alley, thoroughfare, or on any barge, gondola, or boat of any kind!

Most of the streets retain names handed down from ancient times. Just behind St. Mark's Square is the Street of the Assassins, a narrow lane between high houses, with a suitable bend in the middle where the assassins could lurk for their prey. Nowadays it is usually deserted. Several streets recall a sort of bull fight which used to be popular at carnival time. It arose out of a revolt by Ulrich, patriarch of Aquileia, against Venice in the thirteenth century. The Doge, the ruler of the Venetian republic, sent a fleet and took him prisoner with twelve of his canons. They were, however, forgiven and released on condition that their town should send a fine bull and twelve pigs as tribute every year on Carnival Thursday.

A Carnival Custom

The animals were received in great state in one of the salons of the Doge's palace, which was decorated with a number of wooden models of Ulrich's fortresses, the Doge appeared in his robes and solemnly sentenced the bull and pigs to death, and presently martial music heralded a procession of the smiths' and carpenters' guilds with flags and swords. Seizing their victims, they led them into St. Mark's Square where a mob received them with applause. As soon as quiet could be restored, a signal was given for the sacrifice. The bull was more or less released— that is to say, he was tied by a long rope which prevented his charging further than a certain distance. Thereupon amateur bull-fighters danced about with huge, two-handed swords, endeavoring to strike his head off at one blow. Now came the turn of the pigs, which were chased about with swords by the populace. At last the Doge led the way back to the palace, and trumpets were sounded while he destroyed the wooden fortresses with his stick. It was a childish game, but appealed to the humor of the people.

In the old days the carnival of Venice was celebrated throughout the world, visitors flocking to it from all over Europe. Masked balls in theatres and public places, fun and frolic were incessant day and night for a week. Little of all this now remains beyond a few masquerades. Various quarters of the city still keep up many of their old-time local festivals, but modern Venetians dislike the idea.

MC LEISH

THE VENETIAN HAWKER takes his wares from house to house. Though many of the poorer people now live in one or two rooms that they have rented in a once magnificent palace, even the slums of Venice are well served by canals, which are far quieter and pleasanter highways than the tourist finds in other such districts in the larger Italian cities.

COURT OF THE PALACE OF THE DOGES, NOW AN ART GALLERY

The domes are those of St. Mark's Cathedral, which stands behind the palace. Hence the curious mingling of Gothic and Byzantine architecture. The palace was begun about 1300. Some of the biblical and allegorical sculptures can be seen, as also a portion of the delicate pink and white marble diaper work which relieves the heaviness of the superstructure shown at the left.

In the sixteenth century there were no fewer than ten thousand gondolas. Their high prows, called dolphins (resembling sea-horses), were gilded; the little hut in the centre was of velvet; the cushions were of bright silk and satin. But all this dis-play was finally repressed, and the simplicity of the republic revealed in the black wooden fittings and steel prow which characterize the modern gondola. In summer the shelter is replaced by a light awning. There are special arrangements when a

FAMOUS CHURCH OF SAINTS GIOVANNI AND PAOLO

This church, built in 1333–90, is one of the most imposing in Venice. Within its weather-beaten walls are found the monumental tombs of the Doges. On the right is seen Verrochio's bronze equestrian statue of Bartolommeo Colleoni, General of the Republic, of which Ruskin declared: "I do not believe there is a more glorious work of sculpture existing in the world."

gondola is used as a hearse or a prison van; otherwise the boat is standardized.

Nowhere are funerals so impressive as in Venice. In the dazzling sunlight, when the reflections of the rose-colored palaces are dancing in the water, there comes a long file of black gondolas. The first attracts attention by the number of wreaths attached to the prow and a huge silver cross on a black cloth over the cabin, where priests in surplices are murmuring prayers. Immediately behind, propelled by

THE BRIDGE OF SIGHS, in Venice, dating from 1597, is a gracefully arched covered passage built across the narrow canal called the Rio della Paglia. It connects the old law courts in the Palace of the Doges with the grim Carceri or criminal prisons. The name of the bridge comes from the expressed despair of the condemned as they were hurried to their cells.

FELTON

GONDOLAS are used in Venice, a city of 117 islands, for traveling about the city, since canals take the place of streets. The gondola is a long flat bottomed craft with a high, sharply curving stern and bow. The stern is slightly twisted, and acting as a kind of rudder, helps to keep the gondola straight when the gondolier is rowing at one side only.

four gondoliers in black livery, glides a gondola bearing the coffin beneath an awning laden with flowers. A black cross stands out at the helm, and an angel spreads his silver wings at the prow.

To-day gondoliers rely for employment chiefly on their ferries, which have been fixed at certain points from time immemorial and form a kind of trade-union with schools and strict laws and benefits attached. Every gondolier must join a brotherhood, paying certain fees and drawing his share of the profits.

When one wishes to cross the Grand Canal, one can do so by bridge or steamer, but those who prefer old-fashioned ways will find a ferry and step aboard a waiting gondola. Or one shouts "Poppe!" (which literally means "poop") and a boat comes across from the other side. The custom is to deposit fares on the ledge of the boat. The Doge used to be transported through the Grand Canal enthroned on his ivory chair.

Decorated by Great Artists

Weeks could be spent looking at the Doge's palace where lived the rulers of the old republic in the days when it was incredibly wealthy. The outer walls are upheld by arcades of rose marble, the inner walls are gorgeous with paintings by the great Venetian artists. The pillars that support the arcades are rich with carvings. The sculpturing at the top of one pillar exhibits the whole life of man in exquisite miniature—first the baby in a cradle, then a Romeo and Juliet scene at a balcony, a wedding, the appearance of an heir and, finally, a death-bed. Other carvings represent seasons, industries, birds, beasts and fishes, sins and virtues and biblical scenes.

In St. Mark's Square, where streetpeddlers importune the tourist to buy their wares, let us go into one of the old coffeehouses. In winter-time we enter a succession of small, over-heated rooms whose walls are lined with divans of red plush. Here we may see what a coffee-house was like in the seventeenth century. But when spring comes, we may take one of the hundreds of chairs and tables then set far out into the square.

The Cathedral of Gold

The Cathedral of St. Mark's is likely unparalleled in the richness of its decoration. Originally the private chapel of the Doge, it began its career in 828 as a small wooden building erected to contain the relics of St. Mark which had been brought from Alexandria. This church was burned in 976 in an insurrection, but was rebuilt and later altered, on which occasions Byzantine workmen and artists as well as Lombard were employed. The resulting blend represents a unique type of architecture.

As the cathedral became the religious centre of the growing state, it was adorned with spoils brought back from the East and from the mainland of Italy by merchant traders. The general plan of the building is that of a Greek cross, with a dome over the centre and one over each of the arms. The pavement is in part of red and green porphyry mixed with marbles, while walls and ceilings are covered with delicate mosaics set in a background of gold. These mosaics, millions of tiny bits of marble, gold leaf and enamel, colorfully picture the stories of the Bible—the Creation, the Fall of Man, the Flood, Noah's Ark, the Tower of Babel, the story of Moses, the life of Christ, the life of St. John and countless other subjects. Over the doorway at the northwest angle the mosaics show the translation of the body of St. Mark—which now rests within the high altar.

Adventurous Bronze Horses

The Pala d'oro, the retable of this high altar, is one of the finest specimens of goldsmiths' and jewelers' work known. Representing the figures of Christ, the saints, the angels and the prophets, it is set with no less than thirteen hundred pearls, four hundred garnets, three hundred emeralds and an equal number of sapphires. The work was ordered in 976 and was several times enlarged and enriched between that date and 1345.

The four bronze horses over the doors of St. Mark's are said to have come from an arch of Nero, or perhaps to have been

THE WINGED LION OF ST. MARK LOOKS OVER THE LAGOON

In the Piazzetta of St. Mark stand two granite pillars. The nearer one bears a carving of the emblem of Venice, the winged lion of St. Mark, the patron saint of the city, and the farther one a statue of St. Theodore, the patron saint of the republic, standing on a crocodile. This quay was once the Venetian place of execution.

looted from Constantinople. Napoleon carried them off to Paris, but they were brought back after his fall. At the outbreak of the World War they were taken to a place of safety, but have again been restored.

The tall campanile, or bell tower, too, has had its adventures. The foundations had long caused anxiety, on account of their subsidence. Suddenly in July, 1902, the tower collapsed with a mighty roar in

a storm of dust and rubble. Reconstruction was immediately started and was finished in 1910.

On certain high days at the hour of noon the venerable clock over the arch at the entrance to the Merceria, one of the main throroughfares, gives a unique entertainment to the curious. Scarcely have the bronze Moors beaten the hour on a gong than a little trap-door opens and figures of the three wise men emerge,

SCOTT

THE GRAND CANAL, the most important waterway of Venice, laps the steps of St. Maria della Salute, a church that commemorates the great plague of 1630. The S-shaped canal, two miles in length, is spanned by the Rialto Bridge and lined with palaces.

MC LEISH

THE CHURCH OF ST. MARK was named for the patron Saint of Venice. With its marble and colored mosaics, it is one of the world's most magnificent structures. It was modeled after a building in Constantinople. The Campanile collapsed in 1902, but has been restored.

solemnly raising their hats as they pass in procession before the images of the Virgin and Child seated upon a throne.

Venice, with her shining-marble buildings and mirror-like stretches of water, never seems to look the same. Her colors are always changing. Sometimes the whole city seems in mourning, with dark canals, gray palaces and sad lagoons beneath clouded skies. Again canals, lagoons, roofs and windows are red with reflected fire and the pavements are molten gold.

During World War I, there were aerial bombardments during which over six hundred bombs were dropped on Venice, destroying the Church of Santa Maria Formosa, though it has since been restored. (The bronze horses of St. Mark's were temporarily removed to Rome for safety.) In 1917 a Venetian patriarch vowed that if the city were saved he would build a votive temple in honor of the Virgin. The church, located on the Lido, has in its foundations a brick from St. Peter's and a rock from the Grotto at Lourdes where so many miracles of healing have been performed. During the second World War Venice was spared serious damage, though many of her sister cities lost priceless treasures.

McLeish

PIOUS OFFERINGS AT A SHRINE THAT RISES FROM THE LAGOON

Built on piles driven into the bottom of the lagoon, this humble shrine to the Blessed Virgin is especially revered by the fisherfolk of Venice who wish to pray for protection against the perils of the sea. The Venetians were at one time great seafarers, adventuring for purposes of trade to various ports of England, Flanders, Greece and the Levant.

THE JEWEL OF THE MEDITERRANEAN

Sicily's Beauty, Its People and Historic Places

When we look at a map of Italy, which quaintly resembles a booted foot with a high heel, we see, close to the toe, a triangular object which the foot seems about to kick. This is the island of Sicily, for centuries a scene of conflict between East and West. Many races have struggled for possession of the land. Phœnicians, Carthaginians, Greeks, Romans, Vandals, Saracens, Normans, Germans, French, Italians and Spaniards either have had settlements here, or have in turn ruled the island. The ancient ruins with which it is strewn tell its stirring history. The island has a place in modern history, as well. In World War II the Allies made it a stepping-stone for their invasion of Italy from Tunisia. Now peace has settled once more upon this land of olive orchards and orange groves. The chief cities are Palermo, Catania and Messina, all of them on the coast.

AS our steamer plows its way through the blue waters of the Mediterranean, the gray haze seen from a distance out at sea becomes Sicily. Violet shadows fill the valleys, and the vivid green of grass, with the darker shades of the olive groves, complete the brilliant setting. Barely separated from the mainland by the Strait of Messina, two miles wide at one point, Sicily rises on the north in steep cliffs, between which lie Palermo and other good harbors. Here the lower slopes of the limestone mountains blossom into oranges and olives, grapes, lemons and mulberries. The mean temperature ranges between 51½ degrees of rainy January and 77 degrees of sun-drenched July. The one drawback is the parching wind storms of the sirocco, red with dust, which blow from Africa, especially in April and September. The coast to the west and south lies low and malarial between the rising hills and the sea; but the east coast is steep and rocky, save for the plain of Catania and Mt. Etna, whose hardened lava streams radiate for twenty miles in bold promontories. The central plateau is a region of waving wheat fields. Through the northern half there runs a chain of mountains which is regarded as a continuation of the Apennines of Italy. The slopes of the lower hills are everywhere extremely fertile.

The mountains are of volcanic origin. Etna rises over 10,750 feet from the vast plain of Catania, with its lowest slopes, especially toward the southeast, densely populated and clothed with olive groves and vineyards, and is believed to be more ancient than Vesuvius. Higher up, its sides are densely wooded. In winter the peak is covered with snow. An observatory has been built a thousand feet or so below the summit, the ascent to which is usually made from Catania. History records more than eighty serious eruptions of Etna. That of 1928 sent a wave of molten lava three hundred yards in width creeping down the mountainside to meet the sea. This wave piled up, in places, two hundred feet in height and buried the houses in its pathway, while people fled with their livestock through days torrid with the mountain's furnace glow and nights sulphurous with the red stream of destruction. The towns of Mascali and Santalfio were completely buried and parts of Nunziata and Carrabba destroyed.

Not since 1669 had Etna's lava reached the sea. That time it entered Catania. That city has also been laid low many times by violent earthquakes. Messina was destroyed by a big quake in 1908, and 150,000 people killed by an accompanying tidal wave.

In the north of the island there are fairly good harbors. Not one of the Sicilian waterways is navigable for more than a short distance. The people of Sicily have suffered from winter floods and summer droughts. In many cases the rivers dry up altogether so that the plains become parched and arid. Added to these natural causes of misfortune are the people's

TAORMINA, one of the loveliest towns in Sicily, and worth visiting because of its antiquities, was founded southwest of Messina about 396 B.C., under the name of Tauromenium. Here a woman who goes to the spring for water carries her pitcher upon her head, although in other districts the custom is to bear it on the shoulder, or rest it against one hip.

GAILY PAINTED BOATS are drawn up on the beach at Aci Castello, a little town not far from Catania. Near here seven rocks rise out of the blue sea. These are said to have been hurled there by the blinded Polyphemus when Ulysses was escaping.

MONTE PELLEGRINO rises sheer from the sea to the north of Palermo's lovely harbor. Its steep sides, once covered with bushes, are not so bare as they look, for they provide pasture for many sheep. Half way up is the Grotto of S. Rosalia, Palermo's patron saint.

© Cutler

FRESHLY WHITEWASHED WALLS OF A SICILIAN PEASANT HOME

The thick walls help to keep out the heat of a land where the orange and the olive thrive, where the heavy sweet of lemon blossoms perfumes the wind and citrons are a commonplace. The little shrine in the wall, illuminated at night by the lamp hanging before it, is typically Sicilian. Similar ones are found in almost every street.

A REST BY THE WAYSIDE: HOW LEMONS ARE BROUGHT TO MARKET

Near Palermo, on the northern coast of Sicily, is the fertile valley called the Conca d'Oro, or Shell of Gold, where fruit of all kinds, especially citrus, is grown in abundance. The fruit is brought to the high road, along which it is carried to the city in crates roped to the backs of mules, for the tracks are so steep and rough that no vehicle can use them.

375

ANCIENT GREEK TEMPLES of golden stone dating from before the Carthaginian conquests are found at Girgenti. This fragment is called the Temple of Castor and Pollux.

ignorance and indolence. Little reforestation is ever attempted so that Sicily has lost much of the woods for which it was once famous. Surprisingly, in winter many of the mountain towns are swept by bitter winds. Yet the tourist remembers Sicily as a land of roses.

The soil is fertile even in the drier regions, and the vegetation luxuriant. In the southwest there are dwarf palms, and further inland, date palms, Indian figs and prickly pears. Even here diligent irrigation makes it possible to raise groves of lemons and oranges, mulberries and pomegranates, and vineyards of the finest wine grapes. Spring in Sicily is a riot of color, and as the season progresses, quantities of fruit are exported to Italy. Another item of export is copper from the vast mining region at Caltanissetta in Central Sicily.

Glimpses of the Past

At Palermo, on the northern coast, some of the most charming old buildings raise their turrets almost directly out of unspeakably dingy streets. Here and there a fine arched gateway remains standing in good repair, or an old doorway or a colored window demands inspection. The secret of Sicily's appeal lies in these glimpses of bygone days, carrying with them all the charm of ancient legends. Formerly unwashed beggars, descended from countless generations of their calling whined their pleas for alms before every tourist.

As far as it is possible for historians to discover, the first inhabitants of Sicily were a race of people called the Sicani, doubtless Iberians, the Siculi, who dwell along the eastern shore, and a more cultured race, the Elymi, that came to the northeastern part of the island. By 1000 B.C. the Phœnicians had established trading posts along the coast, but were driven out by wandering parties of Greek settlers known as Sikeliots, who during the next hundred and fifty years formed extensive colonies on the east and south coasts and founded the real civilization of Sicily. The Greek colonies included Syracuse, Naxos, Catania, Messina (at first called Zancle), Girgenti (then known as Agrigentum),

Gela and Himera. At first they remained separated from the Siculi, carrying on their own occupations and building after their own style. Many relics of their temples still stand. After some years they gradually intermarried with their Siculi predecessors.

A Succession of Conquerors

In those early times Sicily was over-run by the Phœnicians and the Carthaginians, and later still became the cause of wars between Rome and Carthage. The Romans expelled the Carthaginians in the First Punic War (264-241 B.C.), and in 210 Sicily—then largely a Greek-speaking country—submitted to Rome. For over six hundred years it now remained a part of the Roman Empire. At first a granary for Rome, it came in time to give up the effort of raising corn and allowed the land to revert to pasturage. Palermo (the ancient Panormus), became the leading city, as it is to-day. In the fifth century A.D. the Vandals conquered Sicily but later lost it. For over three hundred years it was a part of the Eastern Empire at Constantinople; and in 878 it was taken by the Saracens. For nearly a hundred years Mohammedan rule was in force. In 1061, came the Normans, at first as plunderers, but afterward as conquerors. Under Robert Guiscard and his brother Roger they over-ran the island for the next thirty years. Robert Guiscard conquered southern Italy and made his brother Count of Sicily. Under Roger's son the by no means unified racial elements of dukedom and county became united as the Kingdom of the Two Sicilies.

Some time later, Sicily passed by marriage to the Hohenstaufen Emperor Henry VI, whose son introduced a high degree of culture to Sicily. But Pope Urban IV, a Frenchman, in 1264 gave the ruling of Sicily to the French Count of Anjou.

The Sicilian Vespers

This period was one of the darkest in Sicily's turbulent history. The Count of Anjou imposed every form of tyranny and taxation upon the people until, in 1282, they massacred almost every man, woman

A SCENE IN THE MARSHY SALT FLATS OF TRAPANI, SICILY

Sicily, part of the Italian Republic, is the largest of the Mediterranean islands. It lies just off the toe of the Italian boot. Salt-manufacture for export is a vital occupation of both the city and province of Trapani; and because the city is the safest port on the western coast of the island it makes an excellent shipping point for the product.

and child of the French population. The massacre took place at Palermo on the evening of March 30, the signal for its commencement being the first peal of the vesper bell. Thus we have the term Sicilian Vespers.

The result of the overthrow of the Angevin power was that Sicily passed into the hands of the House of Aragon, starved, revolted, and eventually became a separate kingdom. Subsequently the island belonged in turn to Spain, Savoy and Austria. Then it was united with Naples in a separate kingdom until the coming of Garibaldi to the island in 1860. He defeated the king, Francis II, and treated the people with great discretion and justice, so that in a short time they and the Neapolitans, with whom they had been linked for centuries, voted to attach themselves to Italy.

Although Sicily once produced a large percentage of the world's sulfur, its output has fallen off in recent years as a result of competition from other countries. The mineral isn't sufficiently valuable to have created great industries. The making and exporting of salt is another industrial activity, particularly on the coasts where sea water can be used. But the island is chiefly agricultural, and many of the people pursue the industries related to farming: canning and preserving of fruits, tomatoes and other foodstuffs, and the making of olive oil. Of late years, Sicilians have started small businesses such as tanning, furniture making, the manufacture of gloves and matches. The fine wines of Marsala have been renowned for hundreds of years. Many Sicilians find employment in deep-sea fish-

A VIEW OF CEFALU, ON THE NORTH COAST OF SICILY

Facing on the Tyrrhenian Sea, a twelve-hundred-foot cliff rising abruptly behind it, Cefalu has limited harbor facilities, but many of its residents earn their living as fishermen. Others work in the marble quarry. The mild climate and the fertile soil of the countryside on the coast near the town are highly suitable for growing grapes and oranges.

ORANGE RINDS FOR ENGLISH MARMALADE

Milazzo, on the northeastern coast of Sicily, is a small port city that exports the citrus fruits and wines of the vicinity. Many Sicilian towns, this one included, were once Greek colonies. Milazzo's ancient name was Mylae. The island of Sicily had its own government until the middle of the nineteenth century, when it became part of the kingdom of Italy.

© Cutler

WHEREVER A FOREIGNER GOES IN SICILY HE IS SURE OF AN INTERESTED AUDIENCE OF BOYS

Poverty does not dampen the spirits of this merry octet of a mountain village high above the malarial districts. They very likely watch their fathers' flocks of sheep and goats, or feed his silkworms, or help in gathering nuts and almonds. For a small tip any one of these boys would act as guide to any place in the district. Most of them can speak Italian as well as Sicilian. Perhaps their fathers work in the sulfur, salt or pumice mines. Sicily produces about one-tenth of the annual world supply of sulfur. Pumice is a kind of hardened volcanic lava.

380

EVENING IN TAORMINA, A TOWN FOUNDED 396 B.C. ON A HILLSIDE ABOVE THE BLUE IONIAN SEA

In the low-lying parts of Sicily there is danger of malaria, and lonely houses may be robbed by brigands, so most of the peasants dwell in little mountain towns. The men often have to journey far to the place where they work, but they usually ride there and back on a fine large donkey, which often shares a poor tumble-down house with its master and all his family. Sicilian peasant women do not wear hats but tie a kerchief, often beautifully colored, over their heads, and little girls wear long frocks almost as soon as they can walk.

AT THE MIDDAY MEAL OF FRUIT AND WINE IN THE REFECTORY OF AN OLD SICILIAN MONASTERY © Cutler

Sicily, a Roman Catholic country, is proud of its beautiful monasteries. Rarely, however, are they now used for their original purpose: the buildings are either deserted or occupied as hotels, schools or agricultural colleges. One of the most famous monasteries is that at Monreale, near Palermo. The Benedictine monastery of San Nicola was originally founded high up on Mount Etna. Later, however, a great annex was built at Catania, and gradually the old building was abandoned and fell into ruins. At one time it was the haunt of a famous brigand chief.

382

CATHEDRAL AT PALERMO FACING THE PIAZZA DEL DUOMO

The Cappella Palatina, the cathedral begun at Palermo in 1176 but many times restored, is a fine example of Norman architecture. The picture shows its four slender towers, its campanile and its modern dome. Within, one can see the panels of the richly gilded and colored nave which bear Arabic inscriptions and thus indicate that they were built by Saracens.

ing, plying their trade as far as the north coast of Africa.

A glance at the map will remind you of the nearness of Sicily to Greece. As a matter of fact, the ancient Sicilian city of Syracuse was a centre of the highest Greek culture. Many leaders in the arts and in government lived here for a period; famous plays were written around her, and some dramas were first produced in the Syracuse theatre before being shown in Greece. Syracuse is one of the lesser cities now; and it is an Italian city. The Sicilian of today in appearance has olive-tinted skin and dark hair, and his features, influenced by the ancient infusion of Grecian blood, are delicately molded.

The agricultural products of this favored island are varied. Shortly after the end of the first World War the farm population of Sicily demanded the use of the uncultivated lands on the large estates and for several months in 1919, and again in 1920 there was such disorder as to create in the hearts of government officials the fear of civil war. Finally the Italian Government took a hand. The estates are being broken up, and a project which includes irrigation of the land and the building of roads and villages has been started.

To-day the prosperous, few in number, prefer living in the big towns. Everywhere the farms are small, except in the plains where are large fields of wheat. Owing to the droughts of summer, it is possible to grow good crops only by using alternate patches of the land, allowing each piece to lie idle, except for grazing, for one or two years, so that it may regain its strength. For so poor does the land become after the summer heat that a single animal requires several acres for a pasture. The farmers live in the nearest villages and their laborers walk several miles each day to and from their work. In the villages and towns a family often lives in a single room, sharing the space with pigs and poultry. The smoke from the fire passes out through a hole in the roof, and rain and wind enter through this crude chimney, making the conditions doubly wretched. Dust, dirt and soot discolor every article in the place. Strips of matting cover the bed, and the only dressing-room these laborers have is the road or a parched plot in front of their dwellings.

For food the Sicilian depends more upon vegetables than meat. Oxen and cows are bred only for plowing and carting, and go to the butcher when they become too old for work. Butter is used only by the rich. The chief items of the peasant's diet are black bread—the staple food of the country—macaroni, beans, herbs and onions, a light wine and a hard cheese which the farmers make from goats' milk. The fruit crops, except prickly pears, are rarely eaten: they are closely guarded for export.

Among the Sicilians there is a great love of poetry, and their language is not unlike the soft Neapolitan, which increases the charm of their folk songs.

Over the distant peaks of the mountains the rose hue of day is fading; the purple is gradually darkening the valleys. We can still see bright color, the yellow from the lemon groves, the greens of the olive groves and mulberry trees. Perhaps, as we gaze over the nodding ears of wheat, we catch a glimpse of the blue waters of the Mediterranean. Sicily, unprogressive as it may be, is yet truly the jewel of the Mediterranean, and no tourist who has ever visited there but longs to return.

© E. N. A.

ETNA SEEN THROUGH THE BLOSSOMING ALMONDS NEAR TAORMINA

The ancient town of Taormina has ruins of a Greco-Roman theatre (shown elsewhere) and of a medieval castle, and it boasts a stirring history of battle, siege and capture that began as far back as 396 B.C. To-day it is unspeakably lovely and peaceful and affords many such views as this of snowy Etna and the blue Ionian Sea.

INDEX FOR VOLUME II

COLOR PLATES IN VOLUME II

INDEX FOR VOLUME II

(General Index for entire work of 7 volumes may be found at the end of Volume 7)

A single star before a page number marks an illustration; two stars are placed before color-plates. The repetition of a page number, first without a star, and then with a star, shows that there is an illustration on the page, in addition to an important text reference.

387